Chicken Soup for the Soul: Age Is Just a Number
101 Tales of Humor & Wisdom for Life After 60
Amy Newmark

Published by Chicken Soup for the Soul, LLC www.chickensoup.com
Copyright ©2020 by Chicken Soup for the Soul, LLC. All Rights Reserved.

The publisher gratefully acknowledges the many publishers and individuals who granted Chicken Soup for the Soul permission to reprint the cited material.

Front cover photo of candles courtesy of iStockphoto.com/Talaj (©Talaj), photo of cake courtesy of iStockphoto.com/juliannafunk (©juliannafunk), photo of balloons courtesy of iStockphoto.com/maikid (©maikid)
Back cover and interior photo of man with beard courtesy of iStockphoto.com/georgemuresan (©georgemuresan)
Interior photos: Woman with white hair courtesy of iStockphoto.com/dragana991 (©dragana991), women doing yoga courtesy of iStockphoto.com/FatCamera (©FatCamera), couple on bike courtesy of iStockphoto.com/monkeybusinessimages (©monkeybusinessimages)
Photo of Amy Newmark courtesy of Susan Morrow at SwickPix

Cover and Interior by Daniel Zaccari

Distributed to the booktrade by Simon & Schuster. SAN: 200-2442

Publisher's Cataloging-In-Publication Data
(Prepared by The Donohue Group, Inc.)

Names: Newmark, Amy, compiler.
Title: Chicken soup for the soul : age is just a number : 101 tales of
    humor & wisdom for life after 60 / [compiled by] Amy Newmark.
Other Titles: Age is just a number : 101 tales of humor & wisdom for
    life after 60
Description: [Cos Cob, Connecticut] : Chicken Soup for the Soul, LLC,
    [2020]
Identifiers: ISBN 9781611590715 | ISBN 9781611593051 (ebook)
Subjects: LCSH: Aging--Literary collections. | Aging--Anecdotes. | Older
    people--Literary collections. | Older people--Anecdotes. | LCGFT:
    Anecdotes.
Classification: LCC HQ1061 .C45 2020 (print) | LCC HQ1061 (ebook) | DDC
    305.26--dc23
Library of Congress Control Number: 2020942106

PRINTED IN THE UNITED STATES OF AMERICA
on acid∞free paper

25 24 23 22 21 20   01 02 03 04 05 06 07 08 09 10 11

AGE IS JUST A NUMBER

101 Tales of Humor & Wisdom for Life After 60

Amy Newmark

Chicken Soup for the Soul, LLC
Cos Cob, CT

Changing your life one story at a time®
www.chickensoup.com

Table of Contents

❶

~The New Normal~

❷

~Try Something New~

3

~Older & Wiser~

4

~Hit the Road~

5

~The Privilege of Age~

❻

~Get Physical~

❼

~Less Is More~

❽

~Love and Love Again~

❾

~Embrace Your Years~

❿

~Second Wind~

⑪

~So Much to Give~

The New Normal

Slips of the Tongue

*I am so clever that sometimes I don't understand a
single word of what I am saying.*
~"The Remarkable Rocket" by Oscar Wilde

"Good morning, Dad. What's new?"

"Oh, hi, Margie. Nothing much. Your mother is doing some online shopping. I think she's ordering a shroud."

"A shroud?"

"Yeah, do you want to talk to her? She'll tell you all about it."

Having overheard my husband and daughter's conversation, I snorted. I took the phone from George's hand but couldn't talk because I was laughing so hard.

"Mom, are you crying?"

"No, laughing," I managed to croak.

"You ordered a shroud?" Margie's voice had risen an octave.

"No, I ordered a bathing suit cover-up. The 'shroud' thing is one of your dad's many malapropisms."

Margie began to laugh hysterically. "I hope you're writing them down."

"I am. I bought a notebook. I swear, since he retired, this speech stumble thing is just crazy. I think it's because he's not having as many interactions with other people. It's entertaining for me because they're getting funnier.

"By the way, we love the Amazon Echo you bought us for Christmas, but Dad has a hard time remembering how to activate it. One day, I heard him call from the kitchen, 'Melissa, Alissa, Melinda…' I came into the room and saw him ready to pounce on the thing. He announced, 'This is infuriating! I am so vivid!'

"'Vivid?' I asked.

"'Yeah, I've never been so mad at a thing!'

"'Her name is Alexa,' I said. He gave me a sheepish look."

Margie burst out laughing again, "You two sure do keep me entertained."

We got off the phone, and I sat down to note the latest incident. I started reading through my collection of George's malapropisms to find they were just as funny as when I first heard them.

One day, he came into the house, shut the front door, and sagged against it. I walked around the corner from the kitchen to ask if he was okay. He held up his hand.

"Don't talk to me right now. I just need ten minutes to decompose."

I walked back into the kitchen, hoping his decomposing didn't make a mess in the recently cleaned foyer. I scribbled keywords of this interaction on a napkin as I tried to laugh quietly.

Our daughter introduced us to the delightful taste of quesadillas. We both love them, but George cannot, for the life of him, remember what they're called. One day, he turned to me after breakfast and asked, "Can we have conquistadors for supper tonight?"

"Conquistadors?" I had no idea what he was talking about. "What are they?"

"You know, Margie made them for us. They're those things in a tortilla that are browned and crunchy on the outside with good meat and cheese inside."

"Ah, I think you mean quesadillas."

"Yeah, those."

"Sure, no problem." I scrambled toward my notebook.

After dinner one night, we gathered all the waste cans in the house to empty them. George tied up the big white bag and, with a flourish of his arm, announced, "Madam, I shall depose this trash." He was out the door in a flash.

I pictured him as a legalistic attorney, recorder on the table, questioning the offending garbage as he collected evidence for a case.

Once he mastered Alexa, George learned he could ask for the music of his choosing. One afternoon, he requested, "Alexa, play Little Big Horn."

From the laundry room, I could hear an argument taking place between my husband and an electronic voice.

"What seems to be the trouble?" I asked.

"I was trying to play one of my favorite country groups, Little Big Horn. It's not working," he said, pointing to the flashing hockey puck.

"Maybe if you asked her to play Little Big Town, you'd get somewhere." He scowled.

I walked toward the desk and my notebook.

Paging through my notes, I came upon the funniest one of all time, but this time George was not the offender. His best friend was, but George was a willing accomplice, hanging on every word.

We were visiting our friends Anne and Bill for a few days. Anne prepared a sumptuous breakfast and had gone into the kitchen to retrieve cinnamon buns from the oven. Friends for over thirty years, the two men at the end of the table began to exchange stories of health issues plaguing men over a certain age. Bill related his experience of having a prostate biopsy. He reassured George, "It didn't hurt because the doctor numbed me, and it only took a few minutes. I never had any side effects, and now all we have to do is wait for the autopsy report."

I had just taken a big mouthful of freshly squeezed orange juice. My eyes widened, and I bolted from the table into the kitchen, bursting through the swinging door. Anne looked up at me as she held a pan of hot buns in her oven mitts. I tried not to choke as I shook with laughter and attempted to swallow.

"What did he say now?" Anne inquired before she burst out laughing. She knew her husband.

I told her. Both of us convulsed as we leaned against the countertops. "Bill's been like this ever since he retired."

Just as I suspected, retirement is the culprit. I rest my case.

— Nancy Emmick Panko —

Forgetting

Does anyone else put things in a safe place and forget
then where the safe place is?
~Author Unknown

Yesterday, I went to the basement and just stood there. Was I there for laundry? No. Extra paper towels? No.

I thought I could reconstruct what sent me down to the basement, so I backtracked through my thoughts. I came up with nothing.

But I wasn't about to go back upstairs empty-handed, so I grabbed a pair of pliers from my husband's workbench. When I got to the kitchen, he was there eating lunch.

"What are you doing with the pliers?"

"I don't know."

"What do you mean you don't know?"

I thought for a moment about making up a story about how he had promised to fix the whatchamacallit months ago but forgot, and so I had to do it myself. But why compound memory loss with lying?

"I went to the basement to get something, forgot what I went to get, so I grabbed your pliers."

Here's where I wish I could say we laughed, split an egg-salad sandwich, and continued in our domestic bliss. But that's not what happened.

He looked alarmed. Granted, his face looked the same as when he was feeling pity, surprise, anger, or any other emotion. That's why he has no lines on his face; it has never been used. But these are the kinds of digressions that got me into this mess in the first place.

He said, "We only have one working memory between us — *yours* — and now *you* can't remember."

I told my friend Linda that I was starting to worry about these senior moments. She's a decade older. Experience matters in these matters. She said, "Oh, that's normal. I've heard experts explain the difference between normal memory loss and dementia: Normal is when you leave the grocery store and can't remember where you parked your car, but you remember after a moment. Dementia is when you leave the grocery store and don't know where you are or how you got there."

I think that's what she said, and I was reassured.

What is it called when you decide that it doesn't matter anyway? After all, I have enough groceries for a week, and I'm pretty sure some of them are in the basement.

— Leesa Lawson —

Old Ladies at the Library

It is sometimes expedient to forget what you know.
~Author Unknown

There is a section in the library for new releases. When I regularly forget to bring my *New York Times Book Review* — on which I have meticulously taken notes — I go and sit on the bench in the new-releases section and browse the new books.

I put a lot of stock in book covers. I absolutely judge a book by its cover. Publishers pay a lot of money to artists and designers of book covers, and I wouldn't want them to feel it was wasted. I believe in the artwork on book covers, although I often wonder about the stuff written on the book jacket. I try not to read the whole thing, although they are never as bad as the Netflix descriptions. Talk about spoiler alert.

Anyhow, I was at the library recently, and a woman was standing next to me holding a book I had recently read. I forget the name now, but I told her it was about a lawyer who decides to defend an eleven- or twelve-year-old boy who murdered a six-year-old girl, and the whole town turns against him and his family, and, well, I don't want to ruin it for you if you decide to read it, but I'd have to remember the name of it first.

I told the woman that she was going to love that book, and she asked me if I had any other suggestions. So, I asked her if she had read the one about the Olympic athlete who was a Japanese prisoner of war in World War II.

"No, no," she said. "What's the name of it?"

I had no idea. "I dunno," I said, "but it was written by the same author who wrote the one about the horse."

She nodded. "Right," she said. "The horse."

"A woman."

"Right. A woman wrote it."

"A racehorse?"

"Right. I loved that book."

"Anyhow, it was written by her." I thought for a minute. "I also liked the one about the girl who was losing her house to foreclosure and a family bought it, but she and her cop boyfriend were working on getting them evicted, and…"

The woman brightened up. "I saw the movie!" she exclaimed. "I loved the old guy, that actor."

"He was magnificent. What's-his-name. Very noble. But if you saw the movie, you probably don't want to read the book."

The woman looked up at the ceiling. "Didn't that end badly?"

I was thinking that the old guy and his wife both die, but I didn't want to tell her that. I nodded at the book in her hand again. "You're going to love that book," I reminded her.

"Well, thanks for your help. It's great meeting another real reader."

She told me her name, which I promptly forgot, but about ten minutes later, I said out loud to nobody, *Seabiscuit!*

— Sherri Daley —

Showing Up

I want to feel my life while I'm in it.
~Meryl Streep

'm seventy-nine years old. Several years ago, I witnessed the sudden and unexpected death of my husband Don after thirty-two years of marriage. Eighteen months later, I met Jim, a gentleman who opened my heart to love again. Sadly, four months after we met, he passed unexpectedly due to a fall.

My grief therapist said one doesn't have to be a soldier to experience PTSD. I felt as if I'd been wounded in combat and wanted to remain hidden in a foxhole.

Now, almost three years later, I have emerged from the foxhole. I feel that life is good again, with no disrespect to loved ones who have passed.

As crazy as it may sound, I give the sport of pickleball a lot of the credit.

After my losses, I was fortunate to have tremendous support from family and friends, but pickleball provided an outlet with unexpected benefits. The obvious one was physical activity, but it delivered so much more.

My husband and I were introduced to the game in 2015 at our summer residence near Flagstaff, Arizona, where the pickleball courts were a two-minute walk from our door. We got hooked on the game but also enjoyed the friendships that quickly developed. Hey, when people see you a few minutes after you wake up with no make-up and accept you, there's an instant comradeship.

When Don passed in April, the first time I went to the pickleball court in May without him was hard. But, once again, fellow picklers pulled me through — and running around the court and working up a sweat surely released precious endorphins, not to mention the release of anger (that often accompanies grief) when you slam the ball as hard as you can.

When I returned to my winter residence in Phoenix, I discovered that the nearby senior center offered pickleball indoors and outdoors. They also had it at my local YMCA. I began to play at each place, and it was easier in some ways because many of these people never knew Don. It was a new circle of friends.

Now, in addition to the physical benefits, here's the *real* secret to the magic of pickleball. It's the social time on the bench or bleachers while you're waiting your turn for a court. You'll meet people from all walks of life with interesting past lives, all ages, and they come in all shapes and sizes. You don't have to be a super athlete to play. It's a short court and a short game; with only eleven points to win, it takes about fifteen minutes per game.

Many mornings, I awoke with a heavy heart after my losses. Some days, I just wanted to burrow back under the covers, but pickleball was an easy option to choose when I was trying to convince myself to go out. I didn't have to sign up ahead of time, and it gave me a reason to get dressed and show up — not just showing up for the game but for life itself. Having a place to go each morning and meeting new people who soon became friends was a great start to each day. It's a great pastime for couples to do together and for singles to meet other singles who have a similar interest.

This year, I've been invited to play in a ladies' pickleball league. We practice each week for our matches with other leagues in the area. Now, in addition to fun, there's a competitive edge and a beautiful comradeship that comes when you are part of a team.

I've played at many different locations and have found each one to be friendly and welcoming to newcomers. When I visited my children in Chicago at Christmas, I found an indoor court at a senior center near their home. Now it's "have paddle, will travel."

My life is so good now that sometimes I feel guilty enjoying myself so much when I've lost two dear people, but perhaps those losses make me appreciate life more. I never take one day for granted and I live life as fully as possible.

—Violetta Armour—

I Blame the Children

Children are a great comfort in your old age,
and they help you reach it faster, too.
~Lionel Kauffman

Back in the early 1980s, the idea of home computers was catching on. I wasn't keen on getting one. In fact, I remember stating that if a computer could clean my house for me, I "might" consider it.

Somehow, I evolved and have owned several computers over the years. None of them cleaned my house. Some days, I loved my computer, but more often than not, I hated it. I didn't grow up with them, and they were a challenge to my mental health. Dealing with modern technology was my introduction to stress, and I know who to blame: my children.

They weren't satisfied that their dad and I finally purchased a computer and learned to send e-mails. We were quite happy with that, but next came a cellphone. Then just talking on the phone was not acceptable; they insisted we learn to text as well. We couldn't get a break.

I remember well the night that Facebook became a household word around here. Those kids of ours showed up at the house for an intervention of sorts, determined to set up a joint account for us. It took some convincing.

After setting up our page, they began scrolling for "friends." They scrolled through many names we knew and many we did not. As they read out the names, we were to approve or disapprove of them as possible friends. That process got old fast. My husband and I would pause and give a great deal of thought to each name. That was hours of our lives that we'll never get back.

"OMG!" our children said in unison. They seemed really frustrated. "You don't have to marry them or invite them to dinner! Just ask them to be friends, for Pete's sake!"

We felt no guilt for grating on their nerves considering the drama they'd sometimes created for us during their teenage years. A little payback wouldn't hurt those two.

More recently, my husband and I were coerced into getting rid of our flip phones and getting smartphones. I will admit that I progressed into appreciating mine. I liked speaking to Siri and finding out what I needed to know in an instant. I enjoyed having Internet access everywhere I went. I felt a sense of accomplishment; my husband — not so much. To this day, he would happily take back his flip phone.

I think of a quote by James Comey, "Technology has forever changed the world we live in." I believe that is true. Back in the 1980s, I would never have guessed that I would own computers or a tiny phone that would eliminate the need for phonebooks, dictionaries, calendars and checkbooks — or that I could learn to use it. Using technology still does not come easy for me. It has certainly changed my world.

Last Christmas, our children surprised us with yet another popular form of technology — Alexa. The girls took our smartphones in hand and got us programmed. Before we fully understood what was happening, we could tell Alexa to turn our lamp on or off, and she would.

To be honest, we were a bit dismayed at having to learn how to use yet another device. After the girls went home, my husband and I discussed this thing called Alexa. We didn't have any business with that thing. We certainly didn't think we needed it. Would it hurt the kids' feelings if we boxed it up and gave it back?

Long story short, we decided to keep it. We mastered turning the lamp on and off, and once again I got the hang of it sooner than my husband did. Alexa would not turn the lamp on for him at first. He would say, "Alisha… turn that lamp on." Or he'd say, "Allison…

put on the lamp."

I became his Alexa coach. When he finally learned the correct name to say, he said it last instead of first. "You have to say her name first," I told him repeatedly. "Say her name first. Say, 'Alexa, turn on lamp one.' Use those exact words… For the love of…!"

"We don't need that lamp on anyway," he'd say.

One night, Alexa did not turn on the lamp when I commanded. I had to get up and manually turn it on. By then, my husband and I were quite spoiled… and sad that our Alexa was broken. We hated to tell the girls but thought we should. Although we'd been querulous about technology, we secretly hoped she could be replaced.

One night, we discovered (all by ourselves) that the device had merely been turned off. We hadn't lost Alexa after all. We had her back with just the flip of a switch. Eventually, we learned how to ask her to add items to a shopping list on our smartphones or to have her call or text our kids. Just think, we reasoned, we are getting to the age when we could fall and not get up. How handy to just yell out to Alexa to call the kids for us.

Thanks to our children and grandchildren, we own tablets and Kindles upon which we can play games or read, obviating actual books. We have tiny contraptions that store music and many charging cords to untangle.

Our children continue to "bless" us with high-tech gifts. We now have Fitbits. Mine sends e-mails when the battery is running low or when I haven't gotten enough steps in for the day. I never meet my exercise goals, it seems. I actually knew that without being told.

I realize there are numerous electronic gadgets out there that our kids haven't tortured us with yet, and many more in the making. I don't know what the technology gurus will come up with next, but I suppose the kids will get us one. Bet it won't clean the house.

— Carol Emmons Hartsoe —

Adventures in a Norwegian Bathtub

I believe that the ability to laugh at oneself is
fundamental to the resiliency of the human spirit.
~Jill Conner Browne

This was a new life. A chance to reinvent myself. All I had to do was figure out who I was at heart and what I really wanted. That can be tricky when you've been half of a whole and are suddenly alone. A year of widowhood passed before I grew confident enough to embark on my adventure — a tour of Norway with a busload of mostly women. What a delight! We began as strangers and ended as friends.

We were constantly on the move, shuttling from museum to village to ancient building in search of folk art, and many of the activities were strenuous. We stopped in a different hotel nightly, and those accommodations were often of historical interest as well as comfortable. Which brings me to a decision that will haunt me the rest of my days.

My muscles were aching despite taking painkillers. And waiting there, in the bathroom of my charming old hotel room, was a tub made for a Viking giant. So inviting. So much longer than I was accustomed to, I just knew I could submerge every throbbing muscle. How good a soak in hot water would feel. I should have known better since I rarely climbed into my tub at home, but that huge porcelain bath was calling my name.

Anticipating a special treat, I ran the water. Wouldn't it be nice to scent it? All I had with me was shampoo, so I added a dollop of that. It smelled heavenly. Cautious, I stepped in. When I went to lower myself, I discovered that the tub was pretty much flush with the wall, so there was nothing to grab onto on that side. I sat down anyway. "Umm. Ahhh." So soothing.

Getting ready to lie back, I tried to reposition my rear end. Uh-oh. What the tub had added in length, it lacked in width. Being a substantial woman, I found myself wedged in! I tried to lift with my arms but there was nothing to grab on the wall side, and the shampoo made the tub slippery. That had been a mistake. Okay. No problem. I'd just let the water out.

Reaching forward, I managed to open the drain. The bath water in front of me ran out. I, however, was doing a Hoover Dam imper-sonation, and half the water was trapped behind me, held securely by my ample derriere! Stunned, I just sat there, thinking about what to try next. If I could get all the water out, maybe I'd be able to get a better grip. Maybe.

By leaning to each side in turn and lifting what I could manually, I managed to free most of the trapped deluge, one splash at a time. I'd wondered why the tub was raised on a pedestal and why the floor had a drain. Now, I understood. I tried to lift my body again and again, but my hand always slipped off that narrow edge. Not a big surprise any longer. The outer tub edge was wide enough for support, but my left arm wasn't strong enough to do the whole job, nor could I maneuver my knees under me by rolling over. I know because I tried. No leverage.

Praying in the bathtub was a new spiritual experience for me, but I gave it my all. Either I had to figure out how to escape, perhaps with divine guidance, or I was going to have to scream for help. The last thing I wanted was for some buff Norwegian Viking named Sven to have to pry me out like the cork in a bottle.

There had to be another way. Maybe if I could turn sideways and reverse directions so my stronger arm bore more weight, I'd be able to stand.

Helping to lift my thighs with my slippery hands, I hoisted one leg over the side of the tub. Then the other. At least fifteen minutes had passed, and I was now sitting sideways within the narrow space, lower legs suspended over the floor, knees hooked on the tub lip. Breathless, I started to smile. This was going to work! I rested a moment, secure in that conviction. Then, I tried to complete the turn.

My legs were loose below the knees, but the skin on my upper back was stuck fast to the opposite wall of the tub!

That's when I lost it. I chuckled, I giggled, and then I roared with laughter until tears were running down my face. There I sat, folded like a legendary corpulent troll, bent double in a narrow Norwegian bathtub. Stuck. My imaginary Sven was going to laugh his head off if I ever managed to actually summon help. Not that I wanted to.

Then, lo and behold, I realized that the jiggling motion of my raucous laughter had loosened part of my back. With a painful twist, I wrenched the rest free. I could move! It was a minor miracle, and I was going to take full advantage of it. Cheeks against porcelain squeaked as I pivoted the rest of me. Now I was on my side, and thankfully the water had all drained out.

Panting and ready to scream "Hallelujah!" at the top of my lungs, I pulled my knees under me. That hurt, too. I didn't care. I was almost free. With my good arm over the wide lip of the tub, I pushed and pulled until I was almost up. I got one foot under me. Then the other. Ignoring that cursed narrow lip by the wall, I put both hands on the wider side and pushed. I was standing! I wasn't going to have to call Sven or his buddies.

All I wanted at that moment was to get out of that death trap. Stepping forward, my toes found no floor, and I was reminded how high off the floor the tub was. Picturing myself in a full body cast as I lunged forward and kissed the far wall, I managed to stay on my feet. Then, I took silent inventory.

I was sore, as tired as a marathon runner after completing a race, and dripping wet with perspiration. There was no way around it. I was going to have to face that tub again, only this time I was taking a shower.

It actually felt pretty good. Under the circumstances.

—Valerie Hansen Whisenand—

As Good as It Gets

The longer I live the more beautiful life becomes.
~Frank Lloyd Wright

"More ham?" I pushed the bag of lunchmeat toward my husband, David.

"No, but pass the pickles."

I slid the food container closer to him and popped the seal. The tangy fragrance of homemade refrigerator pickles displaced the scent of mixed evergreens and deciduous trees around our table. A giant maple leaf drifted lazily to the dirt at my feet.

I grabbed a few baby carrots and tossed one to our senior German Shepherd, Gunny.

Wiping my fingers on an old cloth napkin, my gaze rested on our picnic basket. Once bright and gleaming with varnish and clay sunflowers, its handle and hinges now reflected years of service. I smoothed the tablecloth's tattered edges and sighed.

Things had certainly changed for us over the years. Just as the adage went, we'd started out with almost nothing, and after working hard all our lives we'd managed to keep it.

Gunny flopped onto his side for a nap. Pine needles and soft earth offered the finest bed one could ask for. Murmurs from the nearby stream must have set his mind to dreaming. Lucky dog.

I stifled a yawn, thinking I could easily curl up here, too, despite the crisp edge to the autumn air.

David glanced at our surroundings, and then settled his gaze on me, his lips turning up just a bit at the corners. "Look where we are. This is as good as it gets, isn't it?"

Was it, really? We'd made a life for ourselves, raised our daughter with everything she needed and most of the things she wanted, and we'd supported her marriage to a good man.

We'd traveled all over the world, and gradually our tastes in food, clothing, and lifestyle had come to reflect our comfortable income. For a season, it had been too easy to indulge. And overindulge.

Then the recession hit, and David lost the job he'd worked at for decades. Years of dedication were reduced to a small severance check. A month later, he was diagnosed with a brain tumor, demolishing any shred of hope for the future we'd clung to.

Close to a year after those personal catastrophes, Dave once again found a job, this time as a custodian — but he was different.

In fact, we'd both changed.

I glanced across the table at him. A flannel shirt, jeans and hiking boots replaced the suit jacket he'd worn in the past, and a ponytail took the place of his once styled hair. Yet, he looked better than ever. Relaxed, content, healthy.

Appearance and possessions had once dominated our thoughts, but now we had other priorities. Money mattered, but not for the same reasons. We'd stopped searching for the finest restaurants and swankiest hotels to visit. We'd given up on always reaching for more. At this point, every penny went toward paying a mountain of bills.

Reality had hit us full force. We'd survived what in some circles is called "a humbling." Maybe it was, maybe not. But whatever name we gave that period, we'd learned from it.

My gaze shot to my washed-out jeans, then down to my muddy hiking boots. A week earlier, I'd tried on a pair of the spike heels I used to love wearing. But my feet, now accustomed to sneakers and flip-flops, no longer fit. My soul no longer did, either. It was time to let go of both the old clothes and the old me.

I rose and circled to the other side of the table to sit next to Dave. Facing away from the food, I focused on the glimmering stream as it raced past. Where had it started, and where would its journey end?

The rivulets shifted and flowed, sometimes tumbling over boulders, other times languid and pooling.

I watched as a stray leaf dawdled at the edge of a summer swimming hole. Seconds later, it slipped loose and floated by, carefree as a butterfly on the breeze. It bobbed under the footbridge and disappeared from view.

Maybe, just maybe, life wasn't about the destination at all, but about enjoying the ride — pools, rapids and all.

Muscles in my back relaxed, and my shoulders lowered a notch. I took a deep breath, relishing the chill as it filled my lungs.

David turned to face the same direction. He slipped an arm around my shoulders, and we leaned into each other's warmth. Dappled sunlight broke through the canopy of trees above, creating an enchanting, private world.

Red, orange and yellow leaves broke free and fell, their descent a slow and graceful dance.

My husband poured each of us some wine, and we raised our glasses to toast. Not to four-star resorts and Caribbean cruises, nor to more possessions or living to impress others.

Not even to our glorious past.

Instead, we toasted the beautiful challenge of re-learning a love for things we'd long since forgotten. Things that don't cost a cent or take up space in the garage or on my fingers.

We toasted to dreams hatched during these times of trial. To a love that endured, even thrived through our long walk through the fire, when all that was left were tears and ashes. And us.

We sat drinking silently, without words. No need to waste them. They weren't necessary. Not after thirty years together.

Had I — had we — learned from the hard time?

Yes, but for too long, like snapping a wishbone, I'd kept wishing for a miracle to save us, to return our lives to the way they'd been. It took a while for me to realize a different sort of miracle had occurred. Our lives had been restored. Not our lifestyle, our lives.

My gaze swept the area, taking in the trees, the creek, my dog, and my lifetime mate. My best friend.

David took my hand, bringing it to his lips for a gentle kiss. A moment later, he repeated his signature statement — his mantra. "It doesn't get any better than this, does it?"

I nodded. He was right.

It doesn't. It couldn't.

Life itself, with nothing added, is rich and joyous. And beautiful. Inside, my heart gave a little flip. Yes, he was right.

— Heidi Gaul —

Zooming into the Twenty-First Century

My computer could be more encouraging. You know,
instead of "invalid password," why not something like,
"Ooooh, you're so close!"?
~Lisa Porter

Zooming into the 21st century, COVID-19 hit our senior writers' group with a double whammy. The church in which we met closed its doors, and the state of North Carolina prohibited the gathering of more than ten people. What in the world were we going to do?

Our group is blessed with remarkable, talented people who have been gathering weekly for more than eight years. We've become a tightly knit bunch. It looked like our precious hours together, sharing and critiquing our work, would have to be put on hold indefinitely. As the founder and mentor of the group, I felt a special burden to somehow keep things going but had no idea how. That's when one of our members, Dea, suggested an online meeting service called Zoom that she used in her real-estate work. This would, she assured me, make it possible for us to have a virtual meeting, reading our work to each other just like always.

I thought there was no way I could do this. All I knew about the

Internet was e-mail and the occasional text. I'm seventy-two. I was way too old for this sort of thing.

I mentioned the idea to my twenty-something niece. She lives in Denver and offered to help me long-distance. "It's simple, Aunt Ellen. You'll love it! Between Dea and me, we'll help you get the hang of it."

I had my doubts, but she showed me where the website was and how to start a free membership. It looked easy. "Maybe she's right!" I said to myself as we signed off. "I can do this!" Soon, I was hopelessly lost. They wanted my e-mail address and my Facebook password. I could never remember passwords. I had to get the hang of this, or our beloved writers' group would join the ranks of organizations closed by COVID-19. I was stuck again, so I consulted Dea. She helped me through a few more of the numerous steps to sign up.

"See you tomorrow for our writers' group!" I said breezily. On our Facebook page, I gave everybody the link to use the next day. That night, I decided to take a practice run at signing on. "If you don't receive an e-mail from us," the site said, "try another e-mail address." So, I did. Somehow I managed to open three separate memberships under three different e-mail addresses — complete with passwords!

The next day, I was up before the sun. I'd noticed that the camera on the computer added ten years to my appearance, so I piled on the make-up and picked out a brand-new top to wear. (Now I know that everyone refers to that as their "Zoom shirt.") I was sitting at my computer an hour early when I heard a faint voice. It was our group's resident expert on all things police and military.

"I hear you, but I can't see you," I was told.

I clicked on a tab. Nothing happened. Soon, we were joined by two more members, who both claimed they could see me and each other. A modicum of success. I pressed more tabs. Still no help.

Then Dea came on board. Soon, with her guidance, I was visible in all my glory. Within minutes, we were off and running, joined by four more members, including my niece in Denver. It was just like old times, with each person reading a piece of their work, but the best part was the laughter and fellowship that inspire us from week to week. My prayers were answered. Turns out that a seventy-two-year-old grandma can learn how to do something new on the Internet. I just had to remember how to do it again the next week!

—E.E. Kennedy—

9

Turning Sixty and Crazy

*I think everybody's weird. We should all celebrate
our individuality and not be embarrassed
or ashamed of it.*
~Johnny Depp

When I turned sixty, I decided to shed my reserved nature and allow my sense of humor to peek out. Most people appeared to like the new me, except for my youngest son, Hyrum.

"Mom, you can't be acting all crazy at the wedding shower," newly engaged Hyrum said. "Cara's family isn't used to you. You need to behave."

"Okay," I said, trying not to show that my feelings were hurt.

Hyrum had recently become engaged to Cara, a lovely and vivacious girl. My husband Larry and I were thrilled.

However, Hyrum's admonition that I needed to behave at the shower cut deeply. When had I ever not behaved?

I posed the question to Larry.

He took what was meant to be a rhetorical question and answered seriously. "Well, there was the time that you switched everyone's name tags at your aunt's eightieth birthday party."

"Okay," I said grudgingly. "But people had a great time figuring out who everyone was."

"And there was the time you texted weird messages from your sister's phone, pretending to be her. And the times you made up things for the church bulletin."

I type our church's weekly bulletin. Occasionally, I like to mix things up a bit and add a bit of humor to the otherwise bland announcements.

Larry was definitely on a roll.

I held up a hand to put an end to his litany of evidence. "Okay. Okay. I get it."

Maybe Hyrum had a point. I resolved to be on my best behavior. The night of the shower, I dressed conservatively and put on my game face, i.e., sweet and demure.

At the shower, I murmured hello to Cara's aunt, the hostess, and other members of her family. I made certain that I didn't say anything that could possibly be construed as "crazy."

Over the course of the evening, I sensed Cara looking at me oddly. I sent her a blithe smile and concentrated on the shower game of matching kitchen utensils to people's names.

"Jane, are you all right?" Cara asked when it came time to leave. "You weren't yourself tonight."

"Sure I was."

"I told my family that you were full of surprises, and you didn't do anything even remotely surprising."

"Hyrum told me that I had to behave," I confessed. "I didn't want to embarrass you or him."

Cara's pretty face took on a fierce look. "I'll be talking to him about that."

The following morning, I received a call from Hyrum. "Mom, Cara told me that I ruined the shower by telling you not to act crazy. I'm sorry."

Since then, I have gone back to my crazy ways.

When Hyrum and Cara had their first baby, both sets of grandparents attended the christening.

After Cara's mother held baby Wyatt and cooed over him, Hyrum placed his son in my arms. "This is your other grandma." He lowered his voice. "She's the crazy one."

And that's fine with me.

—Jane McBride—

Chapter 2

Try Something New

10

Realizing a Dream

It's never too late to start something new,
to do all those things that you've been longing to do.
~Dallas Clayton

was standing in a building that resembled a circus ring, looking up at skinny ladders, a maze of wires, and a thin trapeze bar. To the instructors, I looked out of place — not surprising since I showed up wearing pink shorts and a flowered tank top.

"What brings you here?" asked one kindly young man as he wrapped his arm around me in the same way he would comfort his grandmother. In my mind, I could hear him saying, "There, there."

"I'm really fifty years late," I replied. "I should have done this many years ago."

I had signed up for a beginner trapeze class. The instructors were lean and young. So were the other participants. When I signed the release form requesting my insurance information, I put "Medicare."

Ever since I was a young girl doing cartwheels across the back yard and climbing walls barefooted, I'd been fascinated by circus performers — specifically the beautiful ladies on the flying trapeze. I often dreamed of standing on the platform at the top of a tent in a glittering costume, waiting to let loose and swing to the opposite end while performing gravity-defying tricks in the air.

I've always been agile, but the decades have stiffened some of my muscles. So my heart beat rapidly as the participants lined up to try out the stationary bar before climbing the "real" apparatus. As I watched the others, so many questions zoomed through my mind: Could I lift my body up high enough to mount the bar? (I'm short.) Could I flip my body around the bar without letting go? Could I dismount without spraining an ankle?

But I did okay—better than some who were young enough to be my children. That gave my confidence a small boost.

Next, each of us was strapped into a waist harness attached to a wire—in case the worst should happen. Then, one by one, we climbed up the narrow wooden ladder to the platform. The instructor helped position each person as they grabbed the trapeze, leaned forward and waited for the quick "Go" command. We were supposed to immediately lift our legs and hang our knees over the bar on the way out, then release hands to hang upside down. The trapeze slows down when it comes back, and the trick doesn't work well if you're not fast enough. You just have to let go and drop into the net below.

Yes, that's what happened my first time. The sensation of flying in the air was so exciting that I didn't react quickly enough to complete the trick. But we got a second chance to try it, and I did much better.

Then it was time for the main event—fly out, knees up, hands off, and swing upside down for a split second before a hunky acrobat on the other end of the apparatus catches you mid-air.

Whew! Could I do that? I knew that it would take rapid-fire movements, and I still felt so unsure and new at this. My turn came. I could feel my heart beating as I climbed the ladder to the platform. I could barely reach the trapeze without stepping off the platform, but I held on and waited for the instructor to shout, "Go!"

Then immediately, "Knees up!"

"Hands off!"

"Look back!"

All this had to be done on the first swing out. Hesitate, and you miss the grab. Eight seconds to complete the trick.

I did it! I swung out, quickly wrapped knees around the bar and let go. Before I could think about what was happening, I felt two strong hands grasp my wrists as the trapeze swung back toward the platform. I hung on in disbelief for a few seconds until I realized it was over, and it was time to drop into the net.

I did it! That was all I could think when dismounting the tall net by doing a somersault over the edge. The instructor came over, and instead of a "there, there" pat on the back, he raised my arms in victory. His smile was almost as bright as mine.

And that wasn't all. With my unexpected success, the trapeze instructors realized I could do more. So, they taught me some new tricks and let me try those, too.

This was truly a dream come true. But I learned more than how to fly on a trapeze that day. I learned that it's never too late to try new things. Now I'm not afraid to step out of my comfort zone with activities such as ziplining, hang gliding, parasailing, paragliding, Flyboarding, and skydiving. I've traveled worldwide to fascinating places including Antarctica, India, Nepal, Cuba, and seven countries in Africa.

— Beverly Burmeier —

11

Turning Point

*If you're waiting until you feel talented enough
to make it, you'll never make it.*
~Criss Jami, Healology

A s I filled out the form for *America's Got Talent*, I giggled. Here I was, nearly seventy years old, about to make a complete U-turn. I thought back on how my life had been chopped into three distinct pieces.

It started with an amazing childhood. Thanks to a military dad, we traveled all over the world. My life was like the movie *It's a Wonderful Life*, but my wonderful life didn't last.

The next forty years weren't as easy. My problems started with the belief that I was supposed to get married and have kids. In my mind, I didn't have a choice. I had been subtly indoctrinated. Obediently, I got married at a young age and had kids.

It wasn't all bad. Three children, dozens of foster children, reconnecting with God, and a master's degree were the good parts. However, when my second husband and I split, I felt like I was falling and falling with nothing to grab. If I wasn't a wife, who was I? I was a half-person, searching for the other half.

After kissing another disappointing date goodbye, I whined to one of my friends, "Isn't there anyone out there?"

"You know what they say…"

I shook my head. "What?"

"Men our age are looking for a nurse or a purse."

My heart sank, but after thinking about it for several days, a light went on. Did I really need to get married? Maybe I could be a whole person without a husband. It took a year or two to sink in, but when it did, it was a huge turning point!

Watching chick flicks and romantic comedies with my girlfriends was a blast. My grandkids and I got high on the smell of freshly baked chocolate-chip cookies. Teaching Sunday school became a blessing instead of a burden.

Finally, I could look at men as friends, instead of sizing them up as "The Future Mr. Barbara McCourtney." I was an eagle, soaring on an updraft.

One of the best decisions I ever made was taking tango lessons. The clear beat of "Hernando's Hideaway" and the way my partner twirled me around the dance floor made me dizzy with delight. When the singer would end with "Olé!" I would stomp my foot and jerk my head. It was perfect (except I didn't have a rose between my teeth).

Now, instead of hunting for a husband, I had more time to pursue my real passion: writing my first book. An idea had been churning in my head for years, so writer's block was not a problem. When I turned on my computer, it shouted, "It's about time!"

Seven years later, my book, *Does This Diet Make My Butt Look Fat?* was published on Amazon. What a thrill, except my publisher told me I had to do my own marketing. Marketing? I didn't have a clue what that meant, but they threw down the gauntlet and I accepted.

I started with book signings. People poured out praise, but one smiling lady stood out from the rest. "Your book is hilarious," she said. "You should do stand-up comedy." It stuck in my head like a bug trapped in a spider web. Comedy? Maybe… I could use it to market my book, but how?

When I got home, I Googled, "*America's Got Talent* tryouts." I filled out the information, grinning at the question, "What is your talent?" I typed, "Comedian." Next question, "How long have you been doing this?" I answered, "Never," knowing I would be rejected. I called my daughter, and we had a good laugh.

An hour later, I opened my laptop. *America's Got Talent* had responded, "Here's your ticket." My jaw dropped. "Oh, no! I better think of something, quick!"

I sat down and wrote a comedy routine. Later, I performed it for my son and granddaughter. They loved it. After that, I did a different routine for my girlfriends. Everyone laughed and encouraged me. Some had suggestions. I gladly accepted.

On February first, I flew to Los Angeles, and then took an Uber to the Pasadena Pavilion. I wasn't sure if it was the right place, but when I got out of the car, I saw a mustached man wearing a pink tutu. Clearly, I had arrived.

I discovered this was only a precursor to the real thing. In spite of it all, this was the most exhilarating thing I had ever done. The director took about seventy-five of us outside and held a megaphone to her mouth. "Everyone, walk toward the camera over there. Keep walking. Smile and wave. Keep walking." After that, she told us, "Go back and wait for further instructions." We waited together in a tight-knit cluster for twenty minutes. That's when it got interesting.

One guy burst out with "We will, we will rock you," while the rest of us sang along, clapping and stomping. Another guy did a magic act. There was a large group of little girls in sparkling purple dance costumes, chatting and giggling. Someone started singing, "Pretty Woman." We joined in. The harmony was better than The Tabernacle Choir at Temple Square. I met a tiny Asian lady in her nineties who had been a comedian her whole life. Everyone was so talented that I couldn't imagine anyone being eliminated. The director got out her megaphone again. "Okay, everyone! Take two! Action!" It was just like in the movies.

Later, we returned to the pavilion where we waited to perform. Finally, the announcer called my number. I inhaled deeply as I stepped into a room about the size of a high-school gymnasium. Two young ladies sat behind a desk. They introduced themselves and asked a lot of questions. They looked surprised when I told them I had never done this before. Then one of them took out her camera. "Are you ready?"

I nodded and began. "I loved grade school, but junior high wasn't as much fun because I wasn't developing like the other girls. I knew I was flat-chested when I was asked to be the poster girl for International House of Pancakes."

The two ladies howled throughout my routine, making it hard for me to keep a straight face. When I finished, the lady with the camera wiped away a tear and said, "Thank you. Someone will contact you in three or four weeks."

Shortly after I flew home, the COVID-19 pandemic hit. I researched *America's Got Talent*. Their website said, "We most likely will start this summer." It sounded like they didn't know for sure. Finally, after eight long weeks, they said, "Stay home but send us your video." Another chance! My granddaughter came over and recorded my new routine.

I'm still waiting, but whether I make it or not, I'm not worried. I have new goals: polishing my act, backyard barbecues with my family, and writing my next book. As soon as our country opens up, I'm going to start my career as a stand-up comedian. I never knew life could be so much fun.

It took a while to get here, but turning seventy will be the best birthday ever.

— Barbara McCourtney —

12

Pedaling My Way Through Fear

*Nothing compares to the simple pleasure
of riding a bike.
~John F. Kennedy*

"You're going to buy me a bicycle? I don't think so," I replied in horror. "Have you lost your mind or, better yet, have you forgotten how old I am?"

"No, I haven't, and what difference does it make?" my boyfriend said. "We are going on the adventure of a lifetime, and there will be lots of places to ride bikes. Everybody our age who travels full time in a motorhome has bicycles, and they ride them."

I could not believe my ears. We had spent the last few weeks packing up sixty-five years of memories, and it had not been an easy task. Deciding what goes, what stays, and what to store. Selling his house and renting out mine. Buying a forty-foot motorhome. Saying our goodbyes to family and friends.

We were leaving our old life to embrace a new one, and I felt that decision represented enough change for one old gal. So, there was no way I was going to entertain the idea of learning to ride a bicycle, even though I was in pretty good shape.

When I was six years old, a teenage girl from our church was hit by a car while riding a bike. She died instantly, right in front of her home. The entire community was in shock for months, and her parents eventually divorced, going their separate ways to manage their grief and try to make sense of their loss. My parents told me that bicycling would kill me. So, I never had a bike and never learned to ride.

Since we lived on a farm, tractors and pickup trucks became my primary sources of transportation. As I got older, I thought they were way cooler than bicycles anyway.

When I had two children of my own, I championed their desire to own bicycles, and we taught them to ride at an early age. I made sure they were well-schooled in bicycle safety. Of course, I never gave a thought to buying one for myself.

Until now. We were going bicycle shopping at Walmart, where we would pick out a bike, bring it home, and I would have a quick lesson. Then, it would be secured to the bike rack mounted on the rear of the motorhome. My boyfriend made it sound so matter of fact, like picking up the mail, taking out the trash, or walking the dog.

I didn't want to mess up my new life before it started and I knew I needed to face my unrealistic fear, so I decided to go along with this. One is never too old to learn a new skill, I told myself.

As reasonable as it all sounded in my head, I couldn't help throwing out a few alternative suggestions on the way into town. "You know, the three-wheeler seems to be gaining popularity among our age group. That might be a better fit for me, don't you think?"

"Won't fit on the bike rack I bought," he said, parking close to the pick-up lane at the store's entrance.

"How about an electric bike? I hear they are catching on with everybody."

"Too expensive," he said. "Besides, just think of all the exercise we'll get riding our bikes around the campgrounds. And don't forget all the trails we'll discover along the way. Relax. There's nothing to it. It'll be fun."

He had made up his mind. I was getting a "real" bicycle, and as we looked at the gigantic selection, I saw more types of bikes than I ever knew existed. There were mountain bikes, trick bikes, tandem bikes and road bikes, to name a few. And I had to admit that none looked dangerous. After I chose a simple commuting bike, we were on our way to my first lesson.

I had chosen a polished turquoise and hot pink beauty sitting tall on her 26-inch wheels. She sported an adjustable rearview mirror, a large black wire shopping basket, a silver warning bell for passing, and a 10-speed control mounted on the handlebars just above the handbrake that was my new best friend.

With sweaty palms and a racing heart, I awkwardly gripped the handlebars and balanced on those two wheels. There were a few sudden stops and shaky starts over the course of the next thirty minutes, but I did it. I learned how to ride a bike — decades later than the rest of my generation.

Since that day more than seven years ago, I have ridden through the crowded streets of Key West and tackled bumpy, unruly trails in campgrounds throughout Texas, California and Virginia. Bicycling has truly enhanced my retirement years, given me more self-confidence and, more importantly, taught me that a simple courageous act knows no age.

— BJ Whitley —

13

Birthday Balloon

Courage is being scared to death,
but saddling up anyway.
~John Wayne

"We're going where!" It was more of an exclamation than a question. "We're going to do what?" Now that was a real question, because I wasn't sure I had heard right.

And so my daughter repeated it. "We're taking you to Colorado to celebrate your eightieth birthday. And we're all going on a hot-air-balloon ride."

I almost started hyperventilating; my thoughts were spinning. I took a moment to let it sink in. "A hot-air-balloon ride?"

"Mom, don't you want to go? I remember you wanting to on your fiftieth birthday. And I want to help you fulfill your bucket list."

"Honey, eighty is a long way from fifty."

"You're not afraid, are you?"

I didn't want to admit it, but that was the reason I hadn't gone decades ago.

She continued excitedly, "We've got a lodge reserved for your birthday week in July."

Now I was backed in a corner. "Who's the 'we'?"

"It's going to be all girls: me, your three daughters-in-law, and your six granddaughters. I've contacted each of them, and they're all in."

My mind was whirling. My three daughters-in-law! One was local, one in Tennessee, and another in Hawaii.

And my granddaughters—they were scattered even farther, in Arkansas, North Carolina, Tennessee, Alabama, Illinois, and far away Australia.

"Did you say *all*?"

"Yes, all."

The tickets were purchased. The flights were scheduled. The lodge was booked.

To allay any fears, she sent me a link to watch a reporter taking her first ride with the company. I watched as they checked the wind, explained how the balloon was prepared, and finally her experience on the liftoff.

I can do this, I thought. It was time to start making my to-do list:

Pray

Mani/pedi

Lose weight

Pray

— Phyllis Nordstrom —

14

It's Never Too Late

My body is my journal, and my tattoos are my story.
~Johnny Depp

"**M**om, this is something you've wanted to do for as long as I can remember. Come on, it's the perfect time," my daughter avidly demanded as she grabbed my arm, determined to pull me out of the chaise lounge.

Jacqui was right. I'd been dreaming of getting a tattoo for years, so why was the thought suddenly so terrifying when the opportunity presented itself? Excuses gushed from my mouth: "What if it doesn't come out right?" "It might be overly conspicuous!" "I won't be able to go swimming for the rest of our vacation." "Maybe sixty-three is too old for a tattoo."

Admittedly, my excuses were lame. In truth, doing anything on a whim terrified me. Unlike my spontaneous daughter, I needed days to consider every detail before committing to new things.

But, according to Jacqui, there was no time to contemplate. She had not only made extensive inquiries, but she had confirmed my appointment with a well-recommended tattoo artist for 2:00 that afternoon. Not wanting to disappoint my enthusiastic daughter, I let her drag me up to our hotel room where I quickly changed out of my swimming suit into something more appropriate for our hour-long stroll along the streets of Reno toward my first tattoo parlor.

The rest of our group passed on the offer to tag along. Apparently, relaxing by the pool was more appealing than the thought of witnessing my demise.

I'd known for the past few years what my tattoo would be, but I hadn't checked out available designs. Since (for a variety of reasons) we'd always associated a dove with my husband's untimely death, it was definitely going to be a dove. I also knew it would be placed on the outside of my left ankle. Now, I was trusting my daughter to help me decide on the perfect size and image.

My apprehension dwindled with each step along the concrete sidewalk, and eager anticipation began to take over. By the time we entered the front door of the tiny shop, I was steadfast. At first glance, I was taken aback by the multi-tattooed artists and customers, but the intimidation didn't last long. To the contrary, I was captivated by the adventurous atmosphere, even though the majority of the clients and staff were younger than several of my grandchildren.

I thoroughly enjoyed every moment of the experience: choosing the perfect design, the slight stinging sensation of the needle moving across my skin, and the beautiful end result.

My step was a little lighter on our walk back to the hotel where I proudly showed off my new ink. You would have thought I'd won the Nobel Prize!

Perhaps "proud" is not a strong enough word; I remember my granddaughter remarking that I didn't wear long pants for over a year after getting my tattoo. Was I really that obvious?

I did, however, learn that tattoos are addicting. It wasn't long before I had the word "Believe" added to the inside of the same ankle, creating an eloquent bracelet. I've never regretted my decision to follow in the footsteps of some of my children and adult grandchildren. I only wish I'd found that confidence years earlier.

— Connie Kaseweter Pullen —

15

Adventures in Segway-ing

What would life be if we had no courage
to attempt anything?
~Vincent van Gogh

Silent auctions can be full of surprises. That's what I thought last spring at our local food-bank auction when my husband came back to our table and announced that he'd snagged the deal of the century. "I can't believe no one else bid on it," he said, handing me the flyer titled "Segway Scooter Adventure for Two."

Funny thing was, I could believe no one else would bid on it. I'd seen groups of helmeted twenty-somethings roll across intersections near our neighborhood. They looked like robots on a conveyer belt and never moved much faster than pedestrians. How could standing still on a machine qualify as fun or exercise?

Time passed and then several months later my husband reminded me that our Segway tour certificate was about to expire. We had to use it or lose it. He offered to find a more willing partner for the big adventure, but I wasn't about to miss out on a ride that some online reviewers had actually called spectacular, even breathtaking. At the least, I'd see for myself.

The same day I signed us up, my husband's co-worker announced that he was selling his Segway. He'd taken all the neighborhood joy rides he could handle, used it to haul home a few groceries, and now was ready to check that adventure off his bucket list. For a mere three thousand dollars, we could do the same. "We'll take the tour and see what we think," my dear husband added.

"Yeah, right," I snapped back. "I can think of a lot of things that would be higher on my bucket list."

On a warm, sunny morning in September, we arrived early at the Northwest Adventures office where we read and signed pages of waivers. My stomach churned as past athletic failures flashed in front of me. In my thirties, I'd tumbled and skinned my knees trying to balance on Rollerblades. In my forties, I'd taken nosedives into snowbanks learning to ski. Now, in my sixties, was I really ready to do this?

The only physical requirement, though, was the ability to stand up straight for ninety minutes. Surely these upright people-movers were safe and easy.

We met up in the alley behind the office with a much younger couple who were from out of town. Our tour guide, Cliff, explained his years of experience leading all kinds of adventures and told us about the British guy who bought Segway from its American inventor. "Do any of you know what happened to him?" he asked.

"Yup," my husband said with a smirk. "He went off a cliff on a Segway and died."

I glared at him. "No way! That's not true, is it?"

His half-smile faded.

"Why didn't you tell me?"

"Yes, unfortunately, it is true," he admitted to me.

Our guide broke in. "But don't worry. I'm the only Cliff on this tour."

The other couple laughed, and our guide quickly changed the subject. "We're taking the scenic route down to the beach today. One other thing," he said, "be sure not to step off your Segway unless I help you."

It turned out the other couple were experienced Segway riders who had done several tours. "In San Francisco, you're required to take the flat-street tour before you can ride any hills," the woman whispered to me. "I can't believe they're taking first-timers down a big hill."

Yikes! Maybe I could faint on the spot, induce vomiting or drop to the ground in a seizure. Did I dare hope for a natural disaster? A windstorm? An earthquake? Nothing was forthcoming. There was no graceful way to back out. I took a deep breath and donned my helmet as our leader made the rounds to "start our engines." Although he turned the keys on our equipment, they remained eerily silent.

"Don't worry." Cliff must have sensed my anxiety. "We'll stay in 'turtle mode' to begin with. Riding a Segway is intuitive. You will soon become one with the machine."

So, who was this guy anyway — the Dalai Lama? I tried to slow my breathing, grabbed the handlebars and stepped into position.

"Now apply pressure on the foot pad with the balls of your feet, and you will move forward."

Whoa! How could five miles an hour feel so fast?

"Lean back on your heels, and you will slow down."

Okay, but…

"You won't completely stop. Just keep moving slowly back and forth."

"What?" I gasped. *No brakes! Was he kidding?* I rocked my feet slowly. The movement was subtle. Gradually, I felt my body relaxing into the machine. I checked my watch — only an hour and fifteen minutes to go. Maybe I could survive after all.

"Now tilt the handlebars to the left and then the right." Cliff watched as we practiced turns moving up and down on the patchwork of asphalt. "It's like riding a horse."

Minutes later, our little band of Segway riders rolled to the end of the alley. With pretend confidence, I forged ahead as we took to the side streets. "There's very little traffic here, so we'll command the road," our guide said, as we rolled down the street.

When a blue minivan appeared on the horizon, I was riding near the front of the pack. Cliff called out, "Move to the side. But don't get too close to the curb."

I panicked. Suddenly competing with an advancing minivan traveling twenty-five miles per hour, I headed straight for the curb at the breakneck speed of three miles per hour. Instead of turning before

I hit the curb, I rammed straight into it. A millisecond later, I was thrust into a thorny patch of blackberries, trapped under a hundred-pound Segway. The minivan cruised on by, seemingly unaware, as four Segway riders surrounded me, hovering like silent helicopters in a holding pattern.

"Oh dear! Oh dear!" Cliff's voice rose two octaves. He was so alarmed I wondered later if I was his first casualty. Surely this had happened before. "Are you hurt?" He pulled the machine off me. "Are you sure you're okay?"

Except for a twisted ankle and a scraped knee, I was physically fine. Only my ego was bruised, and Cliff's constant questions didn't help. He seemed convinced I was hiding severe trauma.

Fortunately, no more mishaps occurred on our mile-long ride down a back road through the woods to the beach. We encountered only one slow-moving automobile, and I had time to get used to the Segway sensation. Momentum plays no part in the ride; there is no freewheeling. The experience seemed surreal, like how I imagined it would feel gliding on the surface of the moon.

We remained in turtle mode all the way down, and I felt more and more confident by the time we reached the beach. Our rolling contingent turned out to be quite a spectacle for morning walkers when we moved along the boardwalk and stopped on the pier for a photo op. Besides all the curious looks, grins and thumbs up, several people appeared eager to take the tour. "This is the best way to promote tours," Cliff said as he handed out company business cards.

We were just over an hour into our journey when he guided us to his little-known route back. "You'll need the extra power to make it up the hill," he announced as he adjusted our machines to full throttle. We turned onto a narrow street behind several homes and headed up a steep incline. This time, there was no traffic. We accelerated to a top speed of twelve miles an hour and "rip-roared" through the final leg of our trip and back down the alley where it all began.

"So, what did you think?" my husband asked as we headed home after our adventure.

"I guess the reviewers were right," I chuckled. "It did take my breath away when the Segway landed on top of me."

"I'd do it again," he said. "But I think we can cross that one off our bucket list."

"It was never on mine," I reminded him. "At least we can save three thousand dollars."

"Aww, come on. I saw you grinning when we rode along the boardwalk."

"Okay, it was better than I expected, just overrated."

"Speaking of bucket lists...."

Oh, no! One look at my dear husband, and I knew we weren't done yet.

He held up the full-color flyer that he'd picked up in the Northwest Adventure's office. "Look at this. They do parasailing right off the pier downtown. Now that really looks like fun."

—Maureen Rogers—

16

Erma and the Bag Lady

A professional writer is an amateur who didn't quit.
~Richard Bach

I saw the bag of my dreams at the Nutcracker Market in Houston one November. Shaped like a miniature typewriter with rhinestone jewels for the keys and "Once Upon a Time" scrolled across the top, the purse twinkled at me under the fluorescent lights.

The salesclerk had to pry it out of my hands to wrap it in tissue and place it in a shopping bag. "It's our last one." She noticed my tears. "You must really like typewriters."

Embarrassed, I wiped my eyes. "I have to have it," I whispered. "I want to be a writer one day."

I took my treasure home and displayed it on the fireplace mantel in my bedroom, where it gathered dust like a forgotten dream. *One day, I'll use it,* I thought, *even though it's impractical, something to be pulled out for special occasions. One day, I'll be a writer.* But that was impractical, too. In the meantime, I kept my purse and my secret wish carefully hidden at home.

Few people knew I belonged to a writing critique group. Years ago, I shared one of my stories with the members. In my usual self-deprecating style, I read them "Spin Cycle," my story about the horror and humiliation of teaching my first spinning class.

The group howled with laughter at the description of the middle-aged woman sweating on a bike, wearing spandex in a room full of young, fit people, her varicose vein pulsing to the beat of "I Will Survive." Whether they were laughing with me or at me didn't matter. They were laughing, and it warmed my heart.

The leader chuckled. "There's a workshop for humor writers." He tapped something on his laptop and showed me the screen: Erma Bombeck Writers' Workshop.

A spark of excitement ignited in my heart. He scrolled down the page. Dayton, Ohio. My shoulders slumped. Recently divorced with three young children, traveling solo across the country was a work of fiction. I read the fine print at the bottom: "Sold out."

Still, a tiny flame burned deep within me. I slipped the workshop into my mental "One Day" file.

Intrigued, I subscribed to the Erma newsletter and learned the workshop was only offered every two years, and it sold out within hours. In the meantime, my children graduated high school and college. One got married. I remarried.

Almost a decade passed before the timing was right, and everything fell into place like words on a page. I continued following the website and saw the workshop was accepting humorous submissions for an anthology on aging. On a whim, I dug out "Spin Cycle" and sent it in. Then, because I was aging too, I promptly forgot about it.

The day registration opened for the 2018 workshop, my fingers flew across my keyboard. With a flying leap of faith, I clicked "Submit." And waited. My heart soared when the registration confirmation flashed across the screen. I performed a victory dance in my study. My "One Day" was only four months away.

When I joined the Facebook page for attendees and studied photos from past workshops, my courage crumbled. These women were writers, every one of them. They had books and blogs and bios. They had attitude and ambition. More than one wore a tiara on top of her pink hair. I would never fit in. I feared I'd be the oldest, most unfunny woman there.

The morning of my flight, I was wheeling my suitcase out of my bedroom. As an afterthought, I grabbed my typewriter purse off the mantel and stuffed it into my carry-on.

Hours later, I stumbled into the University of Dayton Marriott, weary from travel. In my room, a downy, king-sized bed beckoned me, and more than anything I wanted to disappear under the warm folds of the comforter. Room service would taste a lot better than an awkward dinner with strangers.

But, in honor of Erma, I mustered up my courage, hung my name tag around my neck, and reapplied my lipstick. I pulled out my little typewriter purse. One drink at the bar, one pass through the bookstore, and I'd slip into the dining room and sit in a spot close to the door. I could stash my sparkly purse under the table and crawl down there with it if I was out of place.

I ordered a cocktail, strolled by a table with Erma swag for sale and spotted copies of the anthology I'd submitted my story to months earlier: *Laugh Out Loud*. I drew in my breath. The cover was bright red, with laughing faces framing the title. I quickly turned to the table of contents and searched for my name. Then my heart sank. "40 Women Humorists Celebrate Then and Now... Before We Forget." They'd chosen forty women humorists... My silly spin-cycle story by an unpublished mom from Houston must have crashed and burned on the editing table. My typewriter purse sagged at my elbow.

I was thinking about skipping the banquet when a woman behind me tapped me on the shoulder. She had an engaging smile and a copy of *Laugh Out Loud* in the crook of her arm. "I love your handbag!" Her excited voice carried, and soon a group gathered around, admiring my typewriter. "What a perfect purse for a writer."

Somehow, my bag had introduced me to women who were just my type. Although it was too small to hold much more than a few freshly printed business cards and my room key, it was growing on me. It held my heart and a whole lot of dreams.

The woman gestured to two writers beside her. "Want to sit with us at dinner?"

"Yes!" I smiled, grateful for the invitation.

We entered the ballroom and sat down. As the waiters served us wine, my new friend leafed through the anthology. She checked my name tag again. "Why didn't you tell us you were one of the authors in the book?" She pointed a polished fingernail at "Spin Cycle."

I grabbed her book and turned to the table of contents. It was then I noticed it was divided into two sections, Then and Now. My story wasn't listed in the first part but held a glorious place in the second.

My heart soared. Suddenly, I was more than a middle-aged mom with a Mac. I wasn't just full of wit. I was a writer. What a novel idea! Not only that, I was a humorist. It said so on the cover. And hearing someone say it out loud made me believe it could be true.

A new chapter of my life had begun.

At the end of the workshop, I didn't mind being left holding the bag. In fact, I carried my little typewriter home with pride.

Erma once said, "When I stand before God at the end of my life, I would hope that I would not have a single bit of talent left, and could say, 'I used everything you gave me.'"

I'd like to think she'd add, "Life is short. Buy the handbag. And never stop purse-suing your dream."

— Tassie Kalas —

17

High Flying

The courage to soar to great heights is inside all of us.
~Kerri Strug

On Mother's Day 2002, a few months after I turned sixty-one, my husband planned a special treat for me. He knew how much I love being high in the air. In the prior ten years, I'd been parasailing in Cabo San Lucas, Mazatlán, San Diego and Hawaii, gone hot-air ballooning alongside the Rockies in Colorado, been up in a glider plane, and flown in a bi-plane — leather helmet and all. Before that, I'd stood on top of the Twin Towers and looked over the edge at all the tiny people down below. Even a tall Ferris wheel excites me when it stops, and I'm sitting on top for a few minutes.

My husband drove me out to a wide field in Jamul in Southern California where I soon learned I would be skydiving. Whoopee! He was not about to jump out of a perfectly good plane, but he knew I'd be up for it.

We were led into a room where I was given a stack of papers requiring my initials and signature on each page declaring I would not hold the company liable for my death or dismemberment. I began to wonder if perhaps I should rethink this adventure.

With the paperwork out of the way, I joined a half-dozen other people, mostly men much younger than me, in a room where we were shown a video explaining the how-tos of skydiving. As I climbed into a jumpsuit, the instructor told us not to worry if our main parachute fails to open. He said, "You'll be fine because we have a secondary parachute that's controlled by a computer."

I raised my hand and announced, "I wasn't worried until you mentioned it."

Before I knew it, I was boarding a small plane with the others, mostly military types who did this sort of thing as naturally as I sit on a beach and read a novel. Some of the young men planned to jump solo while others, like me, were jumping in tandem with an instructor.

On the way to the drop spot, the videographer aimed his camera at me and asked how I felt. I grinned wide and said, "I feel great." Then I added, "I'm doing this with thoughts of my mom who went parasailing at age seventy-seven. The thrill of flying high seems to be part of our DNA."

As the plane neared the designated spot, the young daredevils jumped through the door first. Then my instructor attached himself to me, and we inched our way down the aisle and toward the open door.

The wind whipped by me as I stood in the doorway of the small airplane, three miles above the green and brown Southern California fields. The instructor encouraged me to lean back, let go, and step out into nothingness. Easy for him to say. The videographer had already jumped and was floating in the air waiting to film my first skydive.

Without a moment to rethink what I was doing, we were out of the plane and falling through the air. I saw the videographer ahead with his camera aimed at me. What I didn't know until viewing the film later was that my face was highly contorted by the speed, giving me a whole new look. As we freefell at one hundred twenty miles an hour for a full sixty seconds, I felt water from the clouds going up my nose and had the strange sensation of drowning while high in the air. When that feeling passed, I relaxed and began to enjoy myself. I was soaring free as a bird through the sky. (The only difference between me and a bird was that I had a man lying on my back.) I looked around and admired the view spread out below me. How beautiful!

Since everything looked so small, I had no idea how the man attached to me was going to land us at the airfield and not on some roof in Tijuana. Thank heavens that was his job, not mine.

During the ground training, I had asked if there would be a jolt when the chute opened and was told, "No, not at all." I guess when you do it a few times a day, you no longer feel the jolt; however, I felt as though something slammed into us as the chute opened and we started rising.

Then our speed slowed, and we began a gentle descent. As we got closer to the ground, I could see a field below us with colorful parachutes splayed on the ground and people standing around, including the videographer who had just landed. My instructor said, "Okay, we're ready to land, bring your knees up."

"Okay," I said and lifted my knees.

He snapped at me. "I said bring your knees up!"

Obviously, he was used to agile young men and not middle-aged ladies. "That's as high as these old knees will go," I said.

We hit the ground, and it didn't take long to find out why my knees needed to be lifted high. My feet touched land before the instructor's did, and I fell face-first onto the dirt with him spread-eagle on top of me. And the videographer captured it all in living color.

The instructor quickly unhooked himself from me, stood, and offered his hand to help me up. I lay there a while, a little dazed and a whole lot embarrassed. I knew I needed to stand, but my knees and arm were scraped and hurting. Slowly, I rose, brushed the dirt off my face, and limped toward the restroom.

Once inside the ladies' room, the aging woman in the mirror who looked back at me had a smile of delight on her face. After all, I had just jumped out of an airplane and soared through the air — my greatest high-flying experience of all time!

— Linda Loegel —

Going the Distance

Life begins at the end of your comfort zone.
~Neale Donald Walsch

Getting divorced after thirty years of marriage was tough. My kids were grown, so I was suddenly all alone. Each day seemed harder to get through than the last, which is why I was pleased to hear my younger brother's voice on the phone. Rob had experienced a painful divorce himself a few years earlier, so he understood what I was going through.

"Hey, Sis," he said. "Why don't you drive out here and stay in my condo for six weeks?"

Two hours north of Seattle Rob owned a vacation condo at water's edge with Mt. Baker's snowy peak in the background. I lived in Kansas City, 1,836 miles to the east.

"Oh, Rob, I couldn't drive all that way. By myself? It's too far."

"It will be an adventure," Rob said. "Do you good."

Hmmm. If you look up "adventure" in the dictionary, it will read, "unusual, exciting, possibly hazardous activity."

Still, didn't those words define divorce, too? Like it or not, in the second half of life, I was now on my own. Maybe I should test myself.

For a week, I vacillated until finally deciding, *Okay, I'll do it!* And I upped the ante. Our family had camped a lot in years gone by. I still had a two-person tent. More than merely driving across Kansas, Colorado, Wyoming, Utah, Idaho, and Washington, why not camp out the three nights I'd be on the road? And I'd started bicycling again.

Why not strap my bicycle onto my car?

So, I packed my tent, bike, computer, clothes and an armload of books on tape. All I lacked was a phone, but this was 1995 before everyone carried a smartphone.

As I headed out of my driveway, I felt as nervous as I imagined a prairie woman might have felt driving a covered wagon across the plains. My first day took me across Kansas into Colorado. In late afternoon, I headed to a campground in the foothills beyond Boulder, Colorado. Each campsite had a picnic table surrounded by tall pines, and each site was far enough away from the others to feel secluded. I was proud of the way I set up my tent, but as purple dusk turned dark, and I climbed into my sleeping bag, I heard rustlings among the trees. Abruptly, I was gripped with a panicky awareness: What if a bear — or a person — barged into my tent? I remembered a news story about two women who were murdered while hiking the Appalachian Trail.

It was all I could do to keep from pulling up stakes and heading for the nearest Holiday Inn. But I forced myself to stay put. Wasn't my life full of dark unknowns right now? It had been a long day's drive. Even uneasy fear could not keep me awake for long.

When I awoke, the sun was just coming up. I climbed out of my tent, did a big stretch, pulled on my sandals and — suddenly elated — called out, "Good morning, world!" It took me just twenty minutes to break camp, get back on the freeway, find a McDonald's and head west.

On my second night, I found a campground outside Provo, Utah. Campsites were less secluded here, and I enjoyed meeting some of the other campers. Everyone seemed impressed that I was traveling on my own. For the first time, I thought I might be able to navigate this new life I'd been pushed into.

After my third night of camping — this time in Idaho — I met my brother in Seattle, and we caravanned north to his condo near Bellingham, Washington.

"Holly and I will visit on weekends," he promised. "Otherwise, the condo is yours." Holly was Rob's girlfriend, and hearing her name reminded me that love could happen even after a marriage ended.

For the next several weeks, I bicycled the flat back roads around Bellingham. Some nights, I read novels until 2 or 3 a.m., relishing that I didn't need to turn out the light for a sleeping husband. Every morning, I sipped coffee on the condo's wooden deck and relaxed into the quiet. Gradually, I realized I liked my own company. Being alone in Rob's condo felt different from being alone at home. It felt less like an ending and more like a beginning.

Eventually, I returned to Kansas City to deal with financial issues related to my divorce. My tranquil feelings disappeared. Yet I carried with me the memory that in camping and driving to Seattle, I had done something way outside my comfort zone. If I could do this, perhaps I could navigate my new life.

When my next-door neighbor Gloria, whose husband had died the previous year, knocked on my door, I was surprised to see her looking so happy. Gloria was in her sixties, and she and Ralph had been high-school sweethearts. The depth of her grief had been painful to see. But today she was smiling. "I did it, Barbara! And it makes me believe, well, as if I can go on even without Ralph."

And what had she done? Gloria had driven from Kansas City to Topeka, Kansas, a distance of sixty-five miles! She had never driven that far by herself; Ralph always did the driving.

I almost laughed aloud. She thought sixty-five miles was a big deal? Why, I had driven 3,672 round-trip miles all by myself! But as I looked at the sparkle in her eyes and her newly straightened shoulders, I realized something. Whether by divorce or death, when we are thrust out of what we thought was a life in which we would always have a beloved, it is a terrible twist to the heart. And in that place, distance doesn't matter. Getting past the fear matters. It's waking up to the knowledge that: Yes! If I did this, I can do the rest.

I can go on.

— Barbara Bartocci —

Chapter
3

Older & Wiser

Facing My Fears

I'm ever-changing and always evolving,
always trying new things.
~Thomas Rhett

was telling my friend about planning my latest trip. I was going to the Galápagos Islands aboard a hundred-foot yacht. I also told her about how I have this tendency to get seasick.

"Do you notice a pattern here?" she asked.

"What pattern?" I said.

She reminded me that when I went to Machu Picchu, I ended up hugging the side of the mountain half-scared out of my mind because I have a fear of heights. And although I complained often and loudly about how I couldn't stand the hot flashes I was experiencing, I chose to go to Borneo, which, in case I had forgotten, was on the equator and about 180 degrees in the shade.

"I repeat," she insisted, "a pattern."

"Hmmm," I said.

Not a profound response but a thoughtful one. Had I been purposefully doing those things that I most feared? Not long ago, I went hot-air ballooning, knowing that the only way for the balloon to go was up. Up high. I thought I could scrunch down in the basket beneath the balloon, but it was a lot shorter than I envisioned and too crowded for me to sit on the bottom. I imagined falling out and breaking bones I couldn't even pronounce, if I survived at all. It turned out to be pretty tame and incredibly beautiful, but until the balloon was aloft and we were floating calmly above the treetops, I was a wreck.

So why did I go? At this time of my life, when I could be avoiding my fears so successfully, I seem to be rushing headlong into them. My friend was right. I went ballooning quite specifically because I was scared.

Some people do risky things for the adrenaline kick. That isn't my motive. Growing up as a shy child, I spent so many years being afraid of so many things that I figure it's about time I start working through them. That doesn't mean I intend to go downhill skiing or bungee jumping any time soon. I have enough stuff to work around without giving myself a guaranteed heart attack.

I am not the only one doing this. Another friend went parasailing. Her fear was not being up in the air but coming down. What if the boat towing her didn't stop, and she was dragged in the water like a fish trying to get off a hook? Would she get hurt? But she went anyway. I told her next time we would go together so she could calm me down when we went up, and I could buoy her up when we came down.

I'm learning that the physical fears are easier to deal with than the emotional ones. Saying "I'm sorry" for the insensitive things I may have said or done to a dear friend is not easy. Forgiving someone for hurting me and truly letting the hurt go is a toughie. Speaking up for myself is perhaps highest on the list of fears. I don't like dissension. But there are times when it is important not only to stand in your truth but to express it as well.

When I am asked my opinion, I give it. Why not? Maybe I'll be disagreed with, but that is part of the give and take of conversations and makes them more interesting. I don't have to worry about being right all the time.

And I have come to know that I don't need to be perfect. Or the best. Participation is more satisfying than perfection. Chances are that there will be someone better than I am at almost everything, especially when I am learning a new skill. Whatever made me think I had to know how to do something perfectly from the very start? It kept me from doing lots of things. But no more.

Fear has become an amber caution light to me rather than a red stoplight. I look around, and if there isn't an authentic reason to be afraid other than my own reluctance, I may go for it. The best pattern for life may just be no pattern but a willingness to be in the world, whatever comes.

Maybe that is what I have been doing without realizing it — and discovering a new, exciting world in the process.

— Ferida Wolff —

Age Shouldn't Matter

Age is an issue of mind over matter.
If you don't mind, it doesn't matter.
~Mark Twain

He had recently moved up the tennis league's ladder and would compete against someone at a similar skill level. "Do you know who your opponent is?" I asked Allan. My husband explained that although he knew his opponent's name, he had never met him. That's when I saw a young man — about thirty years old — at the other end of the reception area.

The young man had large muscular arms, a well-built physique, and a smooth, shaved scalp. He reminded me of the man in the Mr. Clean commercials, only younger. The young man was using a skip rope at quite a fast pace; I thought he might be warming up for a tennis match. I smiled at my husband and said that might be his opponent. Allan gave me a doubtful smile, remarking it was an unusual way to prepare for a tennis match, as he continued completing his usual warm-up routine.

The league coordinator called out my husband's name, and then she called the young man. I smiled at my husband... the kind of smile wives give their husband when they were right about something. The coordinator gave them their court number. They introduced themselves to each other, shook hands, and headed off.

The young man was dressed in the latest trendy tennis apparel and looked fabulous. With his muscular build, he could have easily passed for a poster-boy athlete. Allan was at least thirty years older, much less muscular, and dressed in an ordinary tennis shirt and decidedly untrendy shorts. Allan's focus had always been on good tennis shoes, socks, and, of course, the almighty tennis racket.

Although the tennis center had twelve courts, Allan and his opponent had been assigned the court closest to the observation window. I had originally planned to read while they played tennis, but since I had a great view of their court, I decided to watch the game. I had noticed that the young man had given Allan the once-over when they met. I wondered if he had prejudged the older man's ability.

When they walked onto their court, it appeared the young man wasn't very keen on the placement of the players' bench. He lifted the bench up with one arm, holding it over his shoulder, and moved it to the other side of the court. I wondered if he was trying to fluster my husband. Allan met my eyes through the window and gave me an amused smile.

Their pre-game warm-up consisted of the usual ground strokes, volleys, overheads and then a couple of minutes of serving at the end. The young man played with confidence. It was almost as if he was showcasing his ability. Allan closely observed his various strokes and powerful serves, while casually returning each shot.

The young man quickly won the first game and was full of confidence at the start of the second game, especially when he won the first point. I watched with amusement as they volleyed the ball back and forth, knowing full well that Allan's mental toughness would prevail even after his slow start. Within minutes, he won the second game, and then he went on to win the first set 6–3. The young man had struggled through the last three games and began to show his frustration when Allan started to play strategic slice shots and volleys.

The young man took a number of risks during the second set and messed up his serve, losing the set 2–6. Although he rebounded during the third set, quickly winning the first two games, the final score was 6–4 in Allan's favor. The young man was visibly frustrated by the end of the match, clearly stunned he had lost to his much older opponent, and so decisively, too!

Allan shook hands with his opponent as they left the court. They were talking to each other as they walked toward the coordinator's desk to record their score. I heard Allan say, "It's only a game — there will be others." The young man asked Allan how long he had been playing tennis. "Forty years or so," Allan replied. The coordinator looked at them both with a smile and said, "Win again, did you, Allan?" She looked at the young man and said, "You'll get over it."

During an interview, Rafael Nadal once said, "As a tennis player, you can win and you can lose, and you have to be ready for both. I practiced self-control as a kid. But as you get older, they both — winning and losing — get easier."

My husband often makes a somewhat similar comment. He says that when playing tennis, losing does get easier as you get older. You just take it in stride. However, there's tremendous satisfaction in knowing that an old guy can still win at this stage of life, no matter the age of his opponent.

— Kathy Dickie —

21

The First Gift Given

When it comes to staying young,
a mind-lift beats a face-lift any day.
~Marty Buccella

For many years, I was too wrapped up in my kids and my life to give a whole lot of thought to how I looked, and the words "low maintenance" described my approach to beauty perfectly. If I remembered to slap on some moisturizer before bed, great. If not, no big deal since I was sure all the Twinkies I'd consumed over my lifetime were going to preserve my youth well into my nineties.

It wasn't until recently, when I had my picture taken for a work ID, that I realized something that most likely had been apparent to the rest of the world for quite some time: I had peaked. About twenty years ago.

The woman in the ID picture looked tired and definitely middle-aged, and no amount of moisturizer, hairstyling or skinny jeans was going to change it. As a matter of fact, the whole picture had a smudged, almost erased quality to it, as if it had been sitting in the bottom of my purse for a few decades.

Looking at it, that's exactly how I felt — faintly erased, as if I didn't quite exist anymore. The "Youth Train" had left the station, and I was no longer on it.

For a few days, I was a little bothered by the fact that I was no longer the sweet, young thing I thought I was. For those few days, I tried a little harder to dress younger, brighter and tighter. I took pains with my hair and added extra eyeliner.

I thought I was succeeding in my quest for a youthful glow until one of my new co-workers casually asked me a question that told me I was fooling only myself. "I don't suppose you know what Facebook is, do you?" she asked, not at all maliciously but with the bluntness of a twenty-five-year-old who has yet to find her first gray hair.

That simple question opened my weary eyes once and for all. Although I'm well acquainted with Facebook and have a passing flirtation with Twitter, to my co-worker I am over the hill and as old as Methuselah's mother. It stung for a few seconds before a revolutionary thought crawled into my head: *Who really cares?*

The best thing of all is that the answer to that question is *absolutely no one*. My family loves me not for my no-longer-shiny hair and once-trim thighs but because I'm the wife and mom. They love me for the part of me that will never change even after my teeth fall out. They love me even when I'm not very lovable.

There's a huge relief in letting go of vanity. Sure, I want to look neat, groomed and smell good, but long lashes and a smooth décolleté? Not going to happen. And that's just fine because the time I spent primping, even though it was always minimal, can now be spent on more pleasurable pursuits like reading and walking the dog. Being with my husband, kids and friends. Enjoying the moment, not obsessing over the wrinkle.

Someone once said that beauty is the first gift given and the first one taken away. I agree but only when it comes to outside beauty. The real beauty, the stuff inside that all of us have, lasts a lifetime.

— Nell Musolf —

22

The View from the Middle Seat

The ability to be in the present moment is a major
component of mental wellness.
~Abraham Maslow

recognize that someone has to sit in the middle seats during an airplane flight, but I end up there more than most. There are two reasons for this: One, my wife likes the window seat, and if I want to sit next to her (and I do), seat B or E is my designated parking place. And two, when I'm alone, I just can't bring myself to shell out the extra thirty-five dollars that's often required to reserve a window.

I find myself in the middle seat even more often these days as my wife and I gradually glide into retirement. In the past two years, we have savored the food and art of Italy, admired the culture and people of Southeast Asia, and visited several new places in the U.S. Most of those trips involved lots of air travel and scenery, so I have become familiar not only with the middle seat, but also with how to use my cell-phone camera to get the best photos from that position.

We also have more time to visit our daughter in Seattle, a city where a camera and an airplane window go together like salmon and capers. Above the Emerald City, a passenger can look down on the waters of Puget Sound and Lake Washington with their lush islands dotting the azure water below. The view also treats fliers to a number of stunning mountain peaks rising from near sea level up to fourteen thousand feet in elevation.

My wife and I still work occasionally, so our schedules don't always coincide, recently necessitating separate flights from Seattle. On mine, I was assigned seat 21E, right in the middle. It was a rare and beautifully clear day, and middle seat or not, I was anxious to get some pictures from the air.

The newer aircraft I was on had a 3D-maps feature as part of its seatback entertainment system, so once in the air I activated it, enabling me to view all the labelled landmarks in our path. As we neared the Cascade Mountains, we made a slow turn to the southwest with both Mount Rainier and Mount St. Helens up ahead. I got my camera ready.

To my amazement, the man sitting in the window seat next to me closed his eyes, totally disinterested in the scenery. The young man and woman in front of me were more interested in one another than in anything outside the plane, and they began passionately kissing, while the obviously embarrassed outsider next to them kept her face buried in a paperback.

I stretched my neck into the personal space of Mr. Dozing Window Seater in order to get a better view outside. Suddenly, into my vision came what was undoubtedly the best image of Mount St. Helens I had ever seen from a commercial flight, the sun's morning shadows falling perfectly on its eruption-torn crater. I immediately picked up my phone and snapped several photos past my sleeping seatmate. I kept taking photos until the mountain was out of sight.

I looked again at the 3D map on the seatback in front of me and saw that Mount Rainier was, at that very moment, visible on the left side of aircraft. Glancing expectantly in that direction, I was horrified. From the exit row in front of me to the entire rear of the plane, every window shade on the port side was tightly closed, the window seat occupants either glued to their phones, reading newspapers or watching action movies on their seatback entertainment screens.

Why? I thought. Why were so many people, some of whom probably paid thirty-five dollars for the privilege of sitting next to a blocked window, voluntarily blind to the majesty only a short distance away?

I might understand the young couple's reluctance to stop making out in the seats in front of me, but what about everyone else? Wouldn't they want to put their movies on pause for a few seconds to view one of God's most magnificent creations?

Shaking my head, I again leaned forward to glance out the window on my right. Just a few dozen miles in the distance was majestic Mount Adams, with its white glacier gleaming in the morning sun. Again, I began to snap photos, thinking how I couldn't wait to show my Facebook friends how I'm spending my retirement.

Suddenly, I put down my camera, a troubling question forcing its way into my mind. While I had been taking pictures of these exquisite mountains, had I paused long enough to really look at them? Was I, in a way, just as guilty of not appreciating their beauty as the passengers with their shades down? I thought about other trips I had taken. I had thousands of photographs from dozens of locations, but had I really seen anything? And why did I insist on posting the pictures on social media? So I could show the world what a great view I missed while I was looking through a tiny viewfinder? Shouldn't I have spent those few seconds gazing at the scene unfettered by technology? Wouldn't that have been more rewarding than a few "likes" on my profile page?

Then I thought about the past. How often had I viewed my kids' birthdays, concerts and dance recitals through the viewfinder of a video camera? And it's not just physical images that get in the way but mental images, too. On a recent train trip along the California coast, I had stared transfixed out the window at the powerful waves crashing onto the rugged coastline, all the while intermittently looking at my watch and worrying about the logistics of getting to our hotel.

My wife has asked me, "When are you finally going to start living in the moment?" Good question. Too often, while I have been in my Walter Mitty alternate universe, there has been a much better world all around me if I would just open my eyes to see it.

So there, in seat 21E, I made a decision: I realized that even in my mid-sixties, I could still learn a new trick. Maybe if I couldn't book a window seat on my next flight, at least I could try to book a window seat on my life. Maybe as I moved into retirement, I could also retire my excess concern with what's to come or what might be in order to better enjoy what's actually set before me. Heck, maybe I should even take a cue from the couple in front of me and better appreciate the company of the person for whom I buy the window seats!

So, I'll apologize to my social-media friends in advance because, in the days to come, I may not be posting as many scenic photos online. But you can be sure that it's not because I have my view blocked. No, this old dog's not going to miss a thing, even if I have to see it from a middle seat.

— Nick Walker —

23

Unlikely Friends

Let us be grateful to people who make us happy,
they are the charming gardeners
who make our souls blossom.
~Marcel Proust

was lucky enough to marry my perfect partner and experience real, true love. I know not everyone gets to have that, and I never took my husband for granted. My love for him was so intense that I thought I couldn't survive if I lost him. And then I did.

When he died unexpectedly at age fifty-five, I was devastated. I always told myself that I would never date again if something happened to him. He was just so perfect for me.

But as my intense grief began to subside, I realized that I wasn't the kind of person who was happy living alone, so I signed up on a few dating websites.

My husband was handsome, funny and kind. He was so well-loved by everyone who knew him that there was standing room only at his memorial service. Since I was a teenager, I had had a list of all the qualities I wanted in my perfect partner, and he checked all the boxes! So, of course, I compared every man on the dating sites to him, and they all seemed to fall short.

Every now and then, I would start corresponding with a man on one of those sites. Usually, it was someone who was creative, funny and enjoyed nature as much as I did. But, eventually, I decided that there just wasn't enough between us to want to meet. He just wasn't "the one" for me.

Since I have always been attracted to men who like to garden, build things and work with their hands, I would sometimes hang out in Home Depot or the plant nurseries, hoping to casually bump into a man and wait for the sparks to fly. Often, I would start a conversation with a man who seemed interesting, only to have his overly protective wife or girlfriend stroll up and possessively take his arm.

I was on and off dating sites for years and never once went on a date with anyone. I just didn't want to face the reality that no one would ever compare to my husband.

Five years after my husband died, I still hadn't been on a single date when a much younger man came to my house to do some work. I wasn't thinking of him in any sort of romantic way because he was a lot younger than me, and he had a long beard and a lot of crazy tattoos. The work he did in my house lasted several hours, and we talked the whole time. Not only did we share the same sense of humor, which led to a rapid back and forth, but we had very similar personalities — sort of introverted, quirky in a way — and we were both nature lovers.

By the time he was getting ready to leave, we felt almost embarrassed because we got along so well. But not long after he left, when he wasn't on company time anymore, he called and told me that he really enjoyed meeting me and wondered if I wanted to keep in touch.

"Why in the world would you want to keep in touch with someone my age?" I asked. And he told me that he didn't usually meet somebody that he got along with that well and, besides, "Age is just a number." So, I agreed.

We developed an unlikely friendship. He was thirty-three when we met, and I was sixty-two. He lived over an hour away from me but began calling me almost daily, and we would talk for hours. Since he knew I was still depressed from the loss of my husband, he tried everything he could to make me laugh, from telling me jokes to teaching me about comedians he liked. He genuinely seemed to want to help me find happiness; it confused me because I hadn't expected to find such a kind friend in the form of a tattooed, bearded, thirty-something man.

He was on several dating sites himself, and he encouraged me to give the sites a chance. "Don't wait for Mr. Right," he would say. "It doesn't have to be true love. Just go out and meet people."

But I never did. In my mind, he just didn't get it. After all, I had lost my one true soulmate. Why would I want to settle for less?

We had known each other for about six months when he called me and said that he wanted to come over and take me on a real date. "What?" I asked. "What do you mean by a 'real date'?" He said that we would go out to lunch, and then we would wander around an antique mall, which was something we both loved to do.

"Why in the world would you want to do that?" I asked.

He told me it was because he wanted to remind me how nice it could be to just go out without it having to mean anything other than having fun.

So, he came over. We knew each other fairly well by then, but since we hadn't seen each other in six months and he had used the word "date," I was somewhat nervous. But he was a perfect, if somewhat goofy, gentleman. We went to a local Mexican restaurant for lunch and then wandered around an antique mall. We talked, laughed and had a really great time. And the afternoon we spent together really proved his point.

Since my husband died, I had closed myself off to anyone whom I didn't feel was perfect for me as a romantic partner. I would categorize everyone by looks or age or some other criteria and deem them unworthy of my time. I had so many requirements for what I wanted, mostly based on what I had with my husband, that I didn't give myself the chance to get to know people.

Before my friend and I had gone on our "date," I had questioned his motives for wanting to be my friend. I don't know why I did, as he had made it clear he had no interest in anything other than friendship.

We've known each other for almost three years now and have become very close friends. We contribute a lot to each other's lives. I add the wisdom of my age, and he adds the carefree spirit of his youth.

It's hard for me to admit that someone half my age taught me such a valuable lesson, but like he said, "Age is just a number." And appearance is nothing but a package that wraps around the soul of some pretty great people.

—Betsy S. Franz—

24

Always Blame the Equipment

Old age is when you resent the swimsuit issue
of Sports Illustrated *because there are*
fewer articles to read.
~George Burns

My husband and I were unexpectedly exploring Australian waterfalls. We were on the trip of a lifetime, spending three months touring Australia in a rented camper. This leg of the trip found us heading up the Eastern coast of Queensland toward the resort town of Cairns. A picnic lunch at a small park had ended in a conversation with some local ladies working the hospitality booth. They suggested that we take a by-road that would allow us to see several waterfalls on our way north.

That conversation was one of those magic moments when something as simple as stopping for lunch turns into a serendipitous adventure. Our travels seldom have a time- or date-specific goal, so a slow trip in the hinterland of Queensland seemed like a good use of a golden day. Our detour ended at a sparkling cascade covering the recessed entrance to a cave. Better yet, this waterfall had a swimming beach bordering the plunge pool. We switched to our bathing suits and headed for the water.

I am a good swimmer. In the water, I am totally relaxed, not fighting my body or the water, moving in sync with the buoyancy. Swimming offers me a transcendental feeling of freedom and tranquility. On the beach, I did a shallow dive and swam to the far side of the pool. I glided under the cascade without hesitation, feeling the pelting water on my back. Once in the cave, I swam to the rocks and sat looking through the sheer veil of water at the blurred images of water and woodland on the other side. After a very few minutes, I swam back, joining my husband on the beach.

Tom was taking pictures the whole time. Later than night, we were looking at the pictures on his computer, and I was delighted with the sight of me in the water. Head down, arms reaching in smooth strokes, I looked as good as I ever did. But fate was playing with me. The next picture showed me coming out of the water. There I was, a sixty-seven-year-old woman: saggy, baggy, covered in cellulite, and wearing an equally old swimsuit.

My mood soured instantly. That picture was like that first time you look at the back of your hand and realize you are looking at your mother's hand. But, just as quickly, I realized that I had a fallback position. In all things related to sports, when I don't like the results, I blame the equipment. Clearly, I needed a new swimsuit.

The next day, I was off to the stores. I went as a lamb to the slaughter.

The first thing the saleswoman offered me was something called a "Miracle Suit." As far as I can tell, these things are made of a Teflon-coated, bullet-proof form of Lycra. Infuse them with iron, and they could be used as suspension rods on the Golden Gate Bridge. The saleswoman promised me it would give me an hourglass shape. Off to the dressing room with that one! And that, as they say, is when the fight started. Trying to get that miracle suit on was a series of pulls, tugs, hops, grunts and desperate wedge maneuvers that soon had me sweating and breathless. And the sweat only made it stick to me even more!

Then, with a sudden snap, the last strap sealed itself to my shoulder. The parts covered in the suit were constricted; in fact, they were immobile. The parts not covered were squeezing out the ends of the suit like extruded modeling clay. That got me worried. What was happening to all the flesh squeezed inside the suit? Where had it gone?

What was it doing? I am science trained, and I know that when things are compressed, they heat up. When things heat, they expand. Was some part of me reaching a critical mass? I envisioned some internal meter with its needle creeping up toward the red zone.

Stand back, she's going to blow!

I had to get that suit off! Immediately!

What followed was a frantic, exhausting and desperate effort. No anaconda ever worked harder to shed his skin. The saleswoman asked twice if I needed help.

Help? I needed deliverance!

Five non-miracle suits later, I found one that fit, looked nice and, if it didn't help my ego, at least it didn't harm it either.

This marathon search for an aesthetic and comfortable suit also gave me a chance to observe all the young women searching for the perfect bikini for their perfect bodies. It caused me some sadness. Not for me. For them. You see, none of them liked what they saw in the mirror either. I wanted to tell them so much, starting with the fact that they were beautiful and every suit they put on was the right one.

I had my own good run at bikinis back in the day. I certainly can't begrudge them their turn. And I was just as self-critical as they were. No amount of positive reinforcement from me, their friends or, God forbid, their mother was going to help.

Had I been asked, I would have told them that while I wish I had the body I did at twenty-two, I don't want to be the person I was at twenty-two. I am a better, stronger, happier person now. I am more confident. I have seen what I can do, especially under pressure. I know what I am capable of, including swimming an easy mile whenever I wish. I am better in every way except when it comes to those darn swimsuits.

You can't have it all. At least, you can't have it all at the same time. Yes, I wish I were young, trim and attractive, but if I can't, I'll be old, fit and happy in my own skin.

Now, there is a real miracle suit.

— Louise Butler —

25

Ducks or Chickens?

*The proper basis for marriage
is a mutual misunderstanding.*
~Oscar Wilde

As we cruised the tree-canopied country road in our new Mustang convertible, my husband and I were savoring the unusual warmth of the early spring day. Mini rivers of melting snow were running down the hillsides, pooling in the ditches on either side of the road. We were enjoying the newfound freedom of empty nesters, each lost in our own thoughts, until we passed an old farmhouse.

"Did you see those ducks?" my husband asked.

To which I replied, "Ducks? They were chickens!"

"No, honey, I am talking about the mama duck with the three ducklings!"

"You mean the mama hen and the three chicks?"

He retorted, "Honey, they were waddling with orange beaks!"

"Oh, come on," I said incredulously. "They had yellow beaks with red crests and were pecking like this." I motioned, moving my head up and down.

Believe it or not, this conversation continued for the next three miles and deteriorated to the point that I shouted, "I am not a stupid woman! I know the difference between a duck and a chicken!"

"Then I am turning this car around because I can't believe you think you saw chickens!"

"Good!" I answered quickly. "Because I can't believe you think they were ducks."

As we crested the hill, the farmhouse came into view, and I quickly pointed up the hill to the yard of the farmhouse. "See, *those* are chickens!" At the same time, my husband was pointing to the roadside gully, saying, "See, *those* are ducks!"

We could not believe our eyes! Indeed, in the same yard were a mama duck with three ducklings playing in the water by the side of the road and, up near the farmhouse, there was a mama hen pecking the ground with her three baby chicks following suit.

We immediately broke into uncontrollable laughter and pulled to the side of the road to gain our composure. We had been bickering for the last ten minutes over something on which we were both correct!

Understandably, my husband's perspective had been restricted to the road ahead while driving. My own perspective had narrowed to the sides of the road as I enjoyed the landscapes and the views of the horizon.

How many times do disagreements occur because of different perspectives? Both parties are correct but fail or even refuse to see the situation through the eyes of the other one.

My husband and I could have chosen to continue to argue and accuse each other of being mistaken. Instead, we decided to take the time to turn around and retrace where we had been in order to increase our understanding of the situation.

Not every disagreement is as easy to solve as our ducks-and-chickens experience. But to this day, my husband and I end many conflicts by agreeing to disagree. I'll say, "It's a chicken," to which he will reply, "It's a duck." Each of us is willing to compromise as we consider the different perspectives of the other and realize that both of us *can* be right. This has taught us in a very real way that not every disagreement has a single solution; we can work out our conflicts with patience and humor. We even have a wooden chicken and duck displayed in our family room as a constant reminder of that day and to not take ourselves too seriously!

— Peg Arnold —

26

College at Sixty-two?

Anyone who stops learning is old, whether at twenty
or eighty. Anyone who keeps learning stays young.
~Henry Ford

Have you ever been archived? I have! I needed a transcript to start my college application process at age sixty-two. I figured I'd get it online, no problem. But my computer screen read: "Unavailable." How could my transcript be unavailable? Didn't they keep them forever? I dialed Michigan State's Registrar.

"Registrar. May I help you?" She sounded about fifteen.

"Yes, I applied online for my transcript, but it said, 'Unavailable.' What does that mean?"

"When did you attend?"

"1967–68."

"Oh... I'm sorry; transcripts prior to 1970 are archived." She did sound sorry; still, I suddenly felt really old.

"But," her voice brightened, "I can manually retrieve it and mail it to you."

"You can't e-mail it?"

"Not if you need a certified copy." Her voice balanced regret and hope.

"I do — I'm applying for admission." I sighed. "How soon can you send it?"

"Are you starting your master's?"

"No, finishing my bachelor's."

"Wow. Good for you! I'll print it from the microfiche and certify it ASAP so I can mail it. Good luck!" I could hear the smile in her voice; it took the sting out of "archived." Instead of old, I felt bold — audaciously planning something unusual.

This pattern repeated many times over the next five years — returning to school juxtaposed the invisibility of age with the welcome of a non-traditional student. My advisor joked I was non-traditional even for a non-traditional. And sometimes, instead of being the invisible older person on a college campus, I was way too visible.

For example, I needed to take placement tests because my SAT scores were so old. I studied for weeks, reviewing online. I wasn't worried about English, but I hadn't used algebra or geometry for anything more serious than hanging curtains in forty years. Nervous didn't begin to describe my feelings when I reported for my testing appointment at the local junior college. The test administrator's reaction didn't help, either.

"You're taking the test?"

After convincing her that I was the "Renny Gehman" taking the placement tests, despite my gray hair and 1950 birthdate, I finally settled in. Finishing an hour and a half later and feeling positive, I went to check out. Again, the testing officials had funny expressions. Handing me an envelope, one of them said, "You need to take this to the Registrar immediately." The other two nodded emphatic agreement.

Since it was almost 5 p.m., I asked, "Today? I thought I'd register tomorrow."

"No," she replied. "They need this right away."

I accepted the envelope and drove to the Registrar's office, where I handed it to the young receptionist and went to sit down. Before I could, she asked, "Is this yours?"

"Yes," I answered. "I just finished the placement tests, and they told me to bring that right over."

"This is yours?" Again, invisibility — after all, I'd just handed it to her.

"Yes, ma'am. Those are mine." Then I thought that maybe something was wrong. "Why, is there a problem?" Suddenly, my heart was racing.

"You got a 55?"

I didn't know; the envelope was sealed. "I guess. Those are mine, right?" Now apprehensive, I wondered what 55 meant. Was it really bad? "Is that bad?"

"I've never seen a 55 before. Just a minute." She phoned someone. What did that mean? I could feel my heart pounding.

Another lady appeared, took my paper from the receptionist, examined it, looked at me, and said, "These are yours?"

I nodded. She turned, calling someone. Another lady appeared. The first lady said, "Look at this," handing my paper to the second lady.

"55?" the second lady said. The other two nodded. A man walking by overheard and said, "Who got a 55?" The second lady pointed at me.

I repeated, "Is that bad?" No one answered, but they called two others to examine my scores.

Enough! I took a deep breath and asked loudly, "Is there a problem? Do I need to do something?"

That got their attention. "Oh, I'm sorry," the first lady said. "It's just... you got 55."

"And ...?" I imagined how much fun taking remedial classes at my age would be.

"I'm sorry," she repeated. "We don't see a 55 often; in fact, yours is the second-highest score ever." Everyone beamed at me. "Would you like to register now?"

I heard someone say, "How old do you think she is?" as I walked into the office.

There's not much information about returning to school at retirement age, but everyone I met — students, faculty and staff — was encouraging. It was challenging, do-able, and full of other humorous moments — like my "American History to 1865" class, where the professor remarked what a resource I would be for the class. I had to laugh. No matter how old I looked, I hadn't lived during the American Revolution or the Civil War.

When I showed up for orientation at the University of North Texas, I had one of those invisibility moments. I was one of ten English department transfers waiting for the TA to hand us schedule forms.

He walked right by me, I thought, hand outstretched for the paper. I was too astonished to say anything, but the young student beside me wasn't.

"Did he just ignore you?" she asked. I nodded, but she raised such a ruckus that quietly obtaining my form seemed impossible. I raised my hand.

"Yes, ma'am?" the TA said, politely.

"Excuse me, I think you skipped me."

"You're a student?" There was no mistaking his incredulity. While my companions were outraged, I took the opportunity to laugh.

I found my young classmates as supportive as my orientation companions—always ready to assist with my smartphone or work on a group assignment. And our shared studies gave us a lot to discuss; age barriers disappeared. The past five years helped me engage with my grandchildren as well. Nothing bonds across generations like studying together!

I graduated in December 2017, fifty years after I began. I wrote "It only took me 50 years!" in white letters on my green cap. A lady in the audience even wanted a picture. I laughed and posed with two millennial friends.

I can't wait for what comes next!

— Renny Gehman —

Slowing Down

Aging is not lost youth but a new stage
of opportunity and strength.
~Betty Friedan

just finished my annual mammogram. I'm not in a good mood as I walk to my car in the maze of the hospital parking lot. Fortunately, I can find it because my daughter taught me to take a picture of the space number with my iPhone. This was excellent advice because I have no sense of direction and often have to wander around pressing the locator button on the remote and listening for the distant beep.

Ah, there it is. I get in, buckle up, and face a new challenge. How do I get out of here? There is construction everywhere. But there are no guiding arrows on the ground or signs to indicate the location of the exit. I take a chance and head down a row that seems to lead to the exit. But no, I am at a dead end. There is no way out.

I put my car in reverse and back up. I spy a space between two cars that looks like a good spot for turning around. I cautiously enter and almost instantly hear a crash as loud as the cymbals in the "1812 Overture." I get out and investigate. I have hit a cement barrier and crushed my rear bumper.

But I still don't know how to escape. I have to calm down. I do my yogic breathing and put the car in Drive. This time, my injured Toyota hobbles down the correct lane. I drive home in tears and shame.

Part of my brain tells me it will be okay while another part catalogues my ever-growing number of fender benders: the lot at the local food co-op, the underground one at the Y, the one near the cleaners. Fortunately, I never hurt myself or anyone else, as my mishaps took place out of traffic. I probably hold a world record: "Most Injuries Ever Inflicted on Cement Poles." What an honor.

"Face facts," my cerebrum is telling me. "Your depth perception is shot. Not only have you vastly exceeded your reasonable quota of collisions, you have also lost your driving confidence. If you're afraid to turn, park, or merge, it might be time to put your license out to pasture."

Could I really stop driving? This is a major life decision. When I get home, I grab a pen and legal pad, make a line down the middle of the page and start listing the reasons "why" and "why not."

Under "Why," I write:
- I'll save a lot on insurance, which is good since I lost my safe-driver discount a long time ago.
- I can always take an Uber.
- I might kill myself or someone else. Yep, those are biggies.

Under "Why Not," I list:
- Loss of independence.

Let's face it, driving equals freedom. The day I got my driver's license was the happiest day of my first sixteen years of life. I grew up in Detroit — Motown. The Motor City. Cars were part of our DNA. I once dated a horrible guy for a few months just because he drove a yellow Corvette convertible.

Also, I lived in a suburb with no public transportation. My parents wouldn't drive me to my friend's house without presenting a legal brief. My driver's license was my "get out of jail free card," and I cherished it.

Loss of independence also means more dependence. This is not me. I cringe at the thought that I will need to rely on my newly retired husband for chauffeuring. The last thing in the world I want is to become a burden to him or to have to make my plans around his golf game.

Can I pretend I live in Manhattan and get everywhere by bus? I live in a city, right? I go online to research public transportation. I print out the routes and stops of every bus I could possibly need. I learn that the local Big Blue Bus can take me almost anywhere. It goes to the gym, my art classes, my volunteer sites, the movies, restaurants and friends' houses. And none of them require more than one transfer.

But, as I review the schedule, I also learn that my usual ten-minute trips will now take about forty-five minutes instead of ten. And what if I miss the transfer? Do I really want to stand at a bus stop for twenty-eight more minutes? I guess I can play "Words with Friends."

I decide to take a trial run of the bus idea. I purchase a senior fare card that lets me go almost anywhere for fifty cents. Transfers are only thirty-five! It's the deal of the century. So, when the #15 bus to my deep-water aerobics class at the Y stops in front of my house the following week, I get on, and the helpful driver shows me how to pay. I am thrilled to discover that the people on the bus do not look scary. In fact, most of them look just like me: old.

During the drive, I begin to think that this bus thing could work out. But I soon worry that it won't always meet all my transportation needs. Some of my need-fillers are pretty far away. How will I get to the doctor who has been taking care of me for forty years? And who will cut my hair? My beautician and I have been through holidays, weddings and my seamless transition from brown with blond streaks to gray. I guess I could try someone else, but she understands my obsession with frizz and knows just how to layer my waves so I don't look like Art Garfunkel.

I return to my list, and the truth hits me. It's simple: "Thou Shall Not Kill" wins. I can't take the chance of hurting anyone. My family, doctor, and hairdresser will all understand. Breaking up will be hard to do, but it is time to end the relationship with my beautiful Prius. Actually, it isn't that beautiful anymore. It, like my confidence, is full of dents and bruises.

The truth is obvious. I am ready to stop driving, and it's going to be okay. In fact, I am beginning to think it will open up a different chapter in my life. I feel a new emotion: relief. I will never have to face another parking lot or change lanes on the freeway. I will never have to have a panic attack when I buckle my grandkids into their car seats. I will never have to call the insurance company again. I am free.

— Maureen Shubow Rubin —

Hit the Road

Free Willie

If happiness is the goal — and it should be,
then adventures should be top priority.
~Richard Branson

My wife, Joyce, and I had just retired from the ministry, and after renting our house to friends, we headed to the open roads for our very first trip in our brand-new motorhome. When it became time to stop for our first night out, I thought it would be easy finding a spot in an RV park. However, after calling several RV parks, no spot was found.

Finally, after being rejected again, I called and inquired with another RV park manager if he had any idea where we could stay. At first, he replied, "Well, now, all the parks in the area are full because so many workers on two major road and pipeline construction projects are staying locally. But I know a place that might have a spot for you."

He gave me the phone number to call. By then, it was after 10 p.m., and I was not hopeful of even getting an answer on the phone, much less a place to stay. To my surprise, though, a nice man answered the phone and told me, "Yes, I have a place for the night." He politely gave me directions to his RV park, agreeing to meet us at the gate and guide us to our spot.

When Joyce and I arrived, he was waiting for us beside a beautiful, fenced-in park with a huge American flag painted on the gate. He introduced himself as Willie. Even though it was a cold night and Willie was bundled up in a coat and hat, I could tell he was at least eighty years old.

Willie guided us to our spot and helped me back into it. He pointed out that there was only one other RV, about thirty feet from us, parked in our section of the park. Willie then said, "Since it's so late, just come to the office in the morning to fill out paperwork and pay."

Joyce and I then got our motorhome set up, and we went to sleep. Early the next morning, as Joyce relaxed in bed, I was drinking a cup of coffee while casually looking out the window toward the RV parked near us. I watched a man come out of that RV and begin to try to light a campfire. The man was totally naked except for shoes, socks, and a baseball cap. I yelled to Joyce, "Come here! You gotta see this! You won't believe it! That guy parked near us is outside completely naked!"

Of course, Joyce didn't believe me, and she didn't come quickly enough to see him before he walked around to the other side of his RV. When he did that, all Joyce could see were his legs. She accused me of making it up because she could see that he had on shoes and socks. I replied, "Honey, I promise you that between those socks and his baseball cap, he does not have on a stitch of clothing." For a few minutes, we sat and discussed how rude and inappropriate it was for that guy to come outside naked.

After breakfast, we packed up and started to drive the half-mile to the office to meet with Willie. As we drove down the narrow road to the office (with a ditch on one side and an embankment on the other side), we noticed a couple in the distance walking up the road toward us. Lo and behold, when they got close enough, we saw that they were completely naked, too. At that point, Joyce and I started to question what kind of park we had wandered into and why it had a spot open for us.

As the walking couple approached our RV, I slowed to a crawl to allow them room to walk past. However, instead of just walking on by, they waved and stopped to talk. Since I had my window down on this warm, sunny day, I could hardly ignore them. As we chatted with the couple for a few moments, all I could think of was, "Don't look down. Just look at their eyes. Just look at their noses."

Finally, they walked on, and we made it to the office to find Willie.

As we started up the steps to the office, I heard Willie's voice call to me from the direction of the swimming pool. "Hey, Donny, come over here." Joyce and I turned to the sound of Willie's voice, and what did we see but eighty-something Willie standing by the pool completely naked!

Now it was confirmed. For our first night on the road in our motorhome, we had stumbled unknowingly into a nude RV park. By the way, I can only imagine the laugh the RV park owner who referred us to Willie's park had after getting off the phone with me. Perhaps he turned to his wife and said, "I got another one, Mildred."

Back at the pool we were introduced to Willie's helper, Chester, who was also naked and almost as old as Willie. Again, all I could think was, "Don't look down. Just look at his eyes. Just look at his nose." Even so, I couldn't help but notice that old, naked Chester had a nasty-looking rash on his bare bottom.

Then we met Willie's naked, aging wife and couldn't help but notice that gravity had not been kind to her. After that, even though we insisted that we had to leave, Willie insisted on giving us a guided tour of the facilities, which meant we had to follow his naked backside all around the park. Finally, Willie led us up a long set of stairs to the office, which meant that his naked behind was now about at our eye level. Once in the office, Willie produced papers for me to fill out. As Joyce and I sat in front of his desk, Willie continued to stand behind his desk, which meant that his naked front was now at our eye level. It was very distracting, and I kept hoping Willie would sit down.

I thought about putting a fictitious name on the paperwork, but Willie required a copy of my driver's license, so I had to put down my real name and address, which worried me. What if I started to get mailers from Willie's nude RV park?

Finally, all the papers and paying were completed, and Joyce and I managed to get back on the road. However, we weren't quite finished with Willie. Two days after telling him goodbye, I noticed that my driver's license was missing. I had left it with Willie. I immediately called him, and he said, "Oh, sure, I got your license. I've been carryin' it with me ever since you left, just waiting for you to call." Hmmm. Where was Willie carrying my license?

I gave Willie the name and address of my brother-in-law in Michigan where we were headed so he could mail it to me there. Now my brother-in-law would be on Willie's mailing list, too.

—Donny Thrasher—

29

A Motorcycle and the Open Road

Remember that happiness is a way of travel —
not a destination.
~Roy M. Goodman

feel guilty for saying this, but I'm happiest when I'm astride my bike. I experience a primitive joy when I ride. It's a feeling that can't be replicated, a sheer pleasure of gunning the throttle and stringing together a dozen or so smooth turns. Even after years of motorcycle insanity, I still chuckle to myself on the twisty stuff.

There's something about experiencing a meandering road, free and uncaged. You can smell nature when you're on a bike, and feel temperatures fluctuate as you pass through shadowy areas. In a car, you're inside a compartment. Watching the scenery through a windshield is like watching TV. You're a passive observer, and everything moves by you unexcitingly, a frame at a time. On a motorcycle, the frame is gone. You are in total contact with your surroundings.

Riding a bike makes me feel young again. Powering into a corner, hugging the turns, sinking into the dips, and powering out are more natural than wrestling an automobile around a bend. The power, the sound, the feel, the acceleration and exhilaration, the sense of control and the freedom — these are just a few of the physical sensations of being one with your machine.

Stress relief! There's that, too. Not that I have as much stress as I did as a younger man. But when I'm on my bike, there isn't anything else on my mind. Riding is meditation, a place where all worldly concerns melt away, and there's just the open road. Being faster than others is not important. I'm not a reckless rider by any stretch. I roll with sufficient pace to make it an enjoyable experience. It may take longer for me to reach my destination, but that's cool. Other motorists are fleeting guests in my world. Slower vehicles are gently and smoothly passed. Faster vehicles zip by, hungrier to reach their destinations.

In my senior years, I've come to enjoy the solitary nature of riding, the oneness of the world. Even when I ride with a group, I'm on my own without a care in the world, living in the moment.

The freedom to explore is another good reason to ride. I've ridden down dirt roads and along narrow highways that I would have never discovered on four wheels.

The sensation of power is an awesome feeling. I enjoy the challenge of trying to perfect my riding skills. I feel like a different person on my bike. My helmet, riding gear, and the adrenaline rush make me feel like a superhero. The bone-numbing cold, the wildlife I see and avoid hitting, the mind-blowing effort that goes into complex overpasses, the simple beauty of a slightly cloudy mid-spring day — it's all there. The only thing really making conscious noise is my brain. No radio, no books on tape, no hands-free conference calls, just me. Whenever I travel on my bike, I enjoy getting there. It's not that I don't feel upset or sad before I kick it down into gear, but those emotions drop away, because I'm doing something that requires a great deal of concentration.

Motorcycle riding has made me a more deliberate person, too. You can only carry so much aboard a motorcycle. Excess baggage is left at home, figuratively and literally. Differentiating between necessity and desire has become much clearer to me.

For this old man, bikes are what make life interesting. They keep things simple and in perspective. A lot of people allow fear to control their lives and stop them from doing the exciting things they enjoy. I'm not one of them. People love to give excuses and call their apprehension something else, but they don't know what they're missing. Motorcycling has changed my life and made it so much better. Tomorrow, I will ride.

— Timothy Martin —

30

The Top of the World

*And so... the greatest journey has always been —
chasing paths where your heart beats and
finding moments that leave you breathless.*
~Mystqx Skye

stood before an eternity of ice, timeless and desolate. There was a bluish-gray mist, and the only sounds were the wind, my breath, and the crunching of my boots as I walked along the deserted Arctic shoreline. It was 9 p.m., but it was late May so I could still see to the distant horizon in the fading light.

It was my sixtieth birthday, and I was fulfilling a personal mission — to visit Barrow, Alaska, now called Utqiaġvik, the most northern city in the United States. I was at the top of the world, far beyond the Arctic Circle.

Not a soul was in sight when I came upon an ancient-looking canoe covered with seal skin. The wind flapped a flag lodged in the center of the boat. I wondered if a similar vessel had carried the first humans to this isolated patch of planet. How could one even consider making such brutal journeys across uncharted seas? I thought of the men and women from times immemorial who had challenged such unimaginable barriers just to survive. Or was it simply to satisfy some innate drive to explore the unknown?

My solitude ended when I heard muted voices and then saw

dozens of snowmobiles parked in the distance on the frozen ocean. It looked like a Walmart parking lot on ice. Scores of people dressed in bulky parkas with fur-lined hoods headed toward a large steel building.

I joined the procession and followed the crowd inside. No one seemed to notice.

I had happened upon the nightly bingo game. A twenty-something man handling the cash box told me to sign in. How many cards did I want? I confessed that I had never been to a bingo game. How many did he suggest? I enthusiastically added that I had just arrived in town all the way from Jacksonville, Florida to celebrate my sixtieth birthday. I admit that I was disappointed when he replied curtly, "Then buy only two cards since you are a beginner." Not exactly the response I had expected.

I took my seat next to an aloof, weathered woman I guessed to be in her seventies. A dozen bingo sheets were spread before her. As I sat down, she barely glanced up. Neither did the others across from me. I intuited that I might be invading their territory. These were some serious bingo players.

I sat in silence waiting to begin. As the numbers began to be rattled off, I did my best to keep up. After stamping her own cards with lightning speed, my dour neighbor peered over at my two sheets and, without a word, jabbed at two squares I had missed. Gosh, she was good. "Thank you," I whispered. No response.

Nobody warns you that "Bingo Fever" spreads quickly. At the break, more cards were sold for the final "winner-takes-all jackpot." With my increasing confidence, I bought several.

When the bingo caller, the same hard-to-impress young man who sold the cards to me earlier, returned to the podium before the big game was to begin, everyone in the room stood up. Was this part of the bingo ritual? Maybe a prayer to the God of Chance to have a winning card? Since the only one sitting was me, I joined the standing crowd.

As he slowly nodded, almost two hundred voices simultaneously began to sing: "Happy birthday to you… happy birthday, dear Claudia…" I was the only one standing as they all sat down.

Misty-eyed, I promised this room full of smiling native Alaskans that for as long as I lived, I would remember this as the most special surprise birthday greeting I ever received. I later learned that the seemingly uninterested young man had gone to each table during the break and organized the sweet serenade to me. Even the reticent woman next to me was beaming.

Now I felt welcome in this remote place where I had felt like an intruder. Bingo!

—Claudia P. Scott—

Once in a Lifetime

Life is not about living the safer option.
Life is about living a life worth living.
~Robert Thier

t all started sedately enough. We had impulsively signed up for a Mexican Riviera cruise. The price was right, the pace was easy, and the weather was good. It was a nice, low-key getaway — that was until I saw the shore excursion for ziplining in the Sierra Madre mountains outside of Puerto Vallarta.

Talk about an opportunity! The brochure couldn't have been more compelling if it had been dipped in chocolate and covered with whipped cream. The experience offered two miles of zipping, rappelling down steep vertical descents, and Tarzan swinging, all in the middle of a jungle.

I was sold, but there was one sturdy obstacle between the jungle and me — my husband. I knew I would have to be my most persuasive.

"So, what do you think we should do while we're in Puerto Vallarta?" I smoothly opened.

"Oh, maybe check out the old town, have lunch and pick up a few things for the kids," he responded. "I don't suppose it's changed much since we were there before."

That was my opening. "You are probably right. I don't imagine it will be much different. Maybe we should try something new."

"New?" There was a note of suspicion in his voice.

"You know, get out of the town and do something exciting."

"Exciting? What kind of exciting?" His antennae were on full alert. He knew me, and he knew this wasn't going to be good.

"Well, I was checking the shore excursions, and there is a great trip into the mountains. It's an eco-tour and gets great reviews." With some trepidation, I handed him the brochure.

"Bird watching, catamaran sailing, dolphin watching... Which one did you have in mind?"

It was the moment of truth. "Actually, I was talking about the ziplining. It's a five-hour tour, really experienced guides, modern equipment, and a chance of a lifetime."

I knew what was coming, and he didn't disappoint.

"Are you flippin' crazy? You want to go flying through the Mexican jungles on cables and ropes? We aren't forty anymore; we aren't even fifty. How about the bird watching?"

But I was relentless. "We need to seize the opportunity; even children participate. The ship wouldn't allow it if it wasn't safe. When will we have a chance like this again?"

I knew I was making progress when he muttered something about our will.

Two days later, we docked in Puerto Vallarta. We lined up with our fellow "zippers" and waited for the guide. The chatter from our cohort was a little intimidating. A couple from Australia was hoping it matched the rush of bungee jumping. A woman from the U.K. who had just finished her fifth marathon was thinking it would be a nice change of pace. You get the idea.

We huddled in the corner next to the only other people over fifty. The husband was celebrating his recovery from heart surgery.

Our guide arrived full of enthusiasm and release forms. We dutifully swore that we were in good health, of sound mind, and would not sue, no matter what. We were off.

A quick trip across the harbor, and we were directed to a row of old military Jeeps. I couldn't contain myself and began to hum the *Indiana Jones* theme song. This was going to be good. Bob was not amused.

We bounced our way across mountain roads and washed-out riverbeds and finally arrived at base camp. Our guide hustled us off the Jeeps and into the equipment room where we buckled, belted and harnessed. Safety helmets and leather gloves completed our gear. We were on to orientation. Six guides were assigned to our crew. They started with an explanation of our equipment and followed with a description of the course and safety features.

Next came basic procedural instruction. We learned how to position our hands and, most importantly, how to brake. This was important to know as you could attain speeds of fifty miles an hour if you don't control the tension. Next, we learned not to brake too soon or you could get stuck in the middle of the cable.

Finally, feet up, relax and have fun. It was time to zip.

The first platform was about 125 feet up, and the distance to the next platform was nearly a quarter of a mile. Bob went first. He stoically gripped the cable and stepped out. He sailed through the air like a pro and landed gracefully on the other side.

I was next. I took a leap of faith and stepped off the edge. It was phenomenal. Below me, way below me, was a riverbed, and all around were century-old trees. Before I knew it, I was approaching the platform at a high speed. I bent my feet and bounced off the tree, grateful to feel the guide grab my harness.

We zipped from platform to platform. After eight "flights," we landed on a somewhat larger space. It was time to rappel the 150 feet to the ground and cross to the next section of the course.

"Mr. Heart Attack" was up first. I've never seen anyone look so scared. He had a death grip on the cable that was wound around his hips and between his legs. Bad idea, the guide informed him. The cable between his legs could do some serious and permanent damage. He reset, wiped the sweat from his brow, and stepped off. The rest of us looked like pros compared to him.

At the bottom, we took a break while the guides explained the next phase. There was also an offer to call it done and head back to the center for margaritas. Thankfully, Mr. Heart Attack took them up on their offer and, surprisingly, so did Bob.

"I'll order you a beer," he said with a smile. "You'll be fine. Enjoy the rest of the course."

I watched him leave a bit wistfully. The fun was really in doing this together, but I was determined to finish, so off I went. At the next platform, we faced our longest and fastest zip yet. I started out just fine but could soon feel myself picking up speed. Nervously, I started braking and found myself stalled six feet from the platform.

"It's okay," said the guide. "Just reach up to the cable and pull yourself in."

Since I have the upper-body strength of a Muppet, that wasn't going to happen. After some finagling, we managed to get me to the platform, safe and sound but exhausted. Two zips later, there was another opportunity to head back. I took a page from Bob's book and called it quits. The experience had been a true adventure, and I decided it was best to quit while I was ahead and in one piece.

I headed back to camp with my appointed escort, one of our charming guides.

"*Señora,*" he said, "you are a strong woman. You did well."

"Yes, well, I'm not so sure, but I had fun, and that's what counts."

"*Si*, you and Mr. Bob did well. He is your husband, right? How long have you been married?"

Well, this was an interesting turn of events. I figured he must be curious because I didn't see how he could possibly be flirting.

"Forty years," I replied.

"You must really love him. Forty years is a long time. I am surprised. If you don't mind my asking, how old are you?"

I hadn't bargained for this part of the adventure, but I forged ahead.

"Let's say a little over sixty."

"*Señora*, that cannot be. You are a beautiful woman. Let me just say this. If you ever decide to leave Mr. Bob, you will not have a problem finding another husband here in Puerto Vallarta." He gave me a huge grin, shook my hand, and led me into camp.

"Have fun?" asked Bob, who was waiting at the bar.

"Fun doesn't begin to describe it. This may be the most exhilarating experience I've had in years. Everything I'd hoped for and more."

Back at the boat, we relived the day and decided it had been a once-in-a-lifetime experience. Bob emphasized the "once," and I was okay with that. After all, how could it get any better?

—Kathy Humenik—

32

Mountain Guide

*A mentor is someone who allows you to see
the hope inside yourself.*
~Oprah Winfrey

I was sitting by the gas-lit fireplace in my local library when a book on a table caught my eye. It was the collected correspondence of Maxwell Perkins and Marjorie Rawlings. As I read their letters, I could hear their long-stilled voices speaking to each other, and to me, across the expanse of decades. I tried to check out the book but was told it was a reject from a book sale. If I wanted it, I would have to buy it, so I did.

At home, I looked up Maxwell Perkins on the Internet. A link led me to rural Vermont and Perkins' granddaughter, the novelist Ruth King Porter. Ruth was giving away her novels, asking nothing in return but that readers post reviews on her website. I sent for Ruth's books, and a correspondence began.

I was scheduled to visit Ruth in spring, when her mother's dying began. I was rescheduled to visit Ruth in autumn, when *my* mother's dying began. My mother was a chronic cancer patient whose condition turned terminal in the autumn of 2013. Instantly, I cancelled travel plans and let go of my already-purchased bus ticket. A local clinic stepped in to provide practical assistance.

Then, a friend offered to drive me to Vermont for the day. Encouraged by my mother, I accepted the offer.

"We are two middle-aged women, both wearing glasses," I wrote to Ruth. "My friend is a blonde with dark roots. I still think of myself as brunette, but there is more salt than pepper in my hair now." Ruth wrote that she would be waiting for me under the clock tower of Montpelier City Hall. I knew what Ruth looked like from the photographs on her website.

My companion and I rode into Montpelier on a glorious Indian summer day at high noon. I saw Ruth sitting on a bench under the clock tower, scribbling in a notebook. Main Street was packed with tourists, and we couldn't stop the car in front of City Hall. We found a parking space down the street. My friend waited in the car while I ran down the block. "Ruth?" The woman on the bench looked up and then leapt to her feet.

Ruth was a pre-hippie back-to-the-lander in her early seventies. At our first meeting, she wore a white work shirt and faded blue jeans. She had slung a black money belt over her shoulder and walked like someone who rides horses a lot.

"Where's your friend?" Ruth called through the crowd of tourists blocking the sidewalk.

"She's waiting in the car!" I called back. I led Ruth to the car and my friend. Ruth then took us on a tour of the golden-domed state capitol. "I hope we don't run into my son." Ruth twinkled. "He'd be embarrassed by the way I'm dressed. My son Louis works as an aide to the governor." When the tour was over, we followed Ruth in her battered old car, out of Montpelier and higher into the Green Mountains, where another world awaited.

I felt as though I'd stepped into a Norman Rockwell painting. Ruth's husband Bill and a second son, Robbie, rode their tractors out of the woods to greet us on the porch of their rambling farmhouse. Taut, lean, Alabama-born Bill wiped the grime off his hands and stepped forward to shake mine. Ruth's daughter Molly, an artist who lived, Thoreau-like, in a cabin she built with her hands, bounded up a hill to join us.

I'm sure they were aware of the situation with my mother, though no one referred to it.

As an early darkness fell, my companion and I crossed back over the fence we call a border, returning to Montreal and my mother's apartment.

"Hello, sweetheart." My dying mother smiled tenderly. "How did it go with the lady in Vermont?"

What could I say? I felt guilty for having left her even for a few hours. I didn't feel like relaying the details of an excursion to Vermont.

Six months later, I returned to Montpelier by bus, alone. Once more, Ruth met me under the clock tower. For a few days in May, I curled under Ruth's wing, sunning on her roof, sleeping in Max Perkins' bed, waking to birdsong, and skimming the staggering array of autographed, out-of-print books dedicated by grateful authors to their engaged and caring editor. "Grieving is hard work," Ruth would greet me when, after a nap, I descended a steep staircase into her dark country kitchen. Standing side by side in the verdant meadow, which was her front yard, Ruth stated, as much in amazement as in sadness, "A year ago this time, both our mothers were alive."

Ruth King Porter is an American blueblood whose ancestry harks back to a woman who held a door for George Washington. I am the Canadian-born daughter of refugees. My mother, a woman who survived three invasions and the Warsaw Ghetto, later in life became prominent in Holocaust education. Ruth and her husband Bill were fascinated by my family history. Ruth did for me what I had done for my mother. She listened and encouraged me to tell my mother's story. When I read a book Ruth recommended, I realized she had a deeper understanding of my background than I thought possible.

Six months after my first extended visit, I was back on the farm. Ruth and her husband Bill acknowledged what would've been my mother's birthday by inserting and lighting large candles into holes carved in a spectacularly tangled chandelier made entirely of logs. As we consumed hot squash and a pot full of peas grown in Ruth's garden, cold autumn rain and wind lashed the last leaves off a forest full of trees outside the wall-sized picture window. Inside, as we ate, the chandelier shone, the tree bark-shaded lamps glowed, and the wood stove burned.

Several weeks later, nearing my birthday, which was a big one, by post I received from Ruth a warm, multi-coloured scarf. Inspired by the gift and the woman who gave it, the next day I bought an attractive hat to wear with the scarf.

I have been back to Ruth and Bill's farm several times since. Between visits, Ruth does for me what her grandfather did for Ernest Hemingway, F. Scott Fitzgerald, Thomas Wolfe — and Marjorie Rawlings. She writes to me and elicits writing from me, reading and critiquing my material, encouraging, cajoling, indicating where and when she believes I have veered off-track, and gently nudging me back.

Clutching the psychic lifeline tossed to me by the descendant of a legendary literary editor, I lived and worked alone in my suburban Montreal apartment. I finished the memoir of my mother.

—S. Nadja Zajdman—

33

Bears in the Woods

Sons are the anchors of a mother's life.
~Sophocles

Day hikes on the Appalachian Trail had taken me across more than 100 miles of rocky inclines, towering boulders, muddy lanes and rough log bridges spanning crystal clear streams. The array of people I encountered through hiking was fascinating, but I was never interested in completing the entire 2,190 miles. Instead, my goal was to spend a single night on the trail.

I was turning sixty, and it was time to confront and conquer my fear of what might be lurking in the darkness of the woods. I had shoulder and neck issues that limited the amount of weight I could carry in my backpack, so I asked my thirty-year-old son, Erik, to assist me. He readily agreed, and now, six months later, we were in Virginia's Shenandoah Mountains preparing to spend a night on the Appalachian Trail.

The morning literally flew by as we ziplined through the woods, a birthday surprise. Unafraid, I sped along on the cable suspended twenty feet above the forest floor. After all, not only could I see any threats that lurked below, but I was well beyond reach! We devoured burgers at a local diner before stationing a car at the hike's end.

Finally, we made our way to our starting point. Our boots did not hit the trail until mid-afternoon. I was not prepared for the intense heat and humidity, far beyond anything I had ever experienced.

The mistake of our delay hung as heavy as the air. The trail began in an open field, under a sun that swiftly sapped my energy. Erik waited patiently as I ducked under small bushes to grab a few inches of shade. My heart pounded against my chest as I gulped down water and inched up the steep incline. I had real doubts that I could finish the first mile, even minus the backpack Erik had already kindly added to his load.

When we finally reached the ridge, the temperature eased in the welcome shade of the woods, and the trail leveled out a bit — small measures of relief, but enough to spur my feet forward. We hiked for another hour before perching on two large boulders to rest. Suddenly, Erik sprang to his feet, pointed down the trail, and blurted out: "Bear!"

Bears were not new to my world. Thirty-seven acres of maple, oak, birch, and cherry had surrounded my childhood home in upstate New York. After bears were relocated there from the Adirondack Mountains, they were seen in back yards and lumbering across roads. One time, our dog had herded my mother, my two brothers and me together in our blueberry lot, and then sat quivering at our feet as we heard loud rustling in nearby bushes.

Bears amplified my already intense fear of the woods and kept my feet in open spaces well into adulthood — until I hesitantly joined a group of friends on a day hike. That day, I discovered the peacefulness that unfolded amidst the trees and the quiet coolness hidden in the shadows I had been so afraid to explore. It was the first of many hikes to follow, and my fear of the woods began to relax — in the daylight.

Now, not thirty feet away, was a huge black bear. Without hesitation, my own "mother bear" instinct kicked in, and adrenaline propelled me between the bear and my son.

"What do we do?" I sputtered.

Erik calmly responded, "Mom, we're just going to walk back the way we came for a little bit."

As we started moving away, the bear crashed off into the heavy brush surrounding the trail. We stopped, held our breath and, to our relief, the sound of small limbs snapping faded away. Cautiously, with eyes jumping from trail to bush to tree, we moved forward.

The sun had already started its long midsummer descent, and we still needed a place to camp. We arrived with the dusk at a campsite, relieved to see two other people there. Maybe they would rush to my aid if I screamed in the night!

We set up the tent, found the tiny, burbling puddle indicated on our map as the only nearby water source, filled our bottles and added the purifying, metallic-tasting iodine pills. Damp wood thwarted Erik's efforts to build a fire in the stone-lined pit. Finally, flames soared, and we sat in a small pool of light. At least now I could see what was coming to get me!

We dined on cheese, fruit, and chili warmed in and eaten from the cans. Then all food was stowed in a bag and hung on the tall, metal post provided to keep it safe from bears. As we walked to our two-person tent, I wondered if I would be as safe as the food.

Erik and I settled into our sleeping bags, in closer proximity than we had been since he was a small boy. We talked a little, and then I fell asleep despite knowing that only a thin nylon wall stood between me and whatever was out there. Each time I turned over in the night, Erik startled awake with a tense "Mom, you okay?!" He would later reveal that he kept dreaming I was outside the tent walking around. My cub was obviously already a protector himself.

Next morning, still in one piece, we retrieved our food from the bear pole and hiked on. We fell into a comfortable mix of silence and occasional exchanges as we walked. This hike was longer than I was accustomed to, and the weather was steamy again. At midday I suddenly felt heavy with exhaustion. I sank onto a nearby tree trunk, and Erik gently encouraged me to keep drinking, even after my thirst had been quenched. Fifteen minutes and two bottles of water later, I felt better.

I had imagined this adventure, the first with my adult son, would be filled with conversations — about him, about me, about life. Instead, his quiet patience, support and concern expressed more — about him, about me, and about life — than I ever expected. I not only made it through the night in the darkness of the woods but did so knowing bears could be lurking outside our tent! And, knowing Erik was by my side, I slept in relative peace. I had hiked thirteen miles in the company of my son and not only faced lifelong fears but discovered unexpected courage within my own heart — along with the depth of generosity and love in his.

—Susan K. Shetler—

And Away We Go!

Travel and change of place impart new vigor
to the mind.
~Seneca

Our kids thought we were nuts. After all, we already had five Corvettes! And we were at the age to retire but we both still worked full time. Most of our friends had already retired and were downsizing. Why did we need another car, let alone another Corvette? A two-seater sports car, low to the ground and fast! Had we lost our minds? Had dementia set in? Our young grandsons, on the other hand, thought we were cool. Way cool. Papa would be driving a new Corvette. And so would I.

My husband Frank has loved Corvettes since he was a boy. We got our first one when we were both in our twenties and had small children — back before seatbelt laws limited where young children could sit. Our family of five went for many drives in that two-seater convertible with Frank and me in the front seats and all the kids lying down in the back. We all loved it.

We added new models to our collection over the years — always adding new ones but never getting rid of the old ones. But now Frank was especially "in love" with the newest Corvette. I tried not to be jealous. But the look on his face and the gleam in his eyes when he looked at the new model reminded me of when we were young. The style, the colors, the performance, the technology… Wow! And the fact that the car gets over thirty miles per gallon on the highway is just a plus.

He was hooked. And I wasn't far behind. We decided to go for it! Why not?

The first thing we had to do was pick our colors — one for the exterior and one for the interior. Then, pulling up a program from the website, we (well really, he) "built" our new car from the frame up. He spent hours and had such fun deciding on the different packages he had to choose from: the exact model, the performance package, the wheels, the style and finish on the hub caps, the exterior trim, and on and on. Who knew there were so many options?

I had a job too. I had to decide on the color for the interior. We chose silver with racing stripes for the exterior and then I went a little crazy. The interior color would be RED!! Bright, dazzling red. Not subdued burgundy or dull maroon. None of that for us youngsters! We were ready. We put in the order.

The day we picked the car up was a day to remember. Frank got up early and got ready — just as if he were going out on a first date! We went to the dealer and there she was — our brand-new silver Corvette with red leather interior. Absolutely beautiful. And she smelled so good, too. When Frank started her up for the first time and heard the rumble of her engine, he was a teenager again.

Every five years the National Corvette Museum in Bowling Green, Kentucky holds a huge gathering over the Labor Day weekend. People from all around the world meet there to celebrate the anniversary of the opening of the museum that honors the one and only true American sports car. The Corvette. And because of my husband's "thing" for Corvettes, we decided we were going to join in on that caravan driving from California across the country to Kentucky.

That is why we were back at the dealer a few weeks later because that was the departure point for the thirteen cars in our Corvette club leaving from our California town. We were committed to driving for five days to get to Bowling Green to celebrate the twenty-fifth anniversary of the opening of the museum.

We were all in different stages of our lives, the common denominator being the car. The oldest in our group was ninety and he was making the trip with his son; the youngest was in her thirties and the rest of us spanned our forties, fifties, sixties, seventies and eighties. Age didn't matter; we all got along beautifully. In addition to our thirteen cars, we were joined by ten cars from Hawaii. These people had had their cars shipped from Hawaii to California specifically to join the celebration and were so excited to be with us. And we all had CB radios so we could communicate with each other. With those radios, it was like we were all together, in one car.

Our first night's stop was in Los Angeles. There we picked up about two hundred more cars. The next morning, when we took off, the local news covered our departure. Police stopped traffic for us until we got on the freeway. Our kids, you know those same kids who thought we were too old to do this, watched on TV from home as Mom and Dad and a few hundred more people pulled out of a parking lot and headed east! And away we went! Bowling Green or bust!

Over the next five days, we drove through Nevada, Utah, Colorado and the Midwest. The route was carefully planned, as were the stops along the way. The routine was that we would depart at 9:00 AM and drive for about three hours. I am the senior editor of Chicken Soup for the Soul and I had deadlines! But I was able to keep working while on the road. During that morning run, I was reading submissions, editing manuscripts, answering e-mails and e-mailing and texting with the people in the office — all of this made possible through wireless technology.

Around noon, we'd all stop a while for lunch. After lunch, Frank and I would switch off and I would take over and do the three-hour afternoon driving duties. The car is so much fun to drive and I love to drive — fast! Then we'd pull into our hotel and stop for the night.

The arrival of the caravan was well publicized in each state we drove through. All along the way, either on overpasses or along the sides of the roads, people were watching for us, waving flags or just waving, holding signs welcoming us to their state. What fun and how exciting. We were celebrities! There were always gatherings each night, put on by either the local Corvette clubs or the car dealers in the area. Dinner, dancing, games and fun. Every place we stopped, we got goodie bags with the local specialties, car accessories and T-shirts included. T-shirts galore! And then the next morning, with more and more cars joining in, we kept driving east and repeated the routine.

By the time we arrived in Bowling Green, there were around 8,000 Corvettes containing 15,000 people, converging from all over North America and beyond... People from Europe, Africa, Australia and other countries participated as well, making it an international celebration of the best car ever: the Corvette.

The fun in Bowling Green was amazing. With all these thousands of people you would have thought it would have been chaotic. But not at all. We had the best time: road trips through the beautiful countryside in Kentucky, visits to local distilleries and businesses, lunch at a hotel built in the 1800s that's said to be haunted, exhibitions, competitions, demonstrations, and much more. We were busy all the time.

The last night there was an outdoor concert. There we all were, sitting on our blankets on the grass under the beautiful Kentucky star-filled night sky in the amphitheater at the Corvette museum, singing along with Jefferson Starship, performing live, on stage. Of course, we knew all the words to the songs; we knew them from years ago but we felt like we were teenagers again!

All too soon the celebration was over, and it was time for everyone to head home. One of our most special memories from the trip is that each morning, before we left on the next leg of our journey, one of the women from the Hawaii group would come on the CB radio and say a prayer, in Hawaiian, wishing us all safe travels. It was very spiritual… and what a wonderful way to start another day of exploring our vast country. What we saw each day was so varied, because the scenery changes often from state to state and even within a state. Each state is unique and beautiful in its own way. From the starkness of the deserts in Nevada to the mountains and rock formations in Utah and Colorado to the green and gorgeous plains of the Midwest, it's all magnificent.

Everyone should take a road trip like this, because you learn that despite the wide variety of environments, as you travel across the country the people you meet are good, kind, generous and friendly.

We look back on our Corvette adventure with such fond memories. And it didn't hurt our reputation at all with our kids and grandkids. They think we're a bit cooler than they had realized. Maybe we'll do it again… in another five years!

—Barbara LoMonaco—

I Belong

*The universal brotherhood of man is our most precious
possession, what there is of it.*
~Mark Twain

This magnificent machine, the baby I call Harley, will help me
forget my troubles. My new moped is waiting on the asphalt
driveway when I walk out the front door. It sits there with its
plastic windshield, black metal frame, silver polished fend-
ers, and Tomos written across the side. There is peace inside me, not
a care in the world.

I don a black helmet and wide goggle sunglasses. My short, sixty-
seven-year-old female body, with its graying hair and degenerating spine,
takes on the appearance of someone composed and self-possessed, like
the bikers in *Easy Rider.* I swing my leg over the seat, move the starter
switch to on, and pedal backward. The engine sputters its putt-putt
noises. Harley and I are bonded, ready to flow as one. I feel power,
something I can control, unlike the feelings I get with my human
children who are now adults.

My feet lift off the ground as I rotate the rubber handle to give it
gas. The air glides over my face, a nice relief on this warm day. I'm on
the road in the town of Poolesville, Maryland, headed for the country.
A group of children on the sidewalk stop walking and turn their heads
to the noise coming toward them. Our eyes meet, and smiles form on
their faces. A ten-year-old boy gives me a thumbs up.

I cruise the country roads, admiring farmhouses and enjoying the coolness in the wooded areas. Then I pass the home of a hospice patient who died this week. Several cars surround her house. It must be the funeral. As a hospice nurse, I know where people are dying. Even when trying to escape from my job, it follows me, reminds me that death is everywhere. I come to an old white church, a small cemetery behind it. There is a fresh mound of dirt with potted gladiolas scattered around a gravesite. A tractor with a front-end loader drops more dirt on top. This must be where she was just buried. I say a prayer, "Peace be with the family."

I continue across a one-lane bridge over a creek. My body sways as I maneuver the curves. I arrive at a country store nestled at the bottom of a hill in the woods. Two old men who look like they are one hundred years old, but are probably in their eighties, sit outside on chairs next to a picnic table. I park the moped and walk up two steps into the old-fashioned general store. It has a wooden floor and seeds in barrels for farmers to buy. Straw is stored in the shed behind the building. I pay for a bottled water, sit outside on a chair near the old men in bib overalls and listen to their country-talk.

Looking at the tall trees, the farmers, and the old store takes me back to the 1960s, to Kankakee, Illinois where I grew up. I think about myself as a ten-year-old. If I'd had a moped back then, riding in the country would have been the most fun in the whole world. Now I can ride every day. Is this why I have such a craving? Is the child inside me coming out?

I finish the water, take a nice long route back to town, and stop at the local grocery store. As I'm locking the moped to go into the store, a woman my age in a baggy housedress approaches me. Her eyes stare at the moped. She asks me many questions about my ride, admiring my bravery. She tells me her husband who died fourteen years ago wanted to buy two motorbikes for them to ride on the country roads, just like me. We have a nice talk, and I tell her we should start a biker group for old ladies. She says, "I might fall off and get killed." I walk into the store thinking I'm the bravest old lady in town.

I tie the groceries on the back of my bike and ride out of town on a different country road, cruising at a speed of twenty miles per hour, with bean fields stretching out across a wide-open field on my right. In front of me, two big, bad Harley-Davidson motorcycles are coming. Their windshields are ten times bigger than mine, with throaty loud noises coming from their exhausts. The riders' legs stretch out near the front tires, and black boots are on the footrests. They wear black leather jackets, matching leather trousers, and helmets with tinted face shields.

I stare at them, wondering if it will happen today. The first biker gets close, and his hand comes off the left handlebar slowly in that "cool-dude" fashion. A leather glove covers his hand, and two fingers point to the side, palm forward. Could this be for me? Oh, my God, it is — a hand greeting from a genuine biker. I don't smile so they will think this happens to me every day. Slowly, I take my hand off the handlebar, imitating that same "I'm cool move." My bare hand gives him the two-finger greeting back. The second Harley rider does the same.

When they are behind me, I smile, and goose bumps cover my body. I've been initiated into the Harley brotherhood, recognized by real bikers, not just ten-year-old children or sixty-year-old women. I finally belong. I straighten my aching spine, lift my head high, and grip the handlebars with pride. Looking up at the baby blue sky with its sparse white clouds, I say the words out loud: "I belong!"

—Susan Randall—

While We're Young

May your years be counted not by your age but by how
you spend your days.
~Catherine Pulsifer

One of the benefits of retirement that I have enjoyed most is the chance to become part of a walking group. No longer do I have to spend solitary hours on the elliptical trainer while watching the Food Network. A walking group makes the regular exercise that is so extolled for its health benefits part of a pleasant social outing.

Our walking group doesn't have any formal membership. It includes anyone who turns up at the front gate of our housing complex to walk on any given morning. Some of us are regulars. Others, not so much. We start out promptly at 8 a.m. and do a brisk five-kilometre walk to our local coffee shop. There, we exchange news and solve the problems of the world before heading home again. Since this takes us close to two hours, it is an activity that only a retiree can indulge in on a year-round basis, and the ages of our walkers reflect that fact.

When you spend time together on a regular basis, friendships develop. In good weather, we sometimes make a day of it and head out for longer and more scenic walks. We have also been known to get together for a glass of wine now and then, and birthdays especially provide an ideal excuse for a bit of a party. In 2012, one of our walkers was bemoaning the fact that she would be turning sixty-five that June. An older member of the group said that was nothing. She would be turning seventy-five the same month. It seemed that two big birthdays demanded some serious celebration, so we put our heads together.

I can't remember who suggested a walking tour in England, but the idea caught on. That June, six of us set off on a self-guided walking tour of the Cornwall Coast Path from St Ives to Lizard, a distance of close to 120 kilometres. What an adventure! The scenic route follows the coastline, so we were treated to some wonderful seascapes and beaches. We saw historical ruins and some quaint villages, but there were also some very long and challenging days. On those days, we might be plodding through mud up past our ankles or scrambling over great rock outcroppings. It sure tested our mettle, and as we got near the end of the route, we were feeling pretty smug about our accomplishments.

We were in this frame of mind the day we met two Austrian women who were doing the trail in the opposite direction. They looked to be about our age and were just starting out. We stopped for a chat. My friend explained that this walk was our celebration of two special birthdays. The older of the Austrian women nodded her approval.

"Yes," she said. "It's good to do these things while you're still young."

I did a double take and looked to see if this was a joke. It seemed not. Her expression was serious and respectful. Her words have stayed with me.

Now, I am the one who is seventy-five years old. My friends and I have booked a tour of the Antrim Coast of Ireland for this coming summer. I plan to celebrate my seventy-sixth birthday on the trail. I have always wanted to see Ireland, and I realize that if I want to do it as a walking tour, it better be while I'm still young.

— Carole Lazar —

Chapter
5

The Privilege
of Age

37

Ball Dude

*You are never too old to set another goal
or to dream a new dream.*
~C. S. Lewis

On August 5, 2003, in my seventh year of retirement, I wore a San Francisco Giants uniform and walked onto the red clay of the third base sidelines of PacBell Park, now known as Oracle Park. I was surrounded by 42,200 fans in the sold-out stadium.

It was around 6 p.m. The players on the field stretched, ran sprints and loosened up before the game. The lights had come on but were not needed yet.

A woman asked me to autograph a ball for her young son.

Was I dreaming? Nope. I had signed a contract and become a San Francisco Giant for one game.

How did a sixty-six-year-old retired teacher get to live his dream to be in the major leagues?

It had started five years earlier with my beautiful daughter, who loves baseball and knows people who know people. She had called and said, "Dad, would you like to be a Ball Dude?"

"Can I start tomorrow?" I said.

She said, "There's a five-year waiting list."

"I'll need a rocking chair by then," I said.

"Why?" she said.

"Before Satchel Paige, the oldest man to ever pitch in the major leagues actually pitched, he sat in a rocking chair in the bullpen."

"You won't be pitching," my daughter said, and hung up.

I said to myself, "What's a Ball Dude?"

A Ball Dude, in 1998, was a senior citizen in a baseball cap, uniform, glove and cleats who sat on the sidelines of either left field or right field during a major league baseball game, retrieved foul balls, and put them in the hands of youngsters.

Five years after my name was put on the wait list, I finally got the call to be in the "bigs." For that night game with Pittsburgh I parked in Lot B with the other employees, bought an official Giants fitted hat from the Dugout Store, and carried a glove instead of a briefcase to work. What a joy to carry that glove. True, it was my daughter's glove, but why tell anyone I had lost my high-school glove?

At age sixty-six, I became the first member of my family of athletes to be on the field during a professional baseball game! Plus, my team-mates were MVP Barry Bonds, All-Star pitcher Jason Schmidt, Gold Glove winner J.T. Snow, and other baseball royalty.

Dick Levy, sixty-five, the other Ball Dude, celebrated his fiftieth birthday in Baseball Fantasy Camp where he batted .571 (8 for 14). He carried his high-school glove and wore his lucky Giants hat for his major league debut.

After changing into uniforms, we were given basic instructions: Stay out of the way of the players and keep foul balls off the playing field. Following a brief tour of the stadium interior — dining room, batting cage, and clubhouse — we heard, "Remember, you are Ambassadors for the Giants."

I remembered that when I noticed a baseball sitting like a little white pearl on a sea of green grass between third base and left field. The fans noticed it. The players ignored it. Dick and I had been told to stay off the grass, but we were Ambassadors, too. I invoked the diplomatic immunity clause, walked onto the grass, and picked up the ball.

A roar came from the stands! The fans begged and pleaded. It was upsetting. So, I handed the ball to Dick and they turned on him instead. He did his job as Ball Dude and placed the souvenir in the hands of a happy child.

Game time rituals commenced: Home-plate umpires accepted line-up cards, players stood along baselines, our national anthem was sung, and an umpire shouted, "Play ball!"

Dick sat on his four-legged stool away from third base. I sat on mine away from first base. As the game progressed, Jason Schmidt's pitching dominated the batters. Of the first eighteen former teammates Jason faced, sixteen of them sat down. I was so immersed in Schmidt's pitching I forgot I was in uniform and simply enjoyed my unique view of a professional baseball game.

In the sixth inning, Dick bolted off his stool and stopped a well-hit ball with his high-school mitt. Dick's efforts flashed on Stadium TV monitors with the announcer's voice, "Great catch! Bad hat." (Dick's hat had been a giveaway at an old Candlestick Park game, but he couldn't see throwing away something he had worn at baseball camp where he'd hit .571.) Giants announcers Mike Krukow and Duane Kuiper gave my hat a "good" rating. (My $25 had been well-spent.)

I relaxed. The Giants played an error-free game. Schmidt pitched a shutout, but a Pirate batter smacked a laser-like ground ball down the first-base foul line. Only when the ball rocketed past me did I remember my job was to catch the ball, not admire how a fan gloved a souvenir.

"Rookie mistake," I told myself, wishing I'd reached out and gloved the ball but comforted that I had not tried and then dropped it.

"I'll get the next one," I reassured my son, daughter and everyone behind me who groaned at my faux pas. I put on my game face, pounded my mitt and leaned aggressively forward. I would do everything in my power to help the Giants win. I hadn't played two years of high-school baseball for nothing.

Ninth inning. Giants 3. Pirates 0. Like Casey Stengel said, "Good pitching will always stop good hitting and vice versa." With one out, the relief pitcher came in. Suddenly, Pirates were everywhere — on all the bases, at bat and in the bullpen — and the game was still one batter against nine players, but that one batter could hit a home run, which would mean Pirates 4, Giants 3.

Tim Worrell, Giants second relief pitcher, entered the game more focused than Schmidt. Worrell pitched one ball. Result: One double play! Giants won their seventieth game.

"I Left My Heart in San Francisco" played over the loudspeakers. The lights dimmed.

I drove home and thought about that ninth inning scare, how baseball really was like life — unpredictable, full of challenges and mistakes, but not quite as much fun as being a Ball Dude.

Caveat emptor: A Ball Dude gets to keep the fifteen-dollar paycheck but not the uniform.

—John J. Lesjack—

38

Reserved for Seniors

My goal is to say or do at least one
outrageous thing every week.
~Maggie Kuhn

was taking my fourteen-year-old granddaughter to soccer practice and I was running behind. As we backed down the driveway,
she drummed her fingers on the armrest.

"What's wrong?" I asked.

"Coach's rule is we have to run a lap for every minute we're late."

"That seems harsh," I said. "But don't worry, sweetie. We'll get
there on time."

I eyed the dashboard clock. The practice field reserved that day
was located at the farthest end of a local high school, just beyond their
outdoor stadium. That added several minutes to our drive.

My granddaughter jiggled her foot while we waited at a red light.

"So, what other rules does your new coach have?" I asked, trying
to divert her attention.

"No earrings. Our shin guards have to be in place, our soccer
shoes tied tight, and he doesn't like us to wear our cleats off the field."
She turned to me. "And we have to be picked up on time."

When the light finally turned green, she twisted her long blond
hair into a ponytail. "Can you drive faster?"

I patted her knee. "Almost there."

Then we ran into a traffic jam. She took off her sneakers and put on her shin guards as we pulled into the parking lot.

Rows of out-of-town buses lined the perimeter. A sign on the marquee announced the school was hosting a regional sports tournament. I drove down row after row searching for an empty space.

With few minutes to spare, my granddaughter pulled on her thick athletic socks and laced up her soccer shoes.

"I thought you weren't supposed to wear your cleats off the field," I said.

"I'm not, but I don't have time to change on the bench. Just stop and drop me off here."

I kept driving. "Hold on. I'm sure we'll find something closer."

As if in answer to my wish, several slots were open near the entrance to the stadium. A sign printed in bold letters read: "RESERVED FOR SENIORS."

"Whew!" I pulled into the closest space.

"You can't park here, Grandma."

"Sure I can." I pointed to the sign. "I'm a senior."

She grabbed her gear and opened the door. "Um, Grandma, these parking places are reserved for HIGH SCHOOL seniors, not senior citizens. You'll get a ticket if you don't move."

I shrugged and smiled. "Don't worry about me, sweetie. See you in an hour."

I rolled down my window and inhaled the scent of freshly cut grass as I watched her trot to her practice field just in time. A wave of nostalgia washed over me as I recalled how fearful I was of getting into trouble when I was her age. My parents were strict, and the nuns at the all-girls' high school I attended were the same. Disobeying rules or questioning authority weren't tolerated.

But I've grown older — and bolder — since then.

If I was asked to move, I'd argue that since the sign didn't specify which type of seniors the parking spaces were reserved for, I wasn't breaking any rules. Feeling sassy, I tuned the radio to a station that played music from my high-school days.

When "Wild Thing" by The Troggs came on, I sang along and danced in my seat, enjoying my rebellious senior moment.

— Donna Volkenannt —

39

Just Socks

The cars we drive say a lot about us.
~Alexandra Paul

My husband Gary is known in our community for his photography skills, so it isn't unusual for him to get a phone call from someone who wants a special picture taken. That is exactly what happened one June day a few years ago.

"Jim asked me to take a couple of photos of something he wants to sell online," Gary announced as he headed to the door, camera in hand.

"What?" I asked.

Gary shrugged. "He didn't say. I'll find out when I get there."

An hour later, my husband returned with love shining in his eyes. Not for me. No, the love was for the red 1990 Mazda Miata that Jim wanted to sell. "I'm thinking of buying it," Gary said.

If he had announced that he was going to fly to the moon, I wouldn't have been more surprised. Us? Buy a sports car? What was he thinking? We're in our seventies. Seventy-somethings do not buy sports cars on the spur of the moment, if at all. I had to talk some sense into him.

In all fairness, I should explain that owning a Miata had been my husband's longtime dream. When our children were growing up and our daughter asked her dad what he wanted for Christmas or his birthday or Father's Day, his answer was always the same. "I want socks," he'd announce to the sighs and eye-rolling of our daughter.

"But," he would quickly add, "the socks must be presented in a special way. They must be packed in the trunk of a Mazda." Needless to say, financial constraints made that wish impossible.

Flash forward to June 2013. "Jim said we can take the car for a test drive," Gary said. "Not today because it looks like rain and Jim never takes the car out in the rain, but tomorrow for sure if the weather is nice."

I prayed for rain the next day. My concern was not the cost of the car. It was whether I'd be able to get my senior body into and out of a sports car without doing physical damage to myself.

In spite of my prayers, the next day dawned sunny and fair, and Gary went to pick up the car. Hoping that my neighbours weren't looking out their windows, I managed to get myself into it, albeit somewhat clumsily. Seatbelts buckled, we took off.

As we headed up a never-yet-explored country road — paved, of course, because you don't drive a sports car on gravel or dirt roads — something magical happened. Low to the ground with the wind blowing in my hair, I felt as though I were one with the countryside. By the time we got back home, the love was shining in my eyes, too.

We bought the Miata that day. For the first time in his life, Gary ordered vanity plates: SOCKBOX.

We spent the next few months exploring the back roads and byways of the surrounding area, finding interesting shops, local produce stands and breathtaking scenery on roads we would likely never have taken in our regular vehicle.

That was not the only gift the Sockbox brought us. We discovered the Trillium Miata Club, based in southern Ontario. Their website included photos taken on tours, showing a group of proud Miata owners with their pride-and-joy vehicles. There were enough grey heads in the group that we knew we would fit in age-wise.

We signed up for Friday evening ice-cream tours, day trips and overnights throughout Ontario and Quebec and into the United States. The tours, organized by members, include winding, hilly roads and spectacular scenery. Overnight stays at hotels or motels include parties in rooms with wine, laughter and socializing. Joining the Trillium Miata

Club was a blessing, a big part of which are the many new friends we have made.

In 2016, we switched to a 2012 Miata, metallic red with a black racing stripe. It has all the bells and whistles because we want to go farther afield on longer trips.

Parting with the original Sockbox was sad, but the license plate on the new one remains the same. We will always be grateful to the amazing little sports car that brought the gift of new friends and adventures into our senior years.

— Marilyn Helmer —

40

Okay, Pops

Growing old is compulsory — growing up is optional.
~Bob Monkhouse

One of our daughters is a schoolteacher, and since she and her husband both work, "Pops" decided to be the caregiver during the school week. Yep, I volunteered. It didn't take much, though, since her two boys, ages one and two, have me wrapped around their little fingers.

The wife said, "Are you sure you want to do this?"

"Hell, yeah," I said. "What's the problem? I'm retired. We can goof around all day. Go on trips to Home Depot and knock stuff off the shelves, dig in the dirt in the back yard. They will be like the sons we never had. It will be a blast."

"Okay," she said. "Just want to make sure you know what you're getting into."

"Please. We raised two daughters. What can be harder than that?"

Oh, boy, when you are in your twenties, it is not a problem. Now, at sixty-two, there is a world of difference, especially with these two knuckleheads. For some reason, the memories of thirty years ago do not coincide with the current situation. For instance, I do not recall the daughters jumping off the top of the couch and landing precisely on Pop's "junk." Never was it necessary to fill up the toys with soggy Cheerios. Oh, and guess who forgot that toddlers do not poop at the same time, or with the same vigor, for that matter.

When the girls were this age, there was *Sesame Street* and *The*

Electric Company, and that was it. Now, thanks to smart TVs, there are literally thousands of hours of kids' programming that we can watch repeatedly. When I say repeatedly, I mean over and over and over again. Don't get me wrong. I like many of the shows they watch, at least the first fifty times.

I know what you must be thinking. "Why not read a book or take them for a walk outside?" Please. Have you ever tried to get a two-year-old boy and a one-year-old boy to sit still long enough to read? It's like waiting for the toast to pop up. You know it's coming, and then, bang, it's off Pops's lap, down on the floor and back to throwing stuff at each other.

To be honest, it's kind of hilarious watching them go at it. That is, until the blood starts flowing. However, we will not be mentioning that to Mommy or Grandma. In fact, there will be a whole bunch of stuff we won't be telling them. Like where they learned the proper technique of the artificial fart under the arm, the lost art of blaming flatulence on someone else, the glorious method of fake vomiting, the poetic beauty of burping the alphabet and, last but not least, the timeless skill of hiding in a closet and jumping out to scare Grandma. You can't learn those things in daycare.

Everything is not all fun and games. Have you ever put together a twelve-piece *Paw Patrol* puzzle fifty times in a row? Maybe you have searched for the TV remote for an hour and finally found it in the Tupperware cupboard. There is also the melodic sound of banging two cookie sheets together. Then there's my favorite: finding your slippers in the kitchen garbage can right next to last night's chicken bones. That happened after they foiled the childproof lock on the can's lid.

You know, I consider myself a very tech-savvy man for my age, but it took me forever to figure out how to turn off closed captioning on the TV after one of them pressed some button on the remote numerous times. I even tried putting it up high on the shelves of the entertainment center until I turned my back for two and a half seconds and the two-year-old had climbed five feet up to get at it.

Thank God for Lisinopril. That is a hypertension medication, by the way. Hey, who hasn't chased down a one-year-old boy scampering across the floor after he has figured out how to take off all his clothes and diaper and decides to pee behind the recliner?

Then there is the pièce de résistance. That is, the mass exodus from the bathtub because someone decided it was the perfect time to poop. You know it makes perfect sense, though. No wiping and no diaper to throw out. To be honest, it was just so damn funny.

Which brings me to my final thoughts… Two years ago, when I took on this most important responsibility, I wasn't sure how it would go. Sure, it had been a long time since I'd watched children this age. I knew it would be different with boys, of course. Then I thought back to when my daughters were this young and how much I missed that age once they grew up; I realized I had been given an amazing gift. I get to spend all this time with my grandchildren without the stress of worrying about work or paying bills. And I get to be a kid again with them.

Spending my days with these two energetic, enthusiastic kids reminds me that even though the world out there seems crazy at times, all of that disappears if I act like them and live in the moment. It can be hard taking care of toddlers, but there's no medication better than a toddler rushing up to me and hugging my leg, or a sleepy little guy falling asleep on my shoulder. So, at the end of the day, I'll put them in their car seats, kiss them goodbye and say, "I'll see you tomorrow, buddies."

And then I hear the sweetest little voices saying, "Okay, Pops."

— D.J. Baumgardner —

41

The Great Smash

Rules should always be bent, if not broken.
It's the only way to have any fun.
~Alyson Noel

thought everyone celebrated their sixty-fifth birthday, not their sixtieth. But my children assured me that turning sixty had to involve some sort of celebration. I vetoed their party idea as I really don't like being the centre of attention. They were determined that something was going to happen and were gracious enough to let me decide what that something would be.

I gave in and suggested a family vacation — maybe a weekend at a cottage in Northern Ontario. That sounded like a good escape to me, and I began making plans. Unfortunately, eight months before the big day, I suffered a head injury. Recovery was slow and painful, but I held onto the hope that I would be well enough to make the journey north.

After several months, we decided to cancel the getaway. I needed to come up with something we could do at home instead. I wanted it to be special, and unusual — something we had never done before.

Then I remembered something I had watched on television a number of years earlier. The couple in the television show were dining in an upscale Greek restaurant. After they finished their meal, they took their plates, bowls and glasses and threw them into the stone fireplace, shattering everything. I remembered thinking that I would love to do that someday.

That was it! Smashing china was what I wanted to do to celebrate my sixtieth birthday. Even though my British relatives love their china dishes, I do not. My children weren't surprised when I told them about my plans. They were used to their mother being weird and thinking outside the box.

Planning was fairly easy. The old, concrete barn foundation on the rural property that I called home would be a great place to hold the event. Dishes would break easily and clean-up would be simple. Where does one search when in need of an item? On social media, of course. Local Facebook buy-and-sell groups worked perfectly. The ad read: "ISO free chipped, cracked, stained, out of date mugs, plates, bowls, glasses. No plastic please. Will pick up."

Members of the groups were happy to part with their unwanted dinnerware. A month before the event, I collected 180 pieces, including plates, bowls, mugs, glasses, teapots and Crock-Pot liners. One specific box contained gold-rimmed china that local thrift stores were unable to sell. Breaking fine bone china was going to be so much fun. I could hardly wait to turn sixty.

The weather didn't co-operate, and the event had to be moved indoors to the unfinished basement. A few days prior to the big day, I practiced breaking dishes just to make sure this idea was going to work. Wearing ear and eye protection and steel-toed work boots, I tossed an old china teapot at the concrete wall. The spout broke off the teapot, so I retrieved the remainder of the teapot and gave it a second toss. That toss proved fatal for the teapot. Hundreds of tiny pieces flew across the basement, landing on the concrete floor. It was so much fun that I just had to do one more. A second teapot met the same fate as the first.

"Research and development," I told myself. That's what I was doing, making everything just right for my family. It was difficult to refrain from throwing more pieces, but I managed to control the urge. I sent text messages to the family about eye and ear protection and proper footwear.

The big day arrived. Balloons were tied to a post at the end of the laneway. The cement steps leading to the front door were decorated with the words: "Welcome to the Great Smash." A poster was hung in the basement with "The Great Smash" written on it. Boxes of dishes of all shapes and sizes were lined up along the wall, ready to be thrown.

My children provided a delicious meal. After eating the cake and ice cream, presents were unwrapped. Then, it was time for "The Great Smash" to begin.

Before any smashing began, everyone had to sign a waiver saying they wouldn't sue me. Actually, it was a guest book. Plates were smashed four at a time, kicked with steel-toed work boots or thrown like Frisbees. Mugs were tossed and batted at the wall with a shovel. Throwing dishes into the corners of the wall shattered them into smaller pieces that travelled farther across the room. The grandchildren could have smashed dishes for hours and were disappointed when the smash was over. But they asked to do it again some time.

Clean-up was easy. With a large broom for sweeping and a shovel for scooping, the job was done. Five boxes were loaded into the back of my car, ready to go to the dump.

The grandkids told all their friends and teachers about "The Great Smash" the next day at school. Word travelled quickly, and some of the friends' parents were interested in smashing dishes. I told them the door is open, bring your dishes, have fun and clean up after yourself.

Saturday at the dump, the attendant gave me a strange look when I told him what was inside the boxes in the back of the car. After I finished telling him about "The Great Smash," he gave me a hug and charged me a two-dollar tipping fee.

My sixtieth birthday celebration was perfect. One more item has been ticked off my bucket list. "The Great Smash" will be held again next Christmas. There's a set of really ugly Christmas dishes that I would like to include in the smash. They are already lined up in the basement.

— Caroline Sealey —

42

Isn't That Something?

God made granddaughters to give our lives variety,
and to keep our hearts young.
~Author Unknown

was watching *Wheel of Fortune* with my husband when my granddaughter called from six hundred miles away in Florida. "Grandma, I'm getting married in a few months."

"Yes, darling, I heard. That is so exciting. We'll be there."

"Grandma, I want you to be my flower girl."

"You mean you want me to help you pick out your flowers? I'll be happy to help you."

"No, Grandma, I want you to carry a basket of petals down the aisle and be the flower girl."

I laughed. "Right. Isn't there an age limit on flower girls?"

"Not in my book. Seriously, I want you, Grandma. I want my family to be in the wedding, and you will be the perfect flower girl." I laughed. Again.

Just to be funny, I asked, "What will I wear?"

"My colors are teals, but you can wear whatever color you want and be comfortable." She was serious.

I told her I would think about it. After all, I was eighty years old. What would people think if, instead of a cute little girl, a gray-haired grandmother came down the aisle throwing flower petals?

I had decided to say no, but I went to the computer and Googled "women flower girls" to gather my evidence. To my surprise, I found a picture of grown women being flower girls. There they were in fancy dresses, women of all ages. The article said it was a growing trend in weddings. *Well, isn't that something,* I thought. *I am going to be a flower girl!*

My granddaughter was stepping out of tradition to have her wedding the way she wanted it. I liked the idea of having what you want instead of what someone thinks you should do. It was like having pizza for breakfast.

The more I thought about the idea, the more excited I became. I told my friends at tennis I was going to be a flower girl. At first, there were some laughs, but then the comments were how wonderful it was and what an honor. I was getting used to the idea. They were interested in what I would wear and offered a multitude of jewelry, shoes and accessories for me to consider. They volunteered to go shopping with me to find the right dress.

I visited many department stores, and even couture secondhand stores, looking for the perfect dress. I even bought one dress, but after my husband said it made me look old, I returned it.

And then I found it. My friend and I were having lunch in a little coffee shop that also sold a variety of unique women's clothing and purses. I saw the light blue dress, and it was in my size. It was a two-piece with a tiered top flowing gently over an ankle-length skirt. I took it into the small dressing room and tried it on. It was just what I wanted. Yes! Lunch and a dress; it was a good day.

My next concern was shoes. My lunch friend and I went shopping for shoes that would be comfortable, but dressy enough to be seen under the skirt. I found a wedge-heeled, toeless dress shoe that felt good to my left-foot bunion. Now all I needed was a pedicure. I never had toenails colored to match a dress before. It was fun. I was finally ready to be in the wedding.

Next up was the wedding rehearsal — the bridesmaids loved the idea of grandmother as flower girl and made me feel special. And then, on the wedding day itself, I glided down the aisle behind the seven bridesmaids. Heads turned, and a murmur went through the church.

When I flipped the first petals from my basket to the floor, gentle laughter arose and followed me. I could feel love and see smiles from the crowd. I enjoyed myself to the hilt as I scattered flower petals on people's laps and down the long aisle.

It was an awesome experience to precede my beautiful grand-daughter who wanted Grandma to be in her wedding party. I reached the end of my journey and sat down in the front row of pews. I looked in my empty basket and smiled.

I was a flower girl. Isn't that something?

— Beverly LaHote Schwind —

43

Stepping Out

It doesn't matter whether you come in first,
in the middle of the pack, or last. You can say,
"I have finished." There is a lot of satisfaction in that.
~Fred Lebow

After my heart attack, a new word entered my vocabulary: exercise. I had no choice. In my mind, walking was the least arduous option. So I began striding with enthusiasm. At first. The exuberance evaporated fairly quickly. I needed an incentive.

Group walks were my literal next step. I would glide in a wave of a bazillion people, swept away by the energy and resolve of events like the Heart Walk, the MS Walk, the ALS Walk, and walks supporting cancer victims. I would get as close to the starting line as possible to let the crowd push me mentally and physically. The large crowd seemed to dilute the number of years I was carrying.

An event scheduled for my own subdivision caught my attention, and my husband liked it because it would be less expensive than those charity walks. I arrived the morning of the walk to a jarring scene. There weren't many in attendance, but those who were there were mainly men wearing thin little running shorts. This former teacher had failed to read the details on the flier. The sponsor was the Bradenton Running Club. I don't run. Or jog. Plus, this was a 10K. I had only done 5Ks. But I had paid, so I edged toward the starting line.

The gun sounded at 8 a.m. Before I had taken four steps, every other person seemed to have advanced a quarter mile down the road. I moved as fast as my seventy-year-old legs would go. They were arguing loudly with my decision to do this. I was still upright, still moving, when I saw my husband on his bike at about the halfway mark. He looked around. "Where is everybody? Are you ahead?"

Ha. A headcase, maybe.

He looked at his watch. "Gosh you better hurry up, honey. Door prizes are going to be given out at 9:30."

As a singer, I know when my lungs have been pushed to their limit. Such was the case as I crossed over that finish line at 9:29 a.m., finishing 250th out of... 250. I dragged myself to a picnic table and collapsed with my head down as the prize ceremony began. No door prizes for me. Then it was time for the medal ceremony. I heard my name.

I didn't even look up, just swatted my hand to say they were wrong. The guy with the medal rechecked his list, continuing toward me. I looked up.

Nope, finished last. Dead last. Head down again.

There were hands on my shoulders, lifting me up as a medal was slid over my head.

No, you don't understand! I finished last place, last... 250th! It was a number I was sure never to forget. Until I heard the next words.

Someone straightened the medal, whispering into my ear, "But, lady, you finished third in your age group."

— Michelle Rahn —

44

Thinking Young

Youth is not a time of life — it is a state of mind.
~Samuel Ullman

stretch in bed, meditating on the pros and cons of reaching my eightieth birthday this month — and marveling how most days I'm startled when I gaze into the mirror and see a woman too elderly to possibly be me staring back.

A triceratops pads into my bedroom. The creature stops near my face and grins. "Hi, Grandma. You awake yet?"

I look into the lovely brown eyes of my youngest granddaughter. She pushes back the hood of her blanket-weight hooded pajamas, designed to vaguely resemble a pink-and-white dinosaur. As I greet her, my youngest grandson dives into my bed and burrows under the covers to get warm.

Their mothers know exactly where to find them and arrive moments later to shoo both in the direction of breakfast. It is a school day for the children and a workday for my daughters. They are on a schedule that I no longer need to keep.

I stay out of the way, taking time to dress, make my bed and straighten up my room. Once they all leave to meet their commitments, I will have a leisurely breakfast while I read the latest news updates on my cellphone, enjoying the decadence of free time.

In the afternoon, I drive to the neighborhood school to bring my grandson home. After his karate lesson or soccer practice, we often hang out together until bedtime. His mom usually comes home from work just before 11 p.m., long after he is asleep. My granddaughter and her mother usually arrive in time for dinner. The grandchildren help me in the kitchen, do homework, and chat about the school day until their bedtime. We laugh together as I attempt to teach them how to use the potato peeler. We giggle over my difficulty in solving their math problems the "new way."

"Were you really a teacher?" they ask, doubt written on young faces.

This isn't the plan I had for my golden years. I never thought five of us would live in the small home where my husband and I planned to finish out our post-retirement lives together. In fact, I still find it difficult to believe that my healthy, athletic husband wouldn't outlive me, but he's been gone nearly ten years.

The unexpected change in plans was stressful in many ways. There were times when I didn't think I could go on, but gradually I adjusted. The life I have now works; I find that I look forward to each new day with enthusiasm.

I value every moment with these two grandchildren and understand from experience just how rapidly they will grow up. I have two great-grandchildren who live in another state; they are preschoolers who hardly know me. I have six adult grandchildren living in different cities, states, and countries. I would love to see them more often, but I did enjoy the luxury of having them near when they were small.

When I crawl into bed tonight, I will be tired and content, looking forward to morning and being awakened by a little triceratops who is accompanied by a lively boy with icy feet.

For now, I will ignore the gray-haired woman in the mirror. She doesn't reflect who I really am.

— Judy Opdycke —

45

Man, Dog, Boat

A man is not old until regrets take the place of dreams.
~John Barrymore

I stood at the kitchen window watching Papa as he sat in the old, aluminum lawn chair staring out at the lake. Ralph, his old black dog, lay on the ground at his side, his eyes following Papa's gaze. Papa's hand absently stroked the head of his old companion as they dreamed the dreams of old men and old dogs in the evening sun. "He does this day after day?" I said to Mama.

She nodded, sadness filling her eyes as she looked to me for answers that I didn't have. "I don't know what to do for him. There is a longing in his eyes that I can't fulfill. A longing for the past." She sighed. "The past can't be brought back to the present. Once days are gone, they are gone forever."

"I'm going down to talk to him," I said.

Mama took Papa's old brown sweater off a peg by the back door. "It's getting chilly outside," she said, handing the garment to me. She poured a cup of coffee into Papa's cracked green ceramic mug that I made for him in third grade. Silently, she held it out to me. My heart melted a little at her tenderness toward the stubborn, old man.

I called out to Papa as I drew near, and he turned in his chair, eyes glowing with delight as usual when he saw me. His beautiful azure-blue eyes looked out of place in the gaunt, wrinkled face of an old man who had spent many long days outdoors in all kinds of weather. Every time I saw those eyes, I wished that I had inherited them instead of Mama's brown eyes. I handed him the cup of coffee and then wrapped the sweater around his shoulders before bending to kiss the top of his head. "What are you and Ralph thinking about all these hours you spend out here?" I asked.

"We're not thinking," he said softly. "We're wishing."

I dropped down in the grass beside his chair. "Wishing for what?"

He sighed. "For the impossible, I suppose."

"You always told me that nothing was impossible if you wanted it badly enough and were willing to work hard enough for it," I reminded him.

He chuckled softly, but there was no amusement in the sound. "But Ralph and I have come to learn that when you reach our age, some things actually are impossible."

"What is it that you want so badly that you spend all your days thinking about it?" I asked.

Papa looked away. "You're going to think I'm a foolish, old man."

"It doesn't matter what anyone thinks," I said. "It's your dream, and you should have it. Maybe I can help you. What do you want?"

He grinned, and his amazing eyes sparkled at the thought of his dream becoming a reality. Just seeing the shine in his eyes made me want to give him what he longed for before I even knew what he wanted. He leaned down and scratched behind Ralph's ears, and Ralph gave him a contented grin.

"Ralph and I want to fix up the old boat in the shed and go out on the lake again." Papa looked out at the lake, and his eyes saw things that I couldn't see. "Ralph and I used to spend all day out on the lake, fishing, drinking beer and eating bologna sandwiches. We'd start for home when the sun went down, totally satisfied with ourselves and with life. And before Ralph, there were other dogs. Good dogs that spent their lives on the lake. But Ralph was cheated because I grew old and had the heart attack while he was young. Ralph deserves one more day on the lake even more than I do." Ralph raised his head and looked at me as if he were imploring me, too.

At first, Mama was appalled at the idea of Papa fixing up his old boat and going out on the lake again. "He's almost eight-five years old.

I'd worry every minute he was gone," she said.

"Mama," I said. "You worry about him sitting in his lawn chair staring out at the lake every day. Worry is worry. And we are all going to die doing something. Isn't it better to die doing something we love rather than die longing to do something we can't do anymore?"

Once Mama gave in, I enlisted my husband and a couple of nephews to help renovate the old boat. The boat was sound, but it was old, and the paint was faded and cracked. The motor was good, but to be safe it was taken in for an overhaul. My two nephews spent several weekends sanding and painting the boat. I replaced the faded and cracked seat cushions. We didn't want the boat to just look okay. We wanted it to be special. We wanted Papa to be proud of the boat as he and Ralph went out on the lake again.

As we all worked together, we were happy to be making an old man's dream come true. We didn't tell Papa that the goal was to have the boat ready by his birthday. We always brushed him off when he asked when the work would be done.

On the day of his birthday, we all gathered at Papa's house early that morning. He was surprised when we all showed up as he was finishing his breakfast.

"It's too early for cake," he quipped.

Then he noticed the cooler that one of my nephews was carrying. "What's this?" he asked, puzzled.

"Beer!" my nephew said.

My other nephew held up a large lunch tote. "Bologna sandwiches, cookies, and dog biscuits."

I stepped forward. "New sunglasses to keep the sun out of your eyes."

My husband grinned. "A new hat in the same colors as your boat." He popped it on Papa's head. Papa's mouth flew open. Mama stepped forward and hugged Papa.

"Happy birthday, honey. You and Ralph are taking your boat out on the lake today."

Papa batted his eyes and fought to hold back tears. It didn't matter because by then all of us were crying. Soon, we all stood by the lake and watched as Papa and Ralph drove away, Papa waving and laughing, looking happier than I had seen him look in a long time. Mama turned to me.

"Look at him. He doesn't look like an old man, does he? Being happy makes him look young again."

I hugged Mama. Papa and Ralph spent many days after that out on the lake where they were always just a man and his dog. They were never old when they were on the lake. They were just happy. Ralph didn't live long after Papa died. He spent most of his remaining days lying in the sun at the edge of the yard gazing out into the lake — remembering, I am sure, the days he and Papa spent together out on the lake.

— Elizabeth Atwater —

Get Physical

46

The Oldest Living Thing in the Building

All progress takes place outside the comfort zone.
~Michael John Bobak

My friend Hedy and I were strolling the path atop the South Rim of the Grand Canyon last fall — she with her nose in a brochure and me wondering how often people fall off the narrow ledges — when she stopped and said, "Want to hike the canyon next fall?"

I laughed, but she didn't. She was serious. Possibly dead serious.

"Hike? As in around, or down to the bottom?"

"Bottom is best. Twenty-five miles in two days with mules to carry the bags." She handed me the brochure as she gazed across at the North Rim. "We need to do this."

Confession: In all my sixty-six years, "Hike the Grand Canyon" has never once appeared on my to-do list: "Learn Piano," "Join a Choir," and "Write a Bestseller" are the things I hope to tick off before I kick off.

But willingly head down into the canyon, confident I wouldn't have to be airlifted out?

Not in a million years.

"Hedy, this seems…"

"Sudden?"

I was about to say "dumb," but then she put a hand on my arm.

"I want to hike the canyon to celebrate my seventieth birthday.

And I want to do it with you."

I'd forgotten she was approaching that milestone. She looked far younger, the payoff of regular workouts. Plus, she'd recently lost weight, which would be inspiring if it weren't so annoying.

She could probably do that hike and live to tell the tale.

Me? Not so much.

I'd settled into a comfortable complacency, accepting a rise in blood pressure and cholesterol as part of the aging process. And that extra twenty pounds? Just growing old gracefully.

"Hedy, I couldn't possibly..." She looked at me expectantly. "Be more excited?"

"Me, too!" She hugged me hard. "I'm so happy right now."

And I was in so much trouble.

Back home, I Googled blog posts by people who had done the hike, hoping for survival hints. The common thread: Get in shape first.

Clearly, this was not a ramble in the woods. If I wanted to hike, I had to get serious. Or take out more life insurance.

I searched "Best exercise for Grand Canyon hike." The same answer came up again and again: circuit training. The only circuits I knew were electrical, but lucky me, there was a center nearby.

I booked a complimentary, no-obligation class, arrived ten minutes before start time, and froze in the doorway.

The reception area was jammed with people, all at least thirty years younger than me.

I was the oldest living thing in the building.

"Lynda?" A young woman smiled and came toward me with a folder. "Welcome!"

No obligations but plenty of paperwork. Any injuries, health concerns, recent bankruptcies?

Waivers signed, a young man led me into the gym with the rest of the crowd, explaining how the program worked as we walked.

"We warm up on the treadmills. An easy 4.5 pace to start, and we work up from there."

"4.5 is my goal."

"You're so funny." He escorted me to a machine. "Five minutes here, then a quick one hundred pulls on a rowing machine and back to the treadmill. We rotate like that for twenty minutes, increasing speed and pulls, and then we hit the weights. Instructions are on the screen at the end of the room." He fastened a black strap around my left bicep. "These monitors send everyone's heart rate to the screens above the treadmills."

Sure enough, my name was halfway down the list, my heart barely in the green zone at eighty beats per minute.

"We want your heart up in the red zone forty percent of the time." He smiled and gave me a thumbs-up. "You'll be great."

Hard to argue with such enthusiasm.

"Let's do this!" he shouted.

A cheer went up, as did the volume on the music, drowning out my yelp when he started my treadmill at 4.5.

Another thumbs-up. "Yay, Lynda."

"Yay," I muttered, already huffing. I was about to lower the speed when who should come to life but my old, competitive spirit, sniffing out the challenge, pushing me to raise the elevation.

Age be damned. I could keep up, right?

Apparently not.

My heart rate zipped right past yellow and was the only one already in the red zone.

Stop, reason whispered, but our leader shouted, "Now, row!" and I was off. Racing to the machines with everyone else, pulling one hundred times, and still the only name in the red zone.

"Treadmill!" the dreaded voice yelled. "Faster, Lynda, faster."

Speed now 5. Elevation up a notch.

Still in the red zone. I lived there now.

Back to rowing, back to treadmill, and suddenly, "Hit the weights!"

I staggered to an empty bench, saw "Jumping Squats with Dumbbells" on the screen at the end of the room, and searched the rack for small weights, three pounds, maybe five.

The starting point was eight.

"You'll need two," my neighbour hollered.

Perfect.

Instructions on the screen: "Squat, jump right. Squat, jump centre. Squat, jump left. Squat, jump centre."

One glance in the mirror confirmed what I instinctively knew: red face, boobs everywhere but where they should be. This would not be pretty.

Fifteen minutes of squats, lifts, curls and flies, red zone all the way. Was that good? Who knew? Who could even think?

"And treadmill! Finish strong!"

I'd be happy to finish at all.

Row and row and walk and walk.

What's higher than the red zone? I wondered and tried not to weep when he finally called, "And we're done!"

"Booya!" the hive shouted, voices ricocheting off the walls.

Stats on the screen. My time in the red zone: ninety percent and holding.

Back in reception, I sank into a sofa and unscrewed the lid on my water bottle with trembling fingers.

As expected, a closer with a clipboard appeared on my right, ready to sign me up. "How great was that?" she asked.

"I may die right here," I managed and brought the bottle to my lips. But my hands were shaking so badly that water spilled down the front of me. Boobs found.

Her horrified expression said it all. *OMG, she's probably right.*

For the first time in fitness history, a closer set the clipboard aside and said, "Can I help you to your car?"

At home, I was still shaking, yet oddly energized. Competitive spirit still alive, I was determined to do that hike and tell the tale. Age is no barrier!

But surely there was a better workout.

After trying everything from Pilates to pole dancing, I finally joined a gym and hired a trainer who was excited that a woman her grandma's age wanted to hike the canyon. We would do this.

Seven months later, my body is stronger, my agility much improved, and my heart doesn't leap into the red zone at the sight of a treadmill.

I've also lost fifteen pounds, which either means it's all working, or I'm in a Stephen King novel and slowly wasting away. I remain optimistic.

Unfortunately, Hedy was recently diagnosed with vertigo. No narrow canyon trails for us for a while.

We're looking at the Cotswolds instead, but one line still waits on our to-do lists:

Hike the Grand Canyon. No airlifts required.

— Lynda Simmons —

Senior Aerobics

True enjoyment comes from activity of the mind and exercise of the body; the two are ever united.
~Wilhelm von Humboldt

When my mother turned ninety, I knew I needed to find a senior fitness class. Not for her — for me. I could see I had it in my genes to live another thirty years, and I wanted to stay in good enough shape to enjoy it.

Yes, I enjoyed walking in local parks, and most days I walked a mile around the neighborhood with my husband. But in my heart, I knew I wasn't as fit as when I was chasing toddlers and working out at the local gym.

I called the senior center. "I'm looking for an aerobics class."

"Talk to Diana," the receptionist said. "She leads a class for us three days a week at a local church."

"What's it like?"

"We hear good things about it."

Diana answered the phone with an enthusiasm that I soon learned was the norm for her. "Come check us out!" she invited. "We start at 10 a.m."

The next morning, I pulled into the parking lot and took a deep breath. Part of me was afraid the class would be too easy and not do me any good. The other part was afraid it would be too hard, and I wouldn't be able to keep up.

Well, there was only one way to find out.

I grabbed my towel and headed for the all-purpose room. Inside, twenty-five folding chairs were arranged in a circle around the sides of the room. People chatted in small groups.

I laid my sweatshirt over the back of an empty chair.

A blond woman in exercise shorts and a bright T-shirt greeted me. "You're new here, aren't you?"

"Yes, first time.

"Welcome. Good to have you here."

Then the music started. Instantly, I felt at home. The moves were familiar from the aerobic dance classes I loved in the 1980s — kick four, two knees, pony back, hustle up — but set to a mix of music dating from the 1940s to modern country. We worked out to Glenn Miller's "A String of Pearls" (1941), swung into "Rockin' with the Rhythm of the Rain" (The Judds, 1985), and cooled down to Roger Williams' "Autumn Leaves" (1955), and "Tie a Yellow Ribbon Round the Ole Oak Tree" by Tony Orlando and Dawn (1973). I recognized some of the songs from my high-school days; others were hits before I was born.

The hour-long workout included aerobics, hand-and-ankle-weight routines, sit-ups, balance exercises, and stretches. The exercise burned off stress and woke up muscles I didn't use in my daily walks. I was hooked.

My classmates ranged from their late fifties to early nineties. Most gave the exercises their own interpretation, doing as much or as little as they were able. Happily, no one was keeping score.

Diana gathered us into a circle. "Today is Pat's birthday," she announced. She launched into "Happy Birthday," and we all chimed in. It reminded me of birthday celebrations when my sons were in preschool — only we didn't ask Pat to hold up fingers indicating how old she was.

I soon learned that physical wellbeing wasn't the only focus of the class. During water breaks, people chatted about the Seattle Seahawks and Mariners or shared family news. Carl, a fellow birdwatcher, told me about nearby bird sightings. Whenever people were absent, we asked around. Were they busy? Or were they in the hospital? We signed get-well cards for those who were ill and sympathy cards for those who'd lost loved ones. I often ran into classmates out running errands or at the grocery store.

As I'd hoped, I'm in better shape now than when I started. But the unexpected gift of joining senior aerobics was in gaining new friendships and feeling more connected to my local community. Studies show that social connections are as vital to our good health as physical exercise. Luckily, my senior fitness class gives me both.

My mother is ninety-three now and just won a gold medal in the javelin throw at the National Senior Games. If I'm going to keep up with her, I may need to hire a personal trainer.

— Christine Dubois —

48

The 1500 Meter

When you put yourself on the line in a race and expose
yourself to the unknown, you learn things about
yourself that are very exciting.
~Doris Brown Heritage

t was the 2019 National Senior Games in Albuquerque, New Mexico, where I'd finally crossed the finish line and collapsed into a yellow chair. There, a paramedic put an ice-cold cloth on the back of my neck and gave me water while my grandson Rio hooked up my oxygen and stood over me with an umbrella to shield me from the blazing sun. My son was saying, "I'm proud of you, Mom… I'm proud of you, Mom… I'm proud of you, Mom…" over and over.

Four times around the track, 1500 meters—almost a mile. Doesn't sound so impossible, even for a ninety-three-year-old couch potato like me. But in advance of that, we'd stood in the 103-degree sun for at least an hour while the committee got the race walk organized. We'd walked almost the full distance of the race getting registered and into position. We'd stood in the sun listening to the directions: heel first, then shift weight to the ball of the foot. We'd be disqualified if we put our toe first more than three times.

There were forty-four other contestants but only two in my age group, ninety- to ninety-four-year-old women, so I was counting on the bronze. I decided to keep my mind on "weight-on-heel, weight-on-ball-of-the-foot, go Jean go."

As I passed the finish line for the first time, my family cheered and yelled, "Go, Jean, go!" By the time I finished another lap and passed the finish line a second time, other people sitting in the stands joined in. I yelled back, "Thanks!"

I was soon being passed by walkers from other age groups. As they went by, they said, "You can do it. Keep going."

I started getting the little red dots at the back of my eyes that signal oxygen deprivation. I kept blinking my eyes, trying to see. I passed the finish line a third time. I was on the last lap.

I tried to change my posture to put the stress in a different place. My cane was having trouble finding the ground. I was heaving for breath.

One of the judges came running toward me. "Don't give up," she said. "You're going to make it." Another judge ran alongside me and told me to move over a lane, which would be slightly shorter. My cane was having trouble again. "It isn't far now," the judge said.

"How far?" I asked.

"Up there, that line of trees."

Might as well be the other side of the world, I thought. But I'd destroyed myself already — I was damn well going to go the distance. Heel-first, weight-on-ball-of-the-foot, gasp, gasp. Then I heard everyone shouting, "You're almost there!" I saw my son and grandson standing by a yellow chair, felt their hands catch me as I fell into it, and heard the judge say, "You're home free." Heard the cheers all around me, "Good job, Jean!" Heard my son say, "I'm proud of you, Mom."

It took another hour to find out if I'd won the bronze. An hour of sitting in the shade breathing in my emergency oxygen. Another hour of strangers stopping to hug me and say, "Good job, Jean!" Another hour to find out I hadn't won the bronze after all — I'd won the silver.

It's on the wall at home now, where I can admire it when I sit in my lounge chair watching TV.

It's next to the gold medal I won in the javelin throw. But that's another story.

— Jean H. Dubois —

49

Don't Call It Ping-Pong!

Table tennis has given me soul.
~Author Unknown

The elderly man shuffled through the door to the multipurpose room, his shoulders hunched, his steps slow. He pulled off his jacket, sank down onto one of the metal folding chairs that lined the wall, and carefully removed a well-worn ping-pong paddle from its zippered case. Then he crossed the room to where I sat watching four other folks play ping-pong.

"That table's empty," he said, pointing to the far end of the room. "Want to play?"

"I'd like that," I said, wondering how a man his age could possibly participate in so physical an activity.

He introduced himself as Ernie and said he was glad I'd come. "We play here at the senior center twice a week for about an hour," he told me. "It's lots of fun. Get a paddle and a couple of balls from that cabinet in the corner, and we'll volley."

It had been quite a few years since I'd played ping-pong (which, I quickly learned, is called table tennis by those who play competitively), but I soon got into the rhythm of hitting back and forth with Ernie.

"Let me know when you're ready to keep score," he said.

"I'm ready," I told him. "You serve first."

Ernie tossed an orange ball into the air and sliced it across the net with his paddle. The ball took a crazy hop. I swung and missed. He served again and fooled me again.

"Gosh," I said. "I guess I'm rustier at this than I thought." Now it was my turn to serve. I'd get those points back for sure. But Ernie returned my serve with ease, and we volleyed a bit before I made a classic rookie error. I hit the ball way too high over the net. He slammed it back so hard that it might have gone down my throat if my mouth had been open. I lost that game 11–2. I did only slightly better in the second game, scoring four points to his eleven. By the time we finished the set, I was breathing hard and covered with sweat.

"Let me ask you something, Ernie," I said, collapsing into a chair. "How long have you been playing ping-pong?"

"Table tennis," he said.

"Okay, how long have you been playing table tennis?"

"Well… let me think." He pulled a handkerchief from his pocket and wiped his face. "I started competing in tournaments when I was thirteen. I'm ninety-three now. So that makes eighty years."

"Wow," I said. "No wonder you crushed me."

Ernie laid a hand on my shoulder. "Don't you worry," he said. "Just keep showing up here on Tuesday and Thursday mornings. The more you play, the better you'll get."

I took Ernie up on the invitation. I never admitted to him or the other table-tennis regulars that I'd actually come to the senior center that morning for a chair yoga class and had wandered into the wrong room. It didn't take me long to discover that table tennis isn't a stroll in the park. It's a sport that requires muscular endurance, cardiovascular fitness, nimble footwork, and flexibility, not to mention intense hand-eye coordination. It also demands singular focus and constant strategizing.

As it turns out, it was exactly the activity I was looking for. These days, I don't miss a Tuesday or Thursday with the table-tennis gang if I can help it.

Table tennis became an Olympic sport in 1988. It's also one of twenty-one sports included in the National Senior Games. To compete in those senior games, you start locally. At our center, we organized a team of six players and signed up for the district tournament. We all committed to competing in singles play. Next, we agreed on partners for doubles and mixed doubles. Then we started some serious practicing — top spin and bottom spin, often with a little side spin thrown in for good measure. Lightning serves. Dinks and slams. Intense defense.

Our team of six players — which included Ernie as honorary team captain — earned sixteen medals, several of them gold, at district competition. We all qualified for the state tournament, which will lead (we hope) to the nationals. I confess it was a thrill I'd never dreamed of when an Olympic medal was hung around my neck.

But that's not really why I play table tennis. Sure, I do it for the exercise. And I do it because it's fun. But mostly I do it because my fellow Olympians — Cyle, Joanne, Paul, Roger and, especially, Ernie — have become some of my dearest friends in the world.

— Jennie Ivey —

50

Happy When I'm Hiking

Walking is the best possible exercise.
Habituate yourself to walk very far.
~Thomas Jefferson

On a breezy March morning, I laced up my sneakers, stashed a PB&J sandwich and water bottle in my ancient day pack, and boarded the senior-center van for my first walking adventure. I was apprehensive but determined. Had I dressed appropriately for the weather? Was I fit enough to participate? Would the other walkers leave me in the dust? Words from an old hiking song I'd learned as a Girl Scout surfaced from my memory and gave me the courage to try. "I'm happy when I'm hiking, pack upon my back."

The group from the Auburn Senior Activity Center welcomed me as if they'd known me for years. We chatted on the drive to our destination: Marymoor Park on Lake Sammamish. I stepped from the van, hoisted my pack onto my shoulders, and took a deep breath of crisp Pacific Northwest air. Ready or not, I joined the group of a dozen walkers and set off behind our leader. The paved path around the lake dazzled us with beautiful views of the water and gorgeous azaleas and rhododendrons along its shores. The outing proved to be an exhilarating opportunity to stretch my legs and increase my heart rate. I had a great time.

As soon as we returned to the senior center, I grabbed a copy of the center's brochure and studied its offerings more closely. As a newbie, my first walk had been a good way to determine if I could keep up with the other participants. I was thrilled that I could, but was I also strong enough for hikes? The brochure's descriptions included each trail's location, length, and how much time the hike or walk would take. Outings that covered fewer than three miles and had no elevation gain were labeled "walks." Hikes would be longer and were rated by difficulty.

As I went on more and more excursions, it didn't take long for me to realize I was poorly equipped. Almost every week, as we rode the bus to a trailhead, conversations included assessments of hiking gear. One hiker demonstrated new trekking poles that can be collapsed until they're small enough to fit inside a backpack. I bought my "sticks" after struggling up a steep, rocky slope at Tolmie State Park. It's amazing how much they help navigate over roots and rocks, up and down hills, and through muddy patches.

Another walker praised the waterproof qualities of a jacket she'd just bought from REI. I discovered the benefits of reliable rain gear on the boardwalks at Nisqually National Wildlife Refuge during an afternoon of relentless downpours. Before our next outing, I purchased a waterproof coat and pants to keep me dry.

A sturdy pair of boots rounded out the ensemble after a stumble on wet rocks at Little Si left me red-faced with mud coating my rear. The latest find by a fellow hiker is a spiffy pair of gloves. They have a special fingertip coating that allows the wearer to tap the screen on her smartphone without having to remove a glove and risk freezing her fingers. Those are at the top of my must-have list.

When my husband raises his eyebrows over my latest splurge on hiking necessities, I remind him it's money well spent, especially when compared to the cost of medical care for "sitting disease." Besides, having the right gear makes my hikes and walks more comfortable and, therefore, even more fun.

"Whatever makes you happy," he then says.

And hiking and walking do give me joy. The jaw-dropping vista of

Mount Rainier filling the horizon on the Naches Peak Loop Trailhead. The roar of water cascading down Twin Falls of the Snoqualmie River (after walking down 104 steps to the viewing platform, and then back up!). The snow-capped peaks at Olympic National Park. The animals, birds, flowers, and berries. All that beauty is part of me now. I've experienced places I never would have ventured to on my own with a great bunch of people who love the outdoors as much as I do. I am stronger physically and mentally as I stretch the limits of what I can achieve.

Now I sign up for almost every walk and hike in the senior-center brochure. I plan to keep hiking and walking as long as I'm able to put one foot in front of the other. My confidence in my ability has grown with each step. I finally have all the necessary gear, although... Lately, I've been hankering for a waterproof hat that keeps showing up on my Facebook feed. It provides protection from the sun's harmful rays and comes in several attractive colors. A bargain at only forty-five dollars.

Whether I buy the hat or not, I know I'll be happy when I'm hiking. "Out in the open country. That's the place for me."

— Sandra R. Nachlinger —

51

The Awakening

None are so old as those who have
outlived enthusiasm.
~Henry David Thoreau

Six months before my sixtieth birthday, I was cycling down a path when a shirtless guy approached on a strange contraption. It looked like he was floating above the trail, and he was propelling himself forward with a single long pole. He wasn't skateboarding or inline skating. I turned around and caught up to the fellow.

"What's this thing called?" I hollered, pointing at his craft.

The man grinned wide. "A land paddle."

"A what?"

"It's called land paddling. Think stand-up paddleboard on land." He must have sensed my curiosity and slowed down by braking with his long pole and came to a standstill on the grass next to the path, allowing me a closer inspection.

The board resembled a skateboard on steroids: fifty-nine inches in length and fourteen inches wide, with four large skateboard wheels. The six-foot pole was braided bamboo with a paddle handle at the top and a six-inch rounded rubber tip at the bottom.

Other than being trim and evenly tanned, with a T-shirt tucked into his back pocket, the man wore no protective gear. He beamed with good health.

"It's an incredible workout," the man said. "You have to propel yourself forward using only your upper body and the pole." Again, the wide grin. "I found it through Kahuna Creations. Have a look online. They always have a sale." With that, the man stepped on his land paddleboard, waved me farewell and propelled himself forward with powerful strokes. The sun painted gold on his flexing muscles as he took the turn and disappeared. I turned around and went on my way, deep in thought.

In six months, I'd be sixty. What if this could spice up my summer-exercise routine?

Later that afternoon, I found the website and got lost in a brave new world. The board and pole cost a little under four hundred dollars—a fraction of the cost of a stand-up paddleboard or a kayak.

Fourteen days later, when the two oddly shaped boxes arrived at my front door, reality set in. What had I done? I couldn't even skateboard!

My significant other rolled her eyes. "Honey, are you having a mid-life crisis?"

"Not so fast," I protested. "It's called a mid-life awakening. If I don't do this, shape up with a land paddle, it will soon turn into a crisis!"

I went back to the drawing board and studied the training videos—over and over again.

I'd start small—on a quiet, tucked-away walking path. I'd gain confidence first.

But I needed some protection. I found a snug-fitting helmet in black, reminding me of a World War II helmet without the brim.

Three times a week, I practiced. The first time lasted only fifteen minutes. Scared to death, I stepped on the board, knuckles white, grasping the paddle pole, forgetting to breathe. I rediscovered the delicate thing called balance.

It hasn't always been like this—me finding enjoyment in staying fit. I fell in love with books in kindergarten and became addicted to reading. Soon, it was like an illness. I turned into a sedentary bookworm who would do nothing but read. Never did I consider any physical activity until my grade nine year. Attending a new school, I took the wrong bus, ending up in the bus terminal late one afternoon. Afterward, I refused to take the bus and opted for cycling to school.

For four years, I cycled fifteen kilometres a day to school. That was only the beginning.

Many of us in Western society have come to accept the flawed philosophy that aging equals decline and loss of function and purpose. Having met and interviewed ninety- and 100-year-olds who were still working fascinated me. Positive aging has since become one of my passions.

A little fun fact: The land paddleboard doesn't come with a brake. No, it's not madness; there are ways to stop. One can drag the rubber tip on the tarmac, swerve from side to side to slow down, or head into the grass next to the little path, praying you retain your balance (my preferred way of stopping).

The technique is to stand with feet planted shoulder-wide but sideways, somewhat toward the back half, propelling forward with the long paddle similar to using a canoe paddle in the water, only pressing with the rounded rubber tip on the tarmac and pushing backward. Steering is by leaning forward on the toes or back on the heels. Simple, right?

There is a learning curve. After about three weeks, my confidence boosted, I took to a busier, paved cycling path with more exciting twists and turns and several baby hills. This beautiful, tree-rich path ran alongside two retention ponds, parallel to a highway, and was 1.2 kilometres long from pedestrian crossing to pedestrian crossing. On a wind-still day, it took seven to eight minutes each way. It soon became my routine: completing eight "laps," taking close to an hour.

After many weeks of land paddling three times a week and cycling twice, I found a rhythm and pace. It was glorious! It came close to the exhilaration of cross-country skiing on a freshly groomed trail.

I have not fallen yet — but have had several close calls.

By the end of September, three months before my sixtieth birthday, I was the proud owner of an authentic six-pack. On unusually hot days, the shirt came off. Could you fault my vanity?

This year, having turned sixty just before the New Year, I couldn't wait for the snow and ice to thaw and disappear. I always first scouted the path by bicycle to determine how feasible the road would be for land paddling.

Unable to wait any longer, I took to the path with the land paddle by late April, with snow still tucked in the shadowy parts beneath the trees. I bundled up, similar as for skiing, and took off.

It is freedom entirely different from cycling, skiing or running.

Don't believe a word that I'm going through a late mid-life crisis — it's an awakening!

—Danie Botha—

The Biggest Trophy

The journey of a thousand miles begins
with a single step.
~Lao Tzu

When my friend Doug asked if I wanted to climb a "vertical mile" of stairs — 423 floors — my first reaction was, "Are you serious?" My second reaction was, "I'm not getting any younger. This could be my last chance to finally prove what I've got inside me."

Baseball, kickball and other sports filled my days in my youth. I dreamed of a big win some day, with a big trophy to go with it. I was skillful and fast, or so I thought. When I started fifth grade at a much larger school, I soon learned I had been a big jock on a small field. During recess, my kickball skills suddenly seemed quite pathetic compared to the bigger, stronger boys who now seemed to occupy every corner of the playground. When I joined the junior-high school track team, the coach penciled me in for the 100-yard hurdles for my first race. My experience in jumping hurdles was, well, zilch. The whistle blew, and I was already in last place before the hard part came — jumping the first hurdle. Turns out, I jumped very few hurdles. I didn't just knock over most of the hurdles; I face-planted twice. Or was it five times? I couldn't remember, as my embarrassment hit full stride even if my legs never did. By the time I stumbled across the finish line, the only recognition I received for my performance was two bloody knees.

In college, I finally got my first official sports win. I signed up for my dorm's intramural swim team and picked the shortest event, the 25-meter freestyle. And, oh, the triumph! Oh, the glory! Oh, the — full disclosure. Turns out I was the only person who signed up for the race. What was I supposed to do — swim hard? Against myself? Instead, I swam leisurely, waving to the crowd, spitting water like a fountain and imitating synchronized swimmers. I figured I might as well make fun of myself before others had the chance.

As an adult, I played on a few recreational softball teams, ran some 10Ks, then 5Ks, then 0Ks when my creaky knees said "enough." Still, I was determined to maintain an active lifestyle as an older adult, and in 2010 I signed up for a stair-climbing challenge: the American Lung Association's Fight for Air Climb fundraiser event. My father had recently died of lung cancer, so this was a meaningful cause for me. I participated in the one-time up, one-time down climbs in a high-rise building in Detroit for nine years. Then, in 2019, the ALA offered an even more challenging climb option: the vertical mile. "Vertical milers" would have three hours to climb up and down twenty-eight floors fifteen times, plus three more floors, which totals one mile up and another mile down.

I trained hard, climbing nearly 7,000 floors over a four-month period. When the challenge started, I felt confident, and after one hour I was ahead of the pace I would need to maintain to finish in time. But soon my legs started feeling heavy, like I was climbing in lead boots, and I began experiencing leg cramps. My progress slowed dramatically as the cramping worsened, and I quickly fell behind. When I came down after finishing lap 14, it was past the three-hour time limit. I had climbed 395 flights of stairs, but my big win had evaded me once again.

Soon after the climb, I struggled to experience the sense of self-satisfaction that would usually come from climbing 395 flights of stairs. I had, after all, set a goal for myself to prove what I was made of, what I had inside me. And what I had inside me was, "Nice try, but you didn't make it." So, a year later, at age sixty-two and after nearly nineteen miles of stair-climbing workouts, I was back at the starting line. Like last year, I was well ahead of pace after an hour and, like last year, I again started feeling some discomfort in my legs. I had told myself this would be my last shot at the vertical mile, and when the cramps in my legs slowed me to a near crawl, I heard myself cry out loud, "Oh, no, not again!" Climbers who had been shouting words of encouragement in passing — "You got this!" — were now asking, "Are you okay?" I kept climbing, but the pain intensified until I finally stopped and sat down on the stairs, feeling quite dejected and wondering if my dream was over. A few climbers stopped to offer help. I was touched by their compassion, putting their personal aspirations aside to help me, but I told them to keep going. Except for one climber. An angel climber, really.

I'm convinced Jessica stopped to help me through a series of divine circumstances. Had my friend Doug not kept after me about getting new running shoes, I never would have met Stephen, the salesman at the running store. And Stephen wouldn't have told me about his friend Jessica, who had also signed up for the climb, and I likely wouldn't have introduced myself to her just before the climb started. And without that connection, she might have climbed past me as I sat on those steps, my legs shaking. But all those things did happen, and Jessica stopped to help.

When she saw I was cramping, she offered me some electrolyte salt she was carrying. I wasn't sure how soon it might help, if at all, but I resumed climbing. I was now behind pace for the first time, with just two laps to go. Time was running out on the clock and on my chance to prove myself, and my legs were feeling like rubber. I stopped Jessica each time we passed, begging for more salt. I remember thinking I was behaving like a drug addict coming off a high, desperately in need of another fix. But Jessica wasn't a drug dealer with no regard for my well-being. She was my angel in the stairwell.

The cramps in my legs finally started to subside. When I made it to the top of the last lap, I felt giddy inside as I realized I was going to make it down in time. As I approached the first floor, I thought of last year's unremarkable ending to my day and the heartache that soon consumed me. This time, my heart was soaring as I crossed the finish line in 2:59:30, just thirty seconds before the time limit! I was met with cheers and high-fives, and a lengthy group hug from two climbers who witnessed my disappointment last year and in whom I had confided that this was my last attempt at climbing the vertical mile. Thinking of the compassion shown by so many who had helped me reach my goal, my emotions overwhelmed me, and I began to cry. My big-time "me goal" had suddenly turned into a big-time "we victory," confirming my belief that there's more inside us than we know, and we're even stronger together. And that turned out to be the biggest trophy of all.

— Marvin Yanke —

53

Chicken Soup for the Soul

Surfing at Sixty

Courage doesn't mean you don't get afraid. Courage
means you don't let fear stop you.
~Bethany Hamilton

've never had great balance. Nor am I crazy about dipping into the frigid Pacific. So when my daughter Emily suggests we head to British Columbia's west coast for some surf time, I'm pretty sure she's flipped her lid. In all my sixty years of living, I've never set foot (or body) on a board—and I'm not sure now is the time to try. But I don't want to let her down. Over the past few months, she's been slammed with work and family demands. And I feel honored that she's chosen me to escape with.

"Check out the wave scale, Mom," she says with a die-hard glee that makes me nervous. "It's extreme!" Sure enough, the arrow on Tofino's rating board is nearly off the chart. For Emily, this is a dream come true. For me, it affirms another goal—to somehow switch my surf lesson to a spa treatment.

After a previous stay at the Wickaninnish Inn, I know both of our wishes will come true. This resort promises "Rustic Elegance on Nature's Edge." As well as being a popular summer haunt, during these winter days, when southeast gales produce mammoth waves, it lures surfers by the drove. My heart does a drum-roll when I think about being included in this mix.

Wanting to get better acquainted with this angry sea before plummeting into it, we stroll along the scalloped beachfront that is sandwiched between an old growth forest of wind-sculpted evergreens and untamed waves. The breakers have tossed up driftwood timbers as though they're as light as toothpicks and have left them strewn all along our sandy path. They've also left behind hundreds of tidal pools that are teeming with sea life. While checking them out and yakking about everything from work challenges to kid issues we're kissed by a fine ocean mist.

It's truly a magical setting and understandably a magnet for many; storm watching aficionados, true-blue romanticists, adventure-seeking families and yes, the crazy surfer crowd who are clad from head to toe in neoprene.

"Are you ready for your big surfing debut, Mom?" Emily says, as I squeeze into my water repellent garb the next morning. "Chill out. You're going to love it."

I'd done some reading to prepare for this wild ride. Wipeouts go with the territory and everyone falls (a lot) when they are newbies. Even concussions are a common hazard. And unlike other sports, surfing has the added danger of drowning if knocked unconscious. The only thing between me and the tumultuous wave action is my five-millimetre-thick wetsuit. I'm praying this protective cloaking also knows how to float. Although feeling more like an oversized seal than a surfer in my second skin, we meet with a dozen much younger and fitter boarder wannabes at Pacific Surf School.

"Paddle like the dickens, and then do the 'pop up' on your board," we're told by our experienced guide. "And don't lose sight of us. The next landmark is Japan!" The common senior quote, "I've fallen and I can't get up," comes to mind. Hopefully I master the pop up and not the pop off!

Our nearby resort is now calling out my name more than ever. But I can't turn back now. With board in tow and Emily by my side, we attack the thunderous waves like whales in mating season. Raging rollers are formed in the distance, their curls navigable only by the pros. Within seconds, they're upon us. One quickly after another. It reminds me a bit of Double Dutch skipping from my youth. When do I make the move? Either I catch a wave or get pummeled by its whitewater wake.

After a few royal washes, my round sixty-year-old neoprene belly melds with the board, and by the end of the lesson, I'm gliding on all fours and going with the flow.

"Next time, you'll figure out the pop-up," Emily later reassures me while we enjoy some pampering at the spa. Beneath a sheltered alcove that fronts the Pacific, we soak our worn and weathered feet, then trail off to our separate sanctuaries for more sublime action. For my daughter, it's a hot-stone massage. For me, it's the Hishuk Ish Tsawalk Awakening Treatment, a whole-meal deal that infuses the elements of life with indigenous traditional techniques.

Under the capable hands of a masseur, my salt-filled pores are exfoliated, cleansed, steamed and rubbed. He says a chant, declaring we are all connected. And while breathing in the heady scent of cedar and listening to the drone of distant waves, I drift off and dream about my next encounter with the surf.

—Jane Cassie—

54

The Grandkid Olympics

Do you know why children are so full of energy?
Because they suck it out of their grandparents.
~Gene Perret

As a lean, mean geezer machine, I have managed to keep my boyish figure all these years by strictly adhering to Zezima's First Rule of Physical Fitness: Exercise and health food will kill you.

That's why my regimen is limited to twelve-ounce curls, which are performed with bottles containing corn, hops, barley, water and other healthful ingredients; the avoidance of all vegetables except, of course, myself; and a daily glass of red wine, which is, according to my doctor, over-the-counter heart medicine.

But I have reached the age (old enough to know better) where I really should be more active than getting up twice a night to go to the bathroom.

That's where my grandchildren come in.

Chloe, who will be six in March; her sister, Lilly, who turned two in October; and their cousin, Xavier, who will be two in March, are the proprietors of Poppie's Gym, a floating health club and potential emergency-care facility that is situated wherever the kids and I happen to be.

The various sites include my house, their houses, the back yards of the aforementioned places, the kiddie pool, the playground, the vineyard, the orchard, the amusement park and whatever store, outlet or mall where my wife and/or daughters are shopping while I am watching or, more likely, chasing the children.

Activities include walking, running, hopping, skipping, jumping, crawling, scampering, splashing, dancing, throwing, batting, kicking and weightlifting. If there were a grandfather competition in the Olympics, I would have won gold in all these events and appeared on boxes of Wheaties, my smiling visage covered with an oxygen mask.

I recently ramped up the exertion level when all three grandchildren visited. It was invigorating, especially when I hoisted Chloe, who weighs almost fifty pounds; Xavier, who tips the scales at thirty pounds; and Lilly, the peanut of the bunch at twenty-three pounds but whose squirminess in my arms amounts to a clean and jerk, the former involving a diaper change and the latter describing me.

Then there was the 100-inch dash, in which I chased Chloe and Lilly across the family room and back again so many times that a calculator would have exploded like the Hindenburg.

Xavier preferred the biathlon, which entailed playing peekaboo and then running around the room with Poppie on his heels. It's a miracle I didn't wear out my heels.

On numerous occasions, all the kids wanted to take my hand and play with me individually. This would require me either to be three people (as my wife would say, isn't one enough?) or to have three hands, which would make it extremely difficult to buy gloves.

After several days, the Olympics were over, and Xavier went back home. My wife and I will soon get on a plane to visit him, and the athletics will continue. We often see Chloe and Lilly, who live only about forty-five minutes away, so Poppie will be sure to keep in tiptop shape.

In fact, shortly after the sporting events had ceased, I went to the doctor for a checkup. My heart rate and blood pressure were perfect, my weight was normal, and overall I was declared a remarkable physical specimen.

"What do you do to stay so fit?" the doctor asked.

"I play with my grandchildren," I replied.

"Keep it up," she advised. "It beats getting up twice a night to go to the bathroom."

—Jerry Zezima—

55

Chicken Soup
for the Soul

See Grandma Run

I don't run to add days to my life,
I run to add life to my days.
~Ronald Rook

I f you ask my children to describe me, they use words like *determined, strong, adventurous...* I don't want to lose those qualities as I age. So, I put up a vision board in my kitchen and started adding things to it that would keep the adventures going, even in my retirement.

I have always been an Olympics junkie. I love watching the games, learning about the athletes, finding inspiration in each story, and marveling at their talent and determination. And, although I competed in sports like badminton and tennis in my youth, I never considered myself "an athlete" or really thought I would ever become one. That was, until I learned about the "Senior Olympics." Not only did I have another goal for my vision board, but I now had an opportunity to become an Olympic athlete myself.

However, I did need to find "my" sport. Track and field seemed like a good place to start. Although I have always walked for exercise, and some may even say that my walking pace counts as a jog, I have never been a runner. But, after reading an article about a ninety-year-old woman who competed in the 50-meter dash at the National Senior Games (as the Senior Olympics are officially known), I figured this could be it. Surely, I could do that, too! After all, I was only eighty, and with two new knee replacements, I was bound to have an advantage.

And I figured my odds of winning were even better if I competed in the 100-meter dash instead of the 50. There might be fewer senior competitors in the longer distances.

I started training at my local middle school's track in May for the state competition that September. In order to advance to the National Senior Games, you must win gold at your state games and meet a qualifying time or distance. Even though he lived hundreds of miles away, one of my sons acted as my coach. He was a runner in high school and advised me that, when practicing, I should walk one loop around the track, then run the 100, then walk another loop, run the 100, etc. As boring as that felt, I followed his routine each time I went to the track.

One day, a young man, probably in his twenties, was there, repeatedly running the 100. I admired his running style and mentioned to my son that maybe I should adopt that training. My son simply replied, "Mom, you should just run whatever way will get you to the finish line." So, understanding his tactful way of reminding me of my age, I kept running my way. I didn't know if less than five months of training would be enough to become an Olympic runner, but that was my hope as I traveled to Springfield, Illinois with my family to compete in the state games.

As I ran the 100 that day, my grandchildren ran the length of the metal bleachers cheering for me and holding up signs that read, "Run, Grandma, Run!" and "See Grandma Run!" My son the coach was standing at the finish line, while my other son ran along the infield of the track, filming my race for those who couldn't be there. Their cheers made me feel like a true Olympian and apparently caused me to run faster than I ever had when practicing. Not only did I win the gold medal in my age group, but I also beat the qualifying time for the National Senior Games!

I did my best to keep training regularly between September and the following June in preparation for Nationals. When the time came, I arrived in Albuquerque, New Mexico, with one of my daughters, two of my granddaughters, and, of course, my coach. As soon as we got off the plane, we saw signs welcoming athletes to the National Senior

Games. More than 14,000 seniors descended on the city. Representatives from every state, as well as from seven foreign countries, were present to compete in one or more of the twenty sports that comprised the games. Similar to the Olympics, there was a torch ceremony before the opening day of competition, as well as a parade of athletes later in the week. Each participant in the games received an official "athlete" identification badge. At last… I was an official Olympic athlete!

All track events required preliminaries. For the 100-meter race, the eight runners with the fastest times would participate in the finals. As we were directed to our lanes for the preliminary race, I was both excited and nervous. In looking at the heat sheets beforehand, I realized that I was the rookie, and most of the other women in the 100 had competed in previous National Games. And then I felt particularly nervous and a bit overwhelmed when the woman in the lane next to me put down a starting block and warmed up by jumping up and down so high that her knees reached her chest. *Yikes,* I thought, *am I truly out of my league?* I can't imagine even walking in track spikes, and I am physically unable to bend my knees all the way, let alone jump while I try.

But I had made it here. I'd earned my place, and I was certainly going to give it my best. I could see my son at the finish line again, and my family in the stands cheering with the same signs.

I placed ninth and missed qualifying by one second. Nonetheless, I was proud of my effort and in having made it to the finish line… especially without falling! Being among senior athletes of all ages in Albuquerque was an extraordinary experience. There were individuals in their nineties and 100s who participated in the running events. I witnessed a ninety-nine-year-old and a one-hundred-year-old compete in the men's 50-meter finals, and marveled at a one hundred-and-three-year-old woman who won gold in the 50-meter and 100-meter races and now holds the world's record in both.

None of these champions was running fast, but they were running. It is definitely apparent that the older one becomes, the fewer competitors there are in that age group. So, perhaps when I reach 100, I will easily make it to the finals and even receive a gold medal in the National Games.

In actuality, the joy of competing in the Senior Olympics is not about receiving a medal. Rather, it is about the camaraderie, the awe-inspiring seniors who participate, and the desire of each to lead a healthy life as one ages. As witnessed by my experience, one does not need to be an accomplished athlete. One only needs the desire to participate in something that will leave them feeling empowered and much younger than their biological age. For me, that was becoming a runner. And despite achieving my goal, the Senior Olympics remains on my vision board. I figure with two new hips next year, I will have an even greater chance of reaching the finals!

— Diana Fischer-Woods —

Less Is More

56

Take Two

For it is in giving that we receive.
~St. Francis of Assisi

When you're my age, you don't get many bridal shower or wedding invitations from your peers. Nieces and nephews, yes. Children of your friends, yes. But not too many wedding bells chime in my age category, especially among those who have already tied the knot once or twice before.

Therefore, when my friend Diane and her beloved, Jack, who are even older than I am, decided to combine their love, lives, children, grandchildren and the paraphernalia of three households (hers, her recently departed mother's and his), the joy among friends and relatives resounded from state to state and across oceans.

In one fleeting, dreamy-eyed moment during the planning of the wedding, Diane said wistfully, "Oh, I hope people don't bring presents. We do not need any more things. Our entire basement is filled, wall-to-wall, ceiling-to-floor, with things we don't need and can't possibly use in this lifetime. Nice things. Well, some of them are nice. Others are, well, too nice to throw away but too sentimental to give to strangers. And I can't bear to have another rummage sale."

Diane kept talking and planning and then she had a great idea: "Wouldn't it be nice to give each guest who comes to our wedding a gift to take home, instead of the other way around?"

I piped up, "Well, I'd be happy to give you a shower, and instead of playing those mindless games, we could wrap all your treasures for you to give away."

Diane practically shouted, "Yes! We'll number each present, and I'll put corresponding numbers on each place card at the dinner tables at the reception." Diane figured she could at least match up some of the more special heirlooms to the people she wanted to receive them.

And so, the bridal-shower invitations went out, requesting that the women bring gift wrap, tape and scissors instead of a gift for the happy couple. We gathered in the basement family room of the house that Diane and Jack had recently purchased.

The first thing the shower attendees got to do was choose three or four gifts from the hundreds in the basement that we, personally, would like to own. We were commanded to take, take, take! It was more fun than 70-percent-off day at the nearest department store. As we chose things we wanted for ourselves, Diane insisted that we take them to our cars immediately so they wouldn't get wrapped for the other wedding guests.

I chose a nice wooden tray that just needed a little lemon oil to remove the water stains, a small lead-crystal candy dish, and a china-faced floppy clown for my granddaughter.

Back downstairs after removing our own treasures, we giggling middle-aged women began to wrap the rest. There were candleholders wrapped in teddy-bear paper. Picture frames and egg cups decorated in purple foil. Decanters in festive holiday paper. Jewelry and mugs in birthday florals. Housewares, glassware, trays, books, linens, silver, and bric-a-brac wrapped to the hilt. One hundred presents in all. "Enough," Diane said, "to give a gift to everyone at the reception with enough left over to share with the wait staff."

While we wrapped, ate, laughed and talked about how we met Diane and what a joyous occasion this marriage would be, Jack sat upstairs with eyes as big as saucers wondering how his friends would perceive this crazy idea of handing out secondhand gifts at his wedding.

As I passed through the TV room where Jack was trying to ignore the cackling downstairs, I bubbled, "Jack, you're not going to believe how much stuff we're getting rid of! We're wrapping one hundred presents!"

"All I'm hoping for is an empty shelf downstairs where I can put a few of my own treasures," he mumbled.

"Jack, when we're finished, the entire basement will be cleaned out! You'll have tons of empty space!"

Diane wrote a poem that was printed and placed on every table at the wedding reception. Two of the five stanzas declared:

We love family and friends without measure.
There are even some things that we treasure.
But as three households merge, there are things we must purge.
So we gift them to you for your pleasure.

You may keep them and use them — or not.
You may love them or trash them or plot
Ways to recycle them, give your own requiem.
Love is wrapped in each piece in the lot!

And so it was that everyone who witnessed the joining of two hearts left with a gift, and a newly married couple went home to a nice empty basement.

— Patricia Lorenz —

57

Saturdays with Jill

There is a bit of insanity in dancing
that does everybody a great deal of good.
~Edwin Denby

With the stay-at-home orders that accompanied COVID-19, our lives changed in what seemed like the blink of an eye. I decided to embrace the opportunity to dig into projects, enjoying the satisfaction of seeing organized closets and tidy drawers. I rediscovered my love of cooking and the aroma that wafted throughout the house. I even finished cleaning the entire garage — an undertaking I began five years earlier and doubted I would ever complete.

But I soon discovered that, while I felt really good about my accomplishments, I began to feel a sadness deep within. My husband had died fourteen months prior, but I was blessed to have family and friends who stepped up. Gradually, I was developing a new normal — returning to my dance group, working out at the gym, and having lunch with friends. But, of course, this abruptly stopped in March 2020 when the pandemic entered our lives.

During this time, my younger daughter, Jill, who is a professional belly dancer, was coming for visits. The two of us have always loved dancing together, so on a whim, we choreographed a number in my driveway to the music of *All That Jazz* using trash cans as props. We filmed it and posted it on Facebook to give people a smile. The response astounded us. The general consensus was that we were inspiring others and making them smile—mission accomplished. This brought us palpable joy, and suddenly we found ourselves on a roll.

In the ensuing weeks, we developed a pattern that was happily anticipated every Saturday. Upon Jill's arrival, we would decide which genre we would tackle. Once we selected the music, the choreography began, with Jill's creativity shining through. Whichever one of us was the "head choreographer" that day would teach the other, and we would practice until we were "camera ready." At age eighty-one, I prayed that I would remember the steps, but thankfully she would softly cue me as we danced. I learned that the world would not come to an end if I made a mistake, which I frequently did, and we ended up getting some good laughs from the "bloopers."

The trash cans became a favorite prop, with us sometimes peeking out from behind one or dancing around them. In our ballet number, they functioned as our ballet barre. For the jazz piece, rakes became canes. And, of course, "Singing in the Rain" wouldn't have been complete without umbrellas.

For the first two months, we were brimming with ideas—tap dancing to "Sweet Georgia Brown," a line-dance number to "Boot Scootin' Boogie," jitterbugging to "Honey Hush," and a few other styles. Then, thankfully, people started posting ideas and requests. Our repertoire now includes reggaeton, which I like to refer to as "Latin belly dance," disco, Gangnam Style and, of course, some hot Latin numbers. We even added some yoga, which included the crow pose, and we challenged each other to a "plank off" as the weather began to creep into triple digits.

Although dancing together was the core of our visits, it included other meaningful moments. After filming our dance, we would rest for a few minutes, then take a long walk, giving us the opportunity for some meaningful, powerful conversations, which were so needed, especially at this time in our lives. Sometimes, we would treat ourselves to a tasty lunch, which would be delivered to my garage. The garage also became the site of Jill's June 24th birthday celebration. As I opened the garage door, she was greeted by birthday decorations and a surprise guest, our dear longtime family friend Samantha. We had a delicious lunch and flowing champagne; it was a birthday that won't likely be forgotten.

As the weeks turned into months, one thing was always constant — Jill's presence. As busy as she was, she never missed a visit, and when she left to go home each week, my spirits were lifted in such a way that could only be provided by this treasured time with her.

How grateful I am to finally have taken the time to clean out that garage.

— Bobbi Silva —

58

The Perfect Pair

A car is not going to change your life, but it will
definitely change your attitude.
~Author Unknown

I stepped back and looked at the cottage at Berry Park I had just rented. Perfect for my remaining retirement years, I decided. It would be hard to leave the house and acreage where my husband and I had raised our four children and lived for forty-two years. But after his recent passing, I needed to downsize while I was physically able.

I wasn't ready for a senior apartment. But a two-bedroom cottage—perfect. I'd have space for my office in the master bedroom. Family could still visit and use the guest room. With a small patio in the back and a porch and flower space in the front, my friends could stop by for a glass of iced tea on a warm day.

Meals were included in my rent if I went to the main building, but I still enjoyed preparing my own. And the cottage had a small kitchen with adequate space for me to do my own cooking.

Oh, and it had a garage. I needed a garage. Oregon winters can be chilly—sometimes even icy. I'd left my car out overnight a few times, and I knew what it was like to scrape ice off the windows on a cold morning. Yes, a garage was important.

My daughter Crystal and her husband Daniel flew in from Israel to help me, and we started downsizing. Day after day, we sorted through my household belongings. "This pile goes to the cottage; this one to

Salvation Army; this one stays for the estate sale." As we worked, we'd take carloads of my belongings over to the cottage. Thankfully, it was only two miles away.

One day, as my Toyota Highlander sat in the cottage driveway, Daniel's forehead wrinkled. "Hmmm," he said. "Your car looks a little wide for the garage door, doesn't it?"

"What?" I screeched. "I can't leave it sitting out all winter."

Distraught, I picked up a box of photos and went inside to ponder what to do. After a while, Daniel came in. "I got the car in the garage," he said, but he didn't look very happy about it. "Barely. There is about an inch of space on each side."

All the breath went out of me. If Daniel could hardly get the Highlander into the garage, I knew I couldn't do it at all. "How could I do it?" I wailed. "I've rented a cottage with a garage door too small for the car. What can I do?"

Crystal and Daniel stared at me for a moment, and then Crystal announced, "Oh, that car is too big for you anyway, Mom. It's about time you buy a smaller one."

"But I don't want a different car," I complained. "Your dad and I bought that one from my friend, and it's just the right size when you kids come home. I don't plan to ever buy another."

Despite my complaints, I knew Crystal was right. I needed to buy a smaller car, and I needed to do it while they were here to help me search. So, that night when Daniel and Crystal huddled in the guest room studying the Internet car market, I didn't interfere. The next day's moving projects were put on hold in favor of finding a vehicle.

Daniel had measured the door width, and Crystal had researched smaller cars with about four inches of space on each side. She thought I could manage that. We looked at a couple of dealerships nearby but didn't find anything interesting.

"What features do you want?" Daniel asked me.

"Seats must be comfortable," I said. "And easy to get in and out of. It would be nice to have a backup camera." I'd backed into cars in my driveway twice — I didn't tell them that.

"What color?" he questioned.

"Oh, I don't care, but it must be very visible."

"There's a car at Beaverton Honda that sounds good," Crystal commented. "Mileage is low, good condition, 2012. I didn't ask the color. Want to go see it?"

"It's almost an hour's drive, but I suppose we may as well," I agreed.

As Daniel drove, I did what I always did before an important decision: I prayed.

Crystal hurried up the steps when we arrived. And when Daniel and I came at my slower pace, she met us. "The salesman I talked with is busy," she said. "So, we'll be talking to someone else."

After introductions, the salesman said, "We have a Chevy Sonic that was just brought in. Sounds like it has all the features you want. Would you like to take a look?"

I nodded. We walked out to the lot, and there sat a cute, little bright red car — the brightest red I'd ever seen.

"Well, it's definitely visible," Daniel said and grinned at me.

"Want to take a ride?" the salesman asked.

I nodded and slid into the driver's seat.

As I drove around the city for a few minutes, the salesman pointed out features that were different from my Highlander. By the time we returned to the dealership, and I had talked with Crystal, Daniel and the salesman some more, I knew that little Sonic was for me. I had fallen in love with it.

As we drove back to the cottage, I smiled happily about my purchase — the first time I'd ever bought a car by myself. And I dreamed a little about the places we could go and the things we could do together — my snazzy little car and me. We'd take short trips. I might drive my granddaughters to the beach and drive to hiking and picnic areas. When we arrived at my cottage, however, I felt a little anxious. Was the garage door really wide enough? Would I really be able to drive the Sonic into the garage? What if the calculations were wrong? What would I do then? I inched up to the narrow opening, looking carefully at one side mirror, then the other. But Crystal's calculations were correct. There were about four inches on each side.

"I did it," I said, smiling as I got out, and I stepped back to look at my car. It was the sharpest little car I'd ever seen, and there was no doubt that it would always be visible. Yes, they were the perfect combination—my perfect car and my perfect little cottage.

—Geneva Cobb Iijima—

59

Attack of Minimalism

*The best way to find out what we really need
is to get rid of what we don't.*
~Marie Kondo

As a probate paralegal, I often encountered family members who were overwhelmed, suddenly left to clean up piles of papers, discard unwanted paintings, and pack away a lifetime of effects. Sometimes, the deceased's treasures were deemed junk and thrown away. Other times, junk became treasure and war would break out over who would get a particular item.

I realized that my own cherished knickknacks had become dust collectors. My treasures had overtaken my home, the furniture was closing in on me, and I had mounds of clothing, some pieces with price tags still attached.

My home had become a prison instead of a haven. My three children had moved to different parts of the world, so now the only occupants of my home were me and my stuff. Each month, I thought about the joy of writing a smaller number on my rent check.

During a two-week solo trip to Thailand during the lantern festival, I met carefree adventurers weighed down only by their backpacks, traveling the world and truly experiencing life. My suitcase suddenly seemed ginormous. My hand-painted fruit bowl would never fit in a backpack, but did I really need to buy a new fruit bowl and carry it all the way home?

An urgent need to break free of the things holding me back overwhelmed me. No longer did I want to be trapped in a larger place because I needed the room for my stuff.

There was the problem of my doll collection. My children's generation do not like to collect things. They might want one or two of my porcelain dolls, but not seventy of them!

It was time to minimize!

At first, making the decision proved easier than carrying it out. I'd come home from work, stand in the doorway, and gaze about at my paintings, favorite chair, and dolls. I would delicately hold and admire an ornamental tea set that, until now, I had long stopped noticing on the shelf.

My doll collection was the biggest hurdle and heartbreak. Getting rid of these porcelain babies I had purposely chosen and lovingly displayed in curio cabinets for so many years felt like a family betrayal. Even though the dolls had "certificates of authenticity," and some were signed by the artists, it didn't feel right to sell them. Something special needed to be done.

I decided to give the dolls to residents at a nursing home.

As some friends and I pulled wagons filled with dolls through the halls of the nursing home, we allowed the patients to pick their favorite ones. We spent the day handing out a variety of babies with ribbons and curls, flouncy dresses and bonnets, in blankets, highchairs, and bathtubs. Eyes lit up as everyone chose a doll, with many of them sharing memories of their own long-ago favorite dolls.

Several residents in wheelchairs gathered together in the hallway, stroking the hair of their babies and smoothing down dresses. As we continued on our mission, a tiny doll dressed in soft fleece pajamas and lying on a fluffy pillow was placed in the eager hands of a blind woman. She let out a squeal of joy as her fingers caressed the soft material and glided over the baby's smile. A bedridden Latina lady gleefully clapped her hands when she claimed the only Latina doll in my collection who, as it turned out, had the same name as she had: Rosie!

Letting go felt really good.

After that experience, I couldn't wait to get rid of the rest of my belongings, which had begun to feel oppressive. This claustrophobia from what once gave me joy actually helped me to part with these things.

A dear friend who was planning a mission trip became the recipient of most of the rest of my things so she could host a garage sale and raise funds. My son took some furniture he needed, and I sold a few items. Within months, I had nothing left but photos, memorabilia, some electronics, and a backpack filled with clothing. And it felt amazing—such a sense of freedom!

Now I am open to more choices and ready to begin a new season of life. I can travel the world, live in a tiny house, be a missionary... (stay tuned).

I've gained so much more by owning less.

— Barbara Shoner —

60

Zen Retreat

Never underestimate the power you have
to take your life in a new direction.
~Germany Kent

"Aren't the residents there using walkers and canes? Don't they just play bingo all day or do crossword puzzles? You are still fifty-five years young! Why would you want to live with a bunch of old people?" I said to my best friend as she was packing up to move to a retirement community.

"It's really nice there. Come out and visit me!" my dear friend I have known since kindergarten said with a smile.

After she settled in, I took a casserole to her in her new "home." As she greeted me at the door, I noticed her large patio with ferns growing and mountains in the background. The living room was very pleasant, although a bit dated. However, I loved the open feeling right away.

"Let's go grab a bite to eat, and I will save the casserole for later," my fit friend said as she put the casserole in the refrigerator. "We have a five-star restaurant right here on the premises."

"What? Here? At the 'old-folks place'? What do they serve? Mashed potatoes and applesauce?" I scoffed.

My friend chuckled and said, "We have the best chef in town."

As we walked over, we saw a covey of quail dart under some agapanthus flowers. Some geese flew overhead, squawking and flying in formation. Then I smelled something delicious from the restaurant kitchen — sautéed garlic.

"Let's eat by the pool," my friend said.

"You have a pool? Aren't they afraid of liability?"

"Nah," she said. "Many residents swim here early in the mornings."

We sat down at a wooden table with an umbrella. Our friendly server mentioned the soups of the day—clam chowder and garlic tomato dill—both my favorites and made from scratch. "There is a gym with new equipment around the corner—I use it three times a week," my friend said.

I noticed a few residents inside the dining room laughing and having a glass of wine with pasta. Another resident was walking by the pool with three little dogs. A slim, handsome man with silver hair sat down to read a book by the pool. I saw two little children entering the pool area with their slender grandma.

"Come on, after dinner let's walk my dog. I will show you the berm."

"What is a berm?" I asked.

"It's a built-up levee where you can walk along the river and enjoy nature—flowers and the mountain views."

After the delicious dinner, we walked the berm, which was peaceful and filled with natural beauty. I grabbed my free cup of coffee in the clubhouse, and I noticed a computer showing all the classes offered: tai chi, yoga, line dancing, and art lessons. There was also an upcoming Fourth of July party. People in the clubhouse were conversing and laughing—and not all were elderly.

Years went by, and there came a time when the owners I was renting from had to sell my place. My friend talked me into looking into her community. Even though I had liked it, I hesitated and started my search instead at a nearby condo. It was dark and small, with a little patio. All the units overlooked a street or parking lot. My friend's condominium, on the other hand, overlooked nature.

"There is a cute studio for sale here," my friend told me. I decided to take a peek.

I immediately felt at home. The sign on the front door said "Zen Retreat," which could not have been more appropriate. The French doors opened to a large patio filled with lemon trees, agapanthus and pink mallow flowers. From inside, there was a view of large cypresses and mountains, making the studio feel larger. There was recessed lighting and a remodeled kitchen. The owner, an artist, had her watercolors of seascapes on display. An artist myself, I felt immediately at home.

I moved in two months later and have not looked back. My significant other now resides here with me. He is a director at a nonprofit that helps the homeless find homes and reminds me how fortunate we are to live here. We have a Sunday brunch ritual with our chef's famous eggs Benedict. I walk every day, and sometimes we take hikes in the nearby mountains, even spotting bobcats.

We have attended Christmas, New Year's and Halloween parties. We have played in putt-putt golf tournaments. I even won a tiara for the best twist dance at a Spring Fling. I felt like the Homecoming Queen. That was a good thing for me, considering I always wanted to be one!

My family celebrated my mom's ninetieth birthday here, and we took photos in front of the large Christmas tree in the clubhouse that I did not have to decorate. I have attended piano and jazz concerts here — for free. We have a small hotel on the premises for guests, and that means I don't even have to change the sheets!

My best friend and I regularly walk together with our dogs. I have been enjoying my two young granddaughters immensely, coloring and painting with them. On our visits, I have taken hundreds of photos of our beautiful flora here — roses, mallows, agapanthus, magnolias, and chrysanthemums, to name a few. I have met lovely neighbors, and we all look out for each other. I love hearing the stories from the older residents about their travels and lives.

I know this is a "retirement community," but many of us still work. I'm only in my sixties now, and I'm finding new adventures even while living here. It is indeed my "Zen Retreat."

— Laurie Muender —

61

Fresh Start

As you simplify your life, the laws of the universe
will be simpler; solitude will not be solitude,
poverty will not be poverty, nor weakness weakness.
~Henry David Thoreau

A s I approach my sixty-eighth year, I have realized that my third child was my old house. The two-story Victorian frame house on the north side of Chicago occupied my free time; I worried about it constantly. I was proud of it, I was ashamed of it, but I always forgave it for any troubles it caused me.

I loved having a space of my own. I fought to keep it and worked hard for it. My heart was broken when I had to leave it. In 2017, I came to the bittersweet realization that I had to sell after living there for thirty years. It was the house in which I had raised my kids, planted flowers, played music, and entertained friends and family. It was the home in which my husband had passed away. It was a starter home in 1985 when I moved in; thirty years later, it was still a "starter home" due to the fact I had never had the money to do a gut renovation.

The house was built in 1897. Victorian charm was evident in the oak staircase, pine flooring, and beautiful carved window casings. The brass doorknobs and clawfoot bathtubs delighted me, as did the heavy iron heating grates.

I listened to my daughter play piano and my son beat on his drums in a small area that abutted the dining room, which I dubbed the "music room." I had a little taste of Downton Abbey in this room.

Its only purpose was to hold books and musical instruments. My sixty-year-old piano and fifty-year-old accordion were its focal points.

Perhaps it was pride that made me hang onto the house for so long after my husband passed away. Perhaps it was because I had grown up in a small, four-room apartment. But, in reality, it was because I had space for the first time in my life. No more tiny college dorm rooms and studio apartments for me. I had a home.

This vintage, two-story house with a small yard resplendent with roses and phlox seemed like paradise. When my kids were small, they had a sandbox and a swing set in the yard. We dragged home the plastic swimming pool from Ace Hardware. The kids played Frisbee and blew bubbles with wands. We made snowmen in the winter and carved pumpkins in the fall. Springtime, we fed the rabbits and put out hummingbird feeders. We had birthday parties and Cub Scout meetings.

To disguise the cracks in the 100-year-old plaster, I painted the walls in vibrant colors: turquoise and pumpkin, violet and magenta. I bought threadbare Chinese deco rugs on eBay and June Cleaver-style vases. On the walls, I hung family photos and Maurice Chevalier posters; I was going for French cabaret shabby chic.

The plumbing was tricky. If the washing machine was running, there was no water on the second floor. It took five minutes for the first-floor toilet to fill, so you couldn't shower. I could have taken a world cruise and gotten a facelift for the amount of money I put into the plumbing. It was epic, finding burst pipes on the back porch and in the basement. Chicago winters can be cruel to old pipes. I often cried in frustration as I mopped up.

When I put the house on the market, I purged thirty-three years of stuff. I gave most of it away to the Salvation Army and appreciative strangers on Craigslist.

I gave away two sets of golf clubs, twenty houseplants, a lawn mower, knitting needles and yarn, three bags of sheet music, pots and pans, lamps and Christmas decorations. The unused dog crate and two sets of dog stairs went quickly. A grateful lady drove crosstown to pick up my dad's wheelchair for her mother.

I gave away my fortieth birthday present — my mink coat — to a young man who wanted to give it to his wife who had been ill. I no longer wore fur; I was glad to share it.

I had 1950s martini glasses that I never used. Off they went in a shopping bag to a young actor who was moving into her first apartment. She had Holly Golightly stars in her eyes.

My wedding dress was given away to a young woman who showed up on my front porch and took the ivory silk and satin dress away with a timid smile. I felt like weeping but was happy someone else would make a memory with it. I hoped the most expensive dress I had ever owned ($285 in 1984) would bring good karma to its next owner.

Moving is emotional, and I knew that I would miss my old house. I hoped it would forgive me; the new owners, my neighbors, were going to knock it down to expand their open space. They had no interest in crumbling Victorian splendor.

I don't travel often, but I felt by moving five miles downtown and offering my possessions to strangers, I had taken a fantastic voyage. I gave and received love as I purged my house of its things.

I am learning new behaviors that give me love. My tap shoes caress my feet, and the sparrows I feed on the balcony look at me with what I hope is recognition and affection. I smile at the new people I meet in my building and in the park when I walk my dogs.

I have started over, and it's all good.

— Felicia Carparelli —

62

Life Is a Journey of Discovery

The purpose of life, after all, is to live it,
to taste experience to the utmost, to reach out eagerly
and without fear for newer and richer experience.
~Eleanor Roosevelt

"Age is only a number." That is what I recently told a granddaughter who felt a bit anxious about turning thirty. What I did not disclose is that I once forgot this important life message. It was when I was about to retire at age sixty-five and realized my pension would only last about fifteen years. I fretted. I stewed. I tried to think of ways to lengthen the time — every way except, of course, altering my lifestyle.

Finally, I accepted what appeared to be inevitable. *It's okay,* I told myself. *When I reach eighty, I will probably be ready to slow down, read the many books I have not gotten to, rest in front of the TV, and just take it easy. I will be fine living off Social Security.* I would stop traveling then.

Yikes! What was I thinking? When I turned eighty, I felt just as energetic as when I was sixty-five. I'm sure it had something to do with spending those years fully absorbed in my passions and, ultimately, my purpose in life.

I finished a day-tripping, picnicking and recipe book that had been oh-so-slowly sprouting for twenty-five years. It was a glorious day when I finally published my book at age seventy. The next three years were spent on an amazing marketing journey that included over 200 book talks at libraries and other local organizations.

When one journey in my life ends, I am compelled to seek out another, having realized that every journey we take — whether across the street, across the country, or across the pages of a book — has the potential to lead to new discoveries that will enrich our lives.

At age seventy-four, I took a solo five-week, 6,400-mile road trip to the West. Everything was a first, from driving to the top of the highest major highway in North America and visiting ten national parks, to staying in youth hostels. In fact, the adventures were so numerous that I was prompted to write a second book. My travel memoir was published at age seventy-nine.

As my eightieth birthday approached, just as I had expected, my pension was almost gone. What to do? Keeping up my home on Social Security alone would be difficult, although I surely could have tightened my financial belt. What eventually became clear, however, is that my life wasn't just about finances. It was more about needing a new purpose and, ultimately, a new lifestyle. Thus, my wanderlust spirit woke up. "So, you're eighty, so what? You are still healthy and active. Why not become a nomad so you can travel full time?"

I loved the vision but wondered how one travels full time on a limited budget. Research provided several options. The most exciting was volunteering at our National Parks. Not only would it be a worthy cause in a beautiful environment, but many of the parks provided free housing.

Shortly after my home went on the market, I secured a four-month position in Yellowstone National Park greeting tourists and helping with projects at the Art & Photography Center. This part-time stint left plenty of free time to roam around the park to view mud pots bubbling, hot springs boiling, wildlife roaming, waterfalls rushing, and rivers roaring. The entire experience was beyond my wildest expectations.

My nomadic lifestyle continued as I drove around the country visiting friends and relatives, housesitting, and renting a room for several months simply to become acquainted with a new city. Along the way, I would occasionally stop at the home of strangers who were willing to accept like-minded travelers for a night or two. Recently, at eighty-two, I even found a way to travel to Honolulu for the first time.

Age should not dictate how we live our lives, especially in the golden years. Whether we are traveling around the country or sitting at home absorbed in passionate hobbies, it is all about the desire and determination to live life to the fullest.

And never forgetting that "age is only a number."

—Jan Mann—

Döstädning

Outer order contributes to inner calm.
~Gretchen Rubin

"Hey, Mom, the house looks great." My grown son nodded approvingly. "Seems like there's a lot less stuff around."

There was.

Two years before, my daughter had introduced me to the concept of döstädning. A recent convert to minimalism — perhaps out of necessity since she lived in a Washington, D.C. apartment — Abigail extolled the benefits of owning less. "Mom, you should try it," she said. "Not having so much stuff to take care of frees up time for better things."

Döstädning.

I might not have remembered it at all if I hadn't bothered to Google the term. Döstädning: Swedish for "death cleaning."

Now that was perplexing, and maybe a tad insulting. I wasn't exactly knocking at death's door.

It turns out that döstädning also means "decluttering." Maybe my daughter had a point. I mean, after three-plus decades of marriage, stuff piles up. Or, in my case, stuff comes in and goes out and comes in and goes out and…

Over the years, my husband and I had endured a half-dozen significant moves. Before any of the moving trucks pulled into the driveway, I divided our worldly possessions into three categories: pack away, throw away, give away. We parceled out van loads. Out went the furniture the children had outgrown. Decor that wouldn't fit well in another home. Coats, hats and boots that would never see another frigid winter. Books, CDs and DVDs, even the potted plants. But the way I found to make the new house a home always pivoted on accessorizing all over again. New pillows and throws. New scented candles. New seasonal decor. You get the idea.

Declutter? I hesitated. I clung to the view Myquillyn Smith teaches the reader to abandon in her book *Cozy Minimalist Home: More Style, Less Stuff*. I worried removing all this would make my home scream cold and cheerless. After all, didn't all my layers of stuff whisper warm and welcoming?

Maybe. Maybe not.

Perhaps, on occasion, I missed the mark trying to achieve that warm and cozy feeling. The time I decided the perfect holiday season included seven Christmas trees, grouped by theme, comes to mind. Or what about those emotion-driven shopping sprees, like when I ended up the proud owner of a porcelain vase collection large enough to fill two curio cabinets?

The same daughter who recommended döstädning had once suggested I add velvet ropes to cordon off rooms in that seven-Christmas-tree home. Maybe all my warm and welcoming accumulations hindered the very environment I strove to create. Maybe there was something to this döstädning.

Maybe.

But I like things. I like admiring them and touching them and, well, just having them. And I was going to need time to adjust to not having them. I made it easy on myself. I headed out to the garden shed and lugged things to the curb for the neighbors to pick up, which they did — with shocking speed. Next (only because most homes in the Deep South don't have basements, so that wasn't an option for me), I headed to the attic and my stash of holiday decor. Who has time for seven trees anyway? After that, I inventoried and culled the closets. Eager young crafters gobbled up supplies requiring nimbler hands and keener eyesight. Clothing refusing to measure well against my more mature self was shown the door (of a local charity).

Like Smith, I now ask myself a few questions about my possessions: Am I using this? Is the care it requires the best use of my time? If I move again, is it worth the cost and effort of packing, transporting and unpacking? Is there someone I know who would appreciate this object?

"No one wants our stuff," my college roommate said recently. Well, no one wants all our stuff all at once, but new homes can be found, piece by piece. Like the Aesop fable teaches, "Slow and steady wins the race." Opportunities presented themselves: a donation call for a church festival, a charity-run used bookstore, a school fundraiser, families in challenging circumstances, "adulting" millennials setting up new households.

And so it occurred to me that while I might not be at death's door, there was no denying that my allotted time on the planet was waning. Suddenly, it seemed selfish to wait for death to pass on heirlooms. Why not gift them now and add another layer to their meaning and history? Why not create new memories with new celebrations?

My goal is one laundry basket a month out the door. Döstädning. Basket by basket. If it's not worth giving away, there is always the recycling bin or, as a last resort, the trash bin.

My daughter hadn't been unkind when she suggested döstädning. For a couple of years, she vehemently denied ever recommending anything related to maternal mortality. She honestly thought döstädning was just Swedish for minimalism.

The process and the journey have been liberating. Even now, my home has more open places, more breathing space. There is less "stuff" clamoring for my attention, more time for living. Cleaning for life, not death!

— M. Elizabeth Gage —

64

One Step Leads to Another

One of the reasons people get old —
lose their aliveness — is that they get weighed down
by all of their stuff.
~Richard Leider

was in a rut. I woke up the same time every day, went to work, came home, ate dinner, and watched TV. Days turned into months. Months turned into years. Before I knew it, almost twenty years had passed, and I was in the same place as when I started.

The beautiful new dream house I had moved into was not so new anymore. The carpet was a mess from years of use and the family pooch's accidents. The hardwood floor no longer gleamed. The paint was fading, the deck was rotting, and the hardware was antiquated. The white GE Profile appliances that were cutting-edge when I moved in looked outdated.

Years of neglect and clutter didn't help the situation. It's amazing the stuff you accumulate over time. Luckily, I had 2,000 square feet of space to store my stuff.

I would never have anyone over because the place was a mess. Frankly, I was embarrassed. I spent a lot of time stressing over it and wondering what happened to my beautiful house. But I didn't do anything about it because it was overwhelming.

Then one day, I decided to replace the old boom box I kept in the bathroom because it took up half the space on the bathroom counter. It was hideous from ground-in grime that would have needed a jackhammer to free it. I found a small, modern-looking radio that filled the space with sound and had a cool blue hue that illuminated the room.

That radio became my impetus for change. It looked so much better than the dinosaur it replaced. I started to wonder how much better the double sinks would look if one of them wasn't filled with junk. There were newspaper clippings, batteries, and other unidentifiable objects strewn about. You name it, it was there.

I decided to dig into the mess and see what came of it, though it was risky without a hazmat suit. I dedicated my day off to the task. Once the sink was clutter-free, I was amazed at the change.

That was the encouragement I needed. Next up was the jumble filling the whirlpool tub. This was no simple undertaking, but I utilized my one day off a week to tackle the mess I had created. Before I knew it, the whirlpool was back to looking like new.

With the bathroom done, I felt empowered to take on the rest of the house. I had thought about selling one day, but I knew that was an impossibility in the condition it was in. So, slowly but surely, I went room by room through years of possessions until the place started to look habitable. There was still plenty of work to do, but the improvement was striking.

After I had made sufficient progress on cleaning up my mess, my girlfriend tackled her possessions, too. Between our efforts, we felt emboldened to call a real-estate agent about putting the place on the market. He introduced us to a contractor, and a few months later the old place looked like new. In fact, it looked so nice that I wondered why we were selling such a beautiful house. But it was all part of the plan.

Selling the house was only the first step. We knew we wanted to stay in the city — for now. After sixty-three years of enduring Chicago's bone-chilling cold, this was going to be our last year in Chicago, and we wanted to go out with a bang.

We ended up moving a mile north, right in the center of all the action Chicago has to offer. The distance was minimal, but we were worlds apart from our previous residence. We moved into a high-rise apartment with a beautiful view of the lake.

The building had amenities for days. I never had so much fun living somewhere. It was like being on vacation, except we never had to leave because we were already home.

My girlfriend is now my wife. We were married by the ocean in Mendocino, California, in September 2018. That was the next step.

In May 2019, we took a road trip to North Carolina and Georgia to see if someplace felt like home. We were looking for a place that called out to us. Charlotte answered the call. It checked off the most boxes on our list, giving us a big-city feel with a small town's warmth.

On the first day of summer, I retired from my career in sales. I received a wonderful sendoff from my friends at work, many of whom are now lifelong friends, but I was ready to move on to the next step, to live the life I always imagined. That started with a final summer in Chicago, in our new apartment. I finally got to do everything I had always wanted to do but couldn't because I was working.

I am a completely different person than who I was growing up. The shy, scared boy has evolved. I couldn't do a pull-up in high school until my senior year. In 2018, I won a physique contest at the Wisconsin State Fair at the age of sixty-two.

I don't know what the road ahead has in store for me, but I am jumping in feet-first, and I know I am ready for anything. Change is good. It all started with something as simple as throwing out an old radio. I look forward to the many steps ahead. This is just the beginning.

— Darrell Horwitz —

Chapter
8

Love and Love Again

65

A Single Yellow Rose

The best thing to hold onto in life is each other.
~Audrey Hepburn

Do you believe a single yellow rose can change someone's life? I do. On a cold November night, I flew into the Denver International Airport after spending a week in my hometown. I always knew I'd go home again someday, but I just had not been ready. It was the place where Richard and I grew up. We had met in first grade, started dating as teenagers, married, raised three children, and lived the company-transfer-lifestyle of the 1970s. We eventually settled in Colorado.

Richard's untimely death the previous year changed my life, and revisiting our hometown by myself was a frightening idea. However, the members of my grief support group encouraged me to take the big step, so I called my daughter and asked, "Would you get me reservations for a week in Iowa in November?"

Before I left Denver, I arranged for my daughter to pick me up at the Denver Airport on Saturday evening. When I called to confirm the time of my arrival, she announced, "Bob D. wants to meet you outside Door 4 by the baggage claim area thirty minutes after you land."

Hmm, that's a surprise, I thought. *I wonder why Bob wants to pick me up.* Bob had been a good friend. In fact, he and his wife had participated in a Bible study group with us, and Richard and Bob had been golfing buddies. Richard had often commented, "Bob is a really nice guy. You should get to know him better."

And I did get to know him better. After our spouses had died within two months of each other, we joined the same grief support group. I discovered why Richard had admired Bob, and because of his kindness, generosity and gentle spirit, he became a good friend and a fellow griever. The week before I left for Iowa, Bob had called and asked, "Since I lost my golfing buddy, would you join me for eighteen holes of golf this afternoon?" He and I discovered laughing and teasing each other was something new for two people who were used to crying together. "Sometimes, I just go to the mall and walk around to be with other people," Bob had told me.

Because of his comments, I wasn't totally surprised about his phone call to my daughter. He could kill some time on a lonely Saturday evening and meet a friend at the airport.

That's when more life-changing events began. On Saturday evening, I stepped out of Door 4, pulling my suitcase. Bob gave me a quick hug, grabbed the case with one hand, and opened the passenger door with the other. While he walked to the back of the car to deposit my luggage, I turned to get into the car. There, lying on the passenger's seat, was a single yellow rose.

"Bob, you brought this for me?" I asked in surprise.

"I thought it was appropriate to bring a rose for my friend," he answered. Then he looked at me and smiled. "I missed you."

I was at a loss for words. *Hmm, is something different here? Do I want something to be different between us? What do I say?*

"How about stopping and getting something to eat?" Bob asked before I could comment.

"Okay," I said, thinking we'd probably stop at a fast-food restaurant on the way to my house.

"Would you like to go to that little café in Parker? It's a nice place with good food," he suggested.

Uh-oh, I thought. *And very appropriate for private conversations. What's wrong with me? It's my friend Bob.* All the while, I was holding my single yellow rose. Still a bit dazed by the turn of events, I inadvertently carried it into the restaurant.

During the previous year in our support group, Bob and I had shared our honest feelings about everything connected with the loss of a spouse, including our anger and disappointment in unanswered prayer. After we settled into a cozy booth, we spent two hours talking about our families, our desire to follow God's will, and our anxiety regarding the future. We were both in our mid-sixties, and we didn't want to stop living. We each had a bucket list of adventures to experience and places we wanted to see.

Wow, are we talking about us? I wondered. *This is Bob, my friend, my buddy.* But there was the single yellow rose in my lap. "We've both suffered tremendous loss this past year. Whatever the future holds, I hope neither of us gets hurt," I commented.

We had always greeted each other and said goodbye with a hug. That night, we hugged a little longer than usual, and it felt good.

"How would you like to go to a movie?" Bob asked me the following weekend.

"Is this called a date?" I asked. "You need to know you're talking a foreign language," I added.

"The same goes for me," Bob laughed. "Wow, I'm going on a date in my sixties!"

Yes, that night was the beginning of a new life for Bob and me. During the next several months, we became a couple. Bob's sons lived miles away. However, Bob kept them apprised of our new "dating" relationship. "We are so happy for you two," was the constant reaction from family and friends.

Since we were very aware of our new motto, "treasure the moment," seven months later, we chose to get married with our children and grandchildren surrounding us. I carried a small bouquet of yellow roses.

"Do you ever regret remarrying when you were in your sixties?" my friend Linda asked me four years ago.

"Never!" I answered. "There are still times of adjustment and compromise, but it's all worth it. We've discovered new hobbies like traveling in a motorhome, spending time at Bob's cabin on the lake in upstate New York, and rounds of golf in new places. We even played at St Andrews in Scotland. Now that we've moved into our seventies, we've learned sitting side by side in our recliners is also a good way to spend an evening."

And it was, until September 2017. Fatigue and weakness in his legs, arms and hands had plagued Bob for over a year. Finally, a neurologist gave us the bad news: "We have ruled out all other possibilities. You have ALS, commonly known as Lou Gehrig's Disease, and it is fatal."

Our love for each other, our faith in God, the prayers and support from our families and friends sustained us during Bob's last months. We often told each other, "I'm glad we decided to get married. It's been a wonderful fourteen years."

Yes, a single yellow rose changed my life when I was in my sixties. However, my life has changed once more. Several months ago, our families and friends gathered to celebrate Bob's life. Once again, I carried a single yellow rose.

— Betty Johnson Dalrymple —

66

Chicken Soup
for the Soul

Speed Dating

When you're open to receiving them,
the possibilities just keep on coming.
~Oprah Winfrey

Edging toward my sixtieth birthday, I realized that I had been divorced longer than I'd been married. And even though I had been engaged twice in that span, I finally came to realize that I was going to be just fine as a single woman "of a certain age."

It was actually rather liberating to let go of the desperate need to find a man to "complete" me.

I had a great career with a private practice in a prestigious clinic. My dream condo had a spare bedroom and bath for my children and their families to sleep over on holidays. My free time was filled with live jazz and art events with good friends, as well as some volunteer activity for my church.

Then, on a rainy weeknight, a business acquaintance called asking for a favor. She and her husband had consulted me for marketing advice for their dating business. Now they needed another woman to even out the numbers for a speed-dating event at a local restaurant. Right away. They even offered to waive the entry fee and buy me a drink!

Hmm, let's see, I thought. *Leftovers and watch some mindless sitcom or a night out for free on a Thursday?*

It didn't take me long to refresh my make-up, spritz on some perfume and say goodbye to the cat.

Now, the way speed dating works is this: Each person gets a name badge with only their first name and a code number. There were fourteen guests: seven men and seven women. All had been pre-screened and were single, available to date, and between the ages of forty-five and sixty.

The ladies sat at high-top tables for two. Every seven minutes, a timer would ding, and the men would move to the next table. Each person had a pad for taking notes. We were allowed to ask about hobbies, favorite date ideas, pets, occupation and general niceties. But we were not permitted to ask for last names, addresses, phone numbers or exact age.

If the woman wanted to know more about the man, she could write his name and number on her pad and submit that request at the end of the event. And if the same man had also submitted an interest in getting to know her, that was considered a "go." The planner would supply the gentleman with the lady's telephone number and suggest he call her to invite her to lunch or coffee.

Well, out of seven men, I asked to meet four guys. And there were five men who wanted to know more about me, including the four I was interested in. So, I had four potential dates.

The first man talked almost two hours on the phone the very next night. After what felt like a friendly job interview, he decided that I was too busy with my family to devote enough time to him. Fine! So long.

The second gentleman was an art professor. We had a lovely lunch, and he invited me to the open-air theater. Since the show changes every two weeks, this was a safe bet for an easy first date. Shirley, a family friend, worked at the concession stand, and I trusted her character judgment. She scowled as soon as he approached her cash register with a thumbs-down. I still cannot recall the play, but I know it seemed like the night would never end. He was so nervous that he talked through the entire show!

The third man was rather quiet and shy, so I offered the summer theater idea again. I was eager to walk this handsome fellow with the easy laugh right up to the snack counter. I ordered popcorn and a diet soda. Shirley took one look at his rosy cheeks and neatly trimmed beard and flashed him a big smile with a thumbs-up! I felt my shoulders relax as we laughed and enjoyed the show. Kenny was so easy to be with that I didn't want the evening to end.

But when this handsome farmer from Topeka asked me out for another date, I had to be honest and say, "Maybe."

I explained that there was one more guy on my list for a coffee date from the speed-dating night.

Kenny just looked down at his shoes and said softly, "Okay."

I asked how many ladies were left on his list. His face turned bright red as he looked into my eyes and said, "Well, you're the only one I wanted to see again."

Yikes, I thought, *no pressure here!*

Kenny looked so sad. I agreed that I would call him right after the last man's date and promised to tell him the truth about a second date for us. He seemed slightly encouraged, but we parted with just a handshake.

The fourth guy took me to see the last play of the season, but he was more interested in the snack bar than me or the show! My friend was laughing as he kept adding items to his order. He acted like we were about to go on a cross-country journey, not watch a two-hour, open-air play. After enduring his lip-smacking and greasy fingers on the arm of my chair, I politely declined his offer for dinner the next night, telling him that I really wasn't looking for daily dinner dates. I guess he was just as happy to move down his list of women.

After my date dropped me off, knowing that Kenny worked the night shift anyway, I couldn't wait to call my "Lucky #3 Guy" and tell him that he was the one for me.

He asked me if I'd like to see a new movie, a controversial docu-drama, and when I instantly agreed, I think we were both surprised.

I just kept thinking that this farmer dude was not a braggart, not a foodie and certainly not like the rude, middle-aged guys I'd met who truly were "just after one thing."

After our movie date, Kenny suggested we grab a bite to eat. I was so relieved because I really didn't want to have to wait another week or so for a next date! As we walked to The Cheesecake Factory, we talked about the film and realized we think alike in politics.

"Wait!" I said, "are you a Democrat in Kansas?"

And with that smile that I've come to adore, he quietly replied, "I sure am."

"And I was the only woman you asked to see again at the speed dating?" I added.

He replied softly, "I saw your eyes light up when you looked up at me, and I thought, 'Wow! I finally got a pretty one.' Why would I look for anyone else?"

I was at a loss for words.

But I was pretty sure that warm glow around my heart was new-found love.

And I was right.

—Valorie Fenton—

67

Finding Love Later in Life

Life can be strange — a person who once was a stranger across the room is now the love of your life.
~Andy Atticus

By the time I reached my sixtieth birthday, I had led a successful, exciting and fulfilling life by most standards. I had worked as an occupational psychologist, a market research consultant, and a helicopter instructor. I had walked round the whole coast of Britain, visited more than eighty countries, and flown almost all types of flying machine. Bucket list? Mine had been completed long ago. There was nothing left that I desperately wanted to do. I lived in a gorgeous country cottage with great views, along with my much-loved cats, and I now earned my living writing about all the things I'd done in the past. I was quite content. After all, what more could I ask for?

However, there was one area of life in which I had been less successful. I had never married, nor really even had a long-term relationship. For many years, I had been too busy with careers and travelling to care about such things. After that... Well, it just hadn't happened, and I hadn't worried that much. But now, as I found myself getting older, things changed. I started to envy those people I knew who had a lifelong companion. I had good friends, but no one really close to me.

Now that I wasn't going out to work, for the first time in my life I started to feel lonely by myself in my little cottage. The idea of sharing my life with someone other than the cats gradually became more attractive. But how could I do that? Surely, it was far too late. Whoever heard of someone meeting their soulmate over the age of sixty? And I knew I couldn't settle for just anyone.

However, I decided to make a last try to meet someone. On the advice of friends, I joined a couple of dating websites. But by 2010, when I was sixty-one, I realised that this was unlikely to work. Most men wanted someone far younger, and I had little in common with the few I met. Many found my background intimidating, and almost nobody could cope with my multi-cat household! It seemed I was doomed to grow old as a lonely, mad cat lady with exciting memories.

Then, just as I was about to let all my subscriptions lapse and give up altogether, I came upon a profile written by a cat-loving man who lived on a canal boat. He wrote well, and he sounded interesting and, well, quite a lot like me. He was a few years younger than I was, but that wasn't a problem from my point of view, although I realised it might be from his. I ignored the profile for a while, but I kept coming back to it, and wondering, just wondering... Should I have one final try?

I decided it could do no harm as I was pretty immune to disappointment by then. So, I wrote to David, telling him about my cats and my life. And he wrote back. We corresponded a bit more, and then we talked on the phone. We seemed to get on well. But that was all that happened for a couple of months as he carried on boating and showed no inclination to meet. I recall saying to a friend that I'd heard from a nice man, but he didn't seem to want to take the friendship any further.

Then fate took a hand. I acquired a new Maine Coon kitten, and David really wanted to see her. So, he came to my house, mainly to meet nine-week-old Xena! But we got on really well and couldn't stop talking to each other. After that, we started seeing each other regularly. I've always joked that it was Xena who really brought us together!

Soon, winter came, and living on the boat became hard, so David accepted my invitation to move in for a while, bringing his cat Cookie with him. After that, he never really left. True, he went back to the boat from time to time for short periods, but that was all. We gradually went from being good friends to being very much more. Eventually, David sold the boat and moved in with me permanently.

We have now been together for ten years. Two years ago, we bought a house together in a nearby town that we both liked and enjoyed fixing up together. We have travelled extensively, and I found out how much more fun it is going to new places with someone to share things with. He introduced me to his children and most recently to his new granddaughter. He took me boating, and I introduced him to cat showing and yoga. We took up ballroom dancing, both of us learning it for the first time. Life together is fun! But, most importantly, we share the same ideas and values, and are still growing closer and closer. He tells me several times a day that he loves me, and I tell him the same thing.

I still can't believe that, at the age of sixty-one, I finally found my soulmate. I am now seventy-one, and life just gets better and better. I consider myself to be very fortunate. So, I always tell people in their forties, fifties and older who lament being alone and say it is too late, my life is proof that this is not the case. You are never too old to find love!

—Helen Krasner—

68

Mom on Match

In the end, we only regret the chances we didn't take.
~Author Unknown

Me? On the Internet? My three daughters were crazy. They knew I hated the computer. Each of them had tried to teach me how to use it and failed. I didn't care if I was Internet illiterate. I had my typewriter and telephone, so I could communicate just fine.

Two of them even came up with the idea of "Mom on Match," which I immediately rejected. Did they really think I, at age eighty-seven, was going to find a date with some old man that way? Never mind that one of the girls had told me earlier about the scammers and criminals out there who prey on older women like me. I wanted no part of that nonsense.

But they wouldn't give up. So, one night, when I felt very tired and wanted to shut them up, I reluctantly agreed to let them put me on Match.com. I didn't have to do anything. They did it all and then instructed me on how to use it. (I didn't take a single note.)

About a month later, all three girls wanted to see the results I'd received from Match.com. None existed! They found out then that I hadn't used it; I didn't even know how. So the one who lived closest took over. She got on the computer, found a gentleman who hadn't given up when I didn't reply on Match earlier, and answered him. Like me, he was a former educator, loved to dance, and enjoyed watching football. After talking on the phone for two weeks, I reluctantly agreed to meet him for lunch. We had much in common, so we continued to meet, had dinner dates (he always brought flowers), enjoyed ballroom dancing (something I hadn't done in years), saw musicals, and went to Indianapolis Colts football games with his season tickets. Spending time together was very comfortable, and we began seeing each other more as the months passed.

Then, one evening, a surprise proposal came in the middle of a dance floor. I love surprises, but I wasn't ready for that one. It did, however, spark some serious discussions about a possible future together. Later, we met with our pastor to examine things further and prepare for a marriage that would bring both of us happiness. We knew we each had a few old habits that should be discussed, and at our age we also had to address possible challenges for the future.

Time passed. We grew even closer together as we explored housing possibilities. My fiancé had a home about twenty miles from my apartment that he would sell. (I had sold my home earlier.) We decided to live in a cottage on the grounds of a senior community that offered all levels of care for the future, if necessary, and a large apartment building with dining, fitness, and ongoing activities we liked. And it was in a perfect central location.

Our small wedding took place a year and a half later, with a reception afterward for family and friends. Then, on our honeymoon cruise, we even won "The Newlywed Game!"

Now, almost two years later, we still feel like newlyweds and have recommended Match.com to others, some of whom have connected. And, yes, I use the computer constantly these days, often to write down such stories as this—which, I admit to my daughters, is a lot of fun.

— Queen Lori —

69

Love Letters

Relish love in our old age! Aged love is like aged wine;
it becomes more satisfying, more refreshing,
more valuable, more appreciated
and more intoxicating.
~Leo Buscaglia

Normally, my husband had a lot to say when he got home from work, but so far he hadn't uttered more than a few words. I waited while he slathered his tacos with a mountain of salsa and sour cream before I finally broke the silence.

"So, how was work?"

"Okay," he shrugged, picking at his food, "except the women I work with called me a lousy husband again."

"What for this time?" I asked.

"Our anniversary," he said. "They couldn't believe I didn't take you out for dinner last night or buy you an expensive gift."

Valentine's Day, Christmas, my birthday—these women loved teasing my husband for not coming through in the "romance department," even though he'd explained several times that I'm the kind of wife who would rather get a bag of Brussels sprouts, a package of gumdrops, or a scenic ride in the car as opposed to a diamond necklace or an expensive dinner. Besides, we loved celebrating at home.

"I hope you reminded those women that I'm not high-maintenance," I answered, shaking my head at their nonsense.

Suddenly, his face lit up like a Christmas tree. "I did remind them.

I also told them that obviously I'm not *that* lousy of a husband since I get daily love letters from my wife — and *their* husbands don't."

I couldn't help but smile. My husband adored his "love letters" and had often mentioned them to the people he worked with, although what he calls "letters" are more like little notes.

Early in our marriage, I'd confessed to my husband that I never wanted to become one of those loving but crotchety wives who barked at their husband over trivial issues. Yet, after wading through several stressful months, that's exactly what I'd done, and I hadn't even realized it. Horrified with my actions, I wanted to ensure that I never turned into that kind of wife again.

Throughout the many years, I've left sticky notes in my husband's cooler for him to read during his lunch hour. He never knows when he'll get one but enjoys my notes and even writes back to me. That gave me a brilliant idea.

Each day, I decided to set aside time to think about my husband and why I was grateful for him on that particular day. On a piece of scrap paper, I scribbled him a note and left it on his nightstand where he'd find it after he got home from work each evening.

My notes are simple but sincere.

"I am grateful for your understanding."

"I'm grateful to you for taking me to my doctor's appointment yesterday."

"I'm grateful for your sense of humor and your laughter on a day when I needed it most."

Once in a while, I get carried away, and his note overflows with mush. I always end the note with "xoxoxoxox."

Of course, my husband thinks that I started the tradition to show him how much I love and appreciate him, but I actually wrote the notes for me.

When life is hectic and disasters abound, when the bills pile up and money is tight, even when all is peaceful and right in our world, I never want to forget the many chapters it took to get us together and on the same page. I feel so blessed to have my husband by my side and never want to take him for granted or forget how I feel about him.

Initially, I planned on leaving him notes for one month, but those little expressions of gratitude meant so much to my husband and made such a difference in my life that they've become a part of our world now. Even though he knows I love him, and I know I love him, it's like feeding the fire one more log—those daily "love letters" keep our love burning a bit warmer and brighter each day.

I think it's pretty neat that my husband tells everyone that he gets daily love letters from his wife, especially since we're old farts who have celebrated thirty-one years of marriage so far. As an added plus, when it comes to his co-workers, his "love letters" are a great defense and prove to those women that no matter what they think, I'm crazy about my husband!

—Jill Burns—

70

The Wild World of Online Dating

Laughter is the corrective force which prevents
us from becoming cranks.
~Henri Bergson

My girlfriends were ganging up on me. We'd met three years earlier in a support group for newly divorced men and women. This program had helped all of us heal from painful breakups. We laughed and cried together, gave each other moral support, and developed long-term friendships. Gradually, we took tentative steps to move forward with life.

At the completion of the course, four of us women got together monthly for dinner. We offered each other encouragement and continued to mend.

I was the only dating holdout of our group.

"I'm almost sixty-two," I complained. "That's way too old to start dating."

"Well, I'm older than you, and I'm doing fine," argued Beth. "So, girl, you've run out of excuses."

Tricia chimed in, "Nancy, online dating is the easiest way to meet men these days. We want you to try it."

Frankly, I was reluctant to dive into the dating pool — or swamp. To me, computer dating was rough country, fraught with minefields and misery. The thought of opening my heart again was terrifying. My career and volunteer work kept me busy. Did I really want to embark on a quest that would probably lead to knowing that my cats adored me most?

But my heart did keep tugging at me.

"There has to be love after divorce," I conceded.

Sensing that I was weakening, my friends pounced and suggested several free online sites that I could browse before choosing one.

"Raise your right hand and promise you'll set up a profile tonight before you go to bed," insisted Louisa. "Just follow the directions."

"And remember to post several nice photos," added Beth.

I raised my hand and halfheartedly agreed, not totally sure I'd follow through.

"I'm going to call you tomorrow to make sure you did it," warned Tricia.

With that, we all said goodnight to each other.

When I arrived home, exhausted from the long day, I ignored my computer. But I had vowed to give this new venture a try, so I finally sat down shortly before midnight and looked over the free dating sites my friends had mentioned. Settling on the one with the easiest instructions, I read a few sample profiles to get a sense of how to present myself to the world.

"This is tougher than I thought," I said aloud. "Let's see — what am I looking for in a man? I'm not even sure anymore."

My profile needed to be short and to the point, clever but not cutesy. Should I write that a sense of humor is vital? Yes. That I'm a singer? My political or spiritual leanings? How about that travel is a favorite pastime?

Oh, yes, it's important to mention my cats in case he's allergic.

Typing and retyping, I yawned and yearned for my bed.

"Select a username," said the instructions. I wasn't supposed to use my real name.

"Let's see," I pondered for a few moments. "I'm a musician. Does 'A Muse' sound okay?"

Composing my first-ever dating profile was grueling.

"Oh, well, it's late, and this is a start," I rationalized. "Thank goodness it can be updated whenever I want."

I had no way of knowing how quickly I would have to do just that.

Finding several pictures of myself, I loaded a close-up, another with my guitar, and one of me on a mountain trail. *That's a pretty good representation,* I thought.

The last category required me to click on my goal for this online adventure. There were quite a few choices listed. "Casual Dating, Friendship, Marriage…"

"Long-Term Relationship sounds best," I decided. A healthy connection with a good man would be heavenly. I clicked on that category and sent my opus into cyberspace.

My cats woke me up the following morning, yowling for breakfast. Pouring a cup of coffee, I logged on to my computer to see if any potential suitors had even noticed me in this new realm.

"Fifty-five replies?" I was astonished. "My friends are going to be so proud of me."

The response was overwhelming. Men from all across the United States had replied. And… oh, my gosh… men from other countries?

"Wow! This is incredible," I gushed.

"Hello, beautiful," wrote one. "I would like to fly you to Italy to spend a week with me."

What?

"Bonjour from Quebec," replied another. "Please come to visit me. I will pay your airfare."

"You are gorgeous," said others. "When can we meet?"

Gorgeous? Me? Didn't these men notice that I'm in my sixties?

Message after message, some flirtatious, some friendly, filled my inbox. All these men wanted to date me. I was flabbergasted. No wonder my girlfriends had forced me into this endeavor.

"Why did it take me so long to go online?" I asked aloud. This world of computer dating was incredibly friendly and filled with such nice men.

As I scrolled down through my messages, my heart was filled with hope for this new chapter in my life. I was honestly touched.

Finally, arriving at the last post, I saw that a cordial gentleman had replied.

"Hello, A Muse," he wrote. "I'm just checking with you because I'm puzzled. You seem like a respectable and upstanding woman. Did you really mean to choose that category as your preference for a relationship?"

"What's he talking about?" I puzzled aloud.

Rereading my profile thoroughly, it seemed fine to me. Then I scrolled down to the Dating Preferences section.

"No!" I gasped. "Oh, no-o-o-o! What have I done?"

No wonder men all over the world wanted to meet me. In my late-night fatigue, I had accidentally clicked on the category just below Long-Term Relationship: Casual Sexual Encounters.

—Nancy Saint John—

71

One Text at a Time

Technology is best when it brings people together.
~Matt Mullenweg

I resisted at first, but my son persisted and I learned to text. Little did I know the huge role my new communications "skill" would play in my future.

Not long after I learned to text, my husband Phil suffered a massive stroke. After he spent a year in a nursing facility, I brought him home and became his full-time caregiver. It was a heartbreaking and exhausting time, but I never regretted giving him the comfort of home and family as he fought for recovery. Sadly, it was a battle won in heaven rather than earth as he received his final healing almost five years following the stroke.

I had actually met Phil at an online site for Christian singles. It had been a good experience, and we were blessed with a loving marriage. And I knew I wanted to find love again. I decided to look online to see if I might discover some Christian widowers who shared my faith, lived close by, and loved the outdoors (and hiking) as much as I did. Because my faith was a big priority, I listed that in my profile.

I made several friends and had a few interesting dates, but nothing serious developed until the day I spotted a profile that seemed to match my desire for a strong faith and my need to be outside. He lived in a city nearby, so I sent a brief comment that we seemed to share similar interests.

Shortly afterward, I received a reply. "I would like to get to know you better. I am impressed with your faith." After a few private e-mails, we arranged to meet at a nearby river park to walk. We exchanged phone numbers... and began texting!

Our first meeting went well. We talked and walked non-stop, and I gave Jim a book I had written containing stories about my life. Jim's wife had died suddenly after over forty years of marriage. Between us, there were seven children and nine grandchildren! As we parted for the evening, we made plans to meet again soon for another hike.

Let the texting begin! In the days that followed, I discovered that Jim's preferred method of communication was text messages. He texted comments and questions in response to my book. As we continued meeting to walk, hike and talk, we considered whether our relationship might have a future. Jim began texting me good morning and goodnight messages to start and close my day. I looked forward to the little "ding" that would tell me he was thinking of me.

Even the first "I love you" came in the form of a text! The morning messages became "Good morning, Sweetheart," and the evenings ended with "I love you most." We connected occasionally throughout the day and "discussed" our plans the same way. Jim owned a goat farm and a part-time shipping business. Our busy schedules required pre-arranging our time together, and texting made it possible to interact at our own convenience without the disruption of a phone call.

As we grew closer and began including our families in our friendship and plans, we used texting to exchange family photos and even the sports schedules of grandchildren. A truly special event was celebrated together by text as we welcomed an additional grandson into my family. Jim awaited the birth announcement via text updates and then rejoiced with us as photos of Josiah Keller Kirkpatrick arrived also by text.

When we are separated and I am traveling, Jim gets "treated" to my experiences on wooded trails or waterfalls and sometimes even my food as I text pictures of my adventures. We have even enjoyed the fun of multi-family texts filled with emojis and sibling banter.

While my marriage proposal actually took place on a mountaintop at a beautiful state park in Alabama (with no cellphone service), many of our wedding plans continue to be made by text. And I recently sent a text picture to Jim of the beautiful wedding bands we had designed after I had just picked them up.

Jim and I will soon begin life together... and there seems no reason to believe the texting will slow down even then. But I cannot even imagine what I could have missed if I had refused to learn how to text! I owe a huge thank you to that persistent son of mine for both his perseverance and his capable tutoring... via text, of course!

—Lettie Kirkpatrick Burress—

72

Miss Matched

*I hate first dates. I made the mistake of telling my date
a lie about myself, and she caught me — I didn't think
she'd actually demand to see the bat cave.*
~Alex Reed

"**A**re you going to keep checking out every guy who walks by?" my dinner companion, Sunny, asked. "I could've gone home from work and spent the night in my pajamas with my cat and the box of wine in my fridge!"

"I'm not checking out every guy!" I scoffed, despite knowing full well that, indeed, I was. She wasn't the only one who had noticed. I'd even caught myself doing it.

"True, it all depends," she replied. "If the guy's wearing a wedding ring, your mind drifts back to our conversation. If not, he gets the major once-over all the way to that big group around the pool tables! Bob's been gone over three years now. If you could ask him, would he want you sitting around, spending the rest of your life alone? Why don't you try some dating websites?"

It wasn't the first time I'd heard that advice. The idea seemed absurd but the seed was planted. A few weeks later I grabbed my laptop and a wine cooler, ignored my skepticism, and made my foray into the world of twenty-first-century dating.

"And where exactly does someone who hasn't been on a first date in almost fifty years begin?" I asked myself. I knew nothing about being a modern-day pursuer! And even scarier was my more pressing concern — my physical change over the years. While I'd turned more than a few heads back in my cheerleading days, the only part of my old uniform that might still fit were the pompoms!

Despite feeling ridiculous, curiosity won, and I logged onto a well-known site. Putting my best creative foot forward, I worked through the questions, trying to sound intelligent and interesting. Once completed, I found an acceptable photo of myself and closed my eyes, finger poised above the "Enter" button. Drawing in a deep breath, I jabbed the key. Regretting it instantly, I shut down the computer and went to bed with my current companion — a good book.

A week later, I checked my responses. I was pleasantly surprised to see several messages. After dismissing anyone living out of state, I spotted a man who lives nearby. At least on paper (or pixels), he looked nice, and we had several things in common. It took a mere thirty-five minutes to compose my two-sentence reply. After progressing to phone conversations for a few days, we agreed to meet. I chose a fast-food place. On a busy street. At 2 p.m.

Walking toward the restaurant where he already sat sipping coffee, I reviewed my opening line. My friend Frank had warned me not to monopolize the conversation, so I'd gone back over the prospect's profile to find an interesting tidbit to ask about.

"I've never met anyone who collects relics," I began. "How do you find them?" I'd retired from providing anti-investment-fraud presentations to groups throughout my entire state, yet I felt like a fish out of water talking to this one person. Frank need not have worried. In such unfamiliar waters, I was very content being the listener this time.

"I just walk through fields," he offered, "and spend the day digging around. Here are some pictures." For the next ten minutes, he swiped his cellphone through dozens of photos to share his finds. To my untrained eye, they all looked like rocks.

Next, he volunteered a history lesson. According to him, the colonists were able to win the Revolutionary War only because the natives taught them about a local plant with which they could drug the British soldiers. Once the troops were stupefied on this loco weed and "running around naked in circles for thirteen hours," the settlers were able to walk right in and make off with the army's muskets, then defeat the enemy with King George III's own weapons!

Now, I admit that history had always been my worst subject in school, but I'm still reasonably sure even I would have remembered such a story. Moments later, he mentioned that very plant grew outside his kitchen window. Actually, it was his sister's house. He just lived there with her. After clarifying that, he suggested making me dinner some night the following week. It was time to head for the hills. Quickly.

Just as I came up with a polite excuse to leave, he recaptured my attention by announcing he'd discovered how to cure diabetes. Having friends and family with the disease, I couldn't resist sticking around for the details. His cure? Diabetics merely need to "walk barefoot, in the grass, on the outer edges of their feet." Who knew? I made a show of checking the time on my phone and bid him goodbye.

During the drive home, flashing constant glances in my rearview mirror, I had three realizations. First, Mr. Match hadn't even asked my last name, saving me from having to invent one. Second, this was assuredly not a match made in heaven, or anywhere else. Third, I wasn't likely to try digital dating again anytime soon.

For now, my retirement days are replete with writing, crafting, volunteer work, and being Uber Grandma to my five youngest grandchildren and their eight activities. But maybe, just maybe, someday I'll make it my mission to bring back dances for those of us who would rather meet people the old-fashioned way — in person.

— Barbara Bennett —

The Girl He Married

Ideally, couples need three lives; one for him,
one for her, and one for them together.
~Jacqueline Bisset

When my husband asked where I wanted to go for my retirement vacation, I had an answer at the ready. "I want to rent a house on the beach in North Carolina," I said. "For a month," I added. "And let's take Annie and make it a road trip."

Annie was the canine only-child in our family of three. The one we promised each other we wouldn't get once the kids were grown and gone. The one we promised would never come as a surprise to the other. The one that wiggled her way into our hearts and claimed her spot in our newly emptied nest. And Ray was the culprit.

"Who's that?" I'd asked him several months earlier, struggling to place the picture of the dark-haired boy clutching a puppy and staring back at me from Ray's iPad.

"It's your new puppy," he said.

"No, I mean who is this?" I asked, pointing to the little boy.

"It's your new puppy," he insisted, a sheepish grin spreading across his face. We had promised each other no puppy surprises. But that was before he thought I needed her. My dad was dying, exacting an emotional toll on our family. "And," he quickly added, weighing the consequences of his infraction, "I've only paid a deposit for her so you can always say no... And, by the way, that cute little boy holding your

Love and Love Again | 241

puppy is the breeder's son."

I loved him for taking that risk. And I didn't say no.

We adored her. And now, four months later as we planned my retirement vacation, only one obstacle remained. I had to retire. As that day drew near, I recalled the opening words of my letter of resignation: "It has been my privilege and honor to serve this organization as its Founder and Executive Director for over twenty-three years. It has truly been a labor of love for me and my family. Therefore, with mixed emotions, and the Lord's peace, I respectfully submit my letter of resignation as Executive Director."

It sounded good, the right way to end. But it wasn't exactly true. It hadn't always been a labor of love. Sometimes, it was hard and conflicted, held together by worn threads of a lifelong mantra: Quitters never win, and winners never quit.

Two years before I submitted my letter of resignation, I knew it was time for someone with a fresh vision and untapped energy to lead. But I wanted to end well. So, I listened, prayed, and watched God's plan unfold.

Then I retired.

A few days later, the three of us left for North Carolina, with Ray and I wondering how this voluntary amputation of a significant role in my life would affect us.

It turned out that I never looked back. Lulled by the soothing rhythm of tires carrying us farther and farther from our former lives, I felt myself slither from the constricting responsibility and persona I'd assumed, escaping the lifeless skin that no longer fit. "There's nobody I have to be anymore," I shared with Ray a few days into our journey. It was the beginning of my coming home to me.

The beach house that Ray found after days of searching on his computer felt perfect: a one-of-a-kind, two-story home with panoramic ocean views and thundering surf at high tide that threatened to unravel the dune on which it sat. Shelves stuffed with an eclectic assortment of books, shells and puzzles lined the walls. Cozy furniture with stories to tell invited us to curl up and stay awhile. And the deck, gated and secure, belonged to Annie when she wasn't chasing seagulls on the beach during morning walks with Ray.

At night, we walked her together, slipping down the back stairs to stroll along the narrow street. Tonight, it was raining. Pulling the hood of my jacket over my head, I cowered, resisting the inconvenience before stepping into the downpour. Wet gravel scrunched beneath our feet as we dodged puddles on our way to the deserted corner lot.

Somewhere between the back door and the corner lot, we glanced at each other and erupted into laughter — soaking wet, drenched heads tossed back, and rain coursing down our faces — a belly laugh long overdue. Pure joy. Deep connection. In that moment, the stress of a quarter-century cracked and broke loose from my soul.

Ray knew it, too. "I feel like I got the girl back that I married," he whispered. We were in love and having a blast, daring to dream about our empty-nest future.

Seventeen months later, Ray died.

As I sift through memories of the slow dance of our lives, this one settles things. I feel loved and forgiven. It nourishes and comforts my soul in the dark nights of this long goodbye. I ended well in the eyes of the one who mattered most.

Ray's words gave me the gift of knowing our love came full circle — the validation of more than four decades of marriage. From being deeply in love when we married, through the challenges and chaos of parenting seven children, and enduring countless career ups and downs, we were more in love when we ended than when we began.

And buried beneath the distractions of life was the girl he married. I'm thankful we both got her back.

— Paula S. Freeman —

74

And Always One More Time

Have enough courage to trust love one more time
and always one more time.
~Maya Angelou

I have a framed quote from Maya Angelou sitting on my desk that became my mantra after I was suddenly widowed. It was that quote that gave me the courage to try online dating. I had to admit that my fear of being alone outweighed my fear of online dating. So, with a little nudge from my persistent friends, I began weeding through profiles.

The process was interesting. It wasn't difficult to meet men — several showed interest. But at this phase of my life, it proved nearly impossible to make a lasting connection. I had a few relationships that were a little more than casual, but nothing ever felt right. It always felt like I was trying to force a piece of a puzzle that did not fit. Now, later in life, I wasn't willing to settle or, worse yet, change. As I endured these missteps, I would go through periods of feeling hopeless, believing that I was destined to be alone for the rest of my life. Then, hearing Maya's voice say, "Have enough courage to trust love one more time and always one more time," I'd become hopeful.

Near the end of my three-month subscription on a senior dating website, I finally read a man's profile that intrigued me. "I enjoy indie music and indie movies," it read. I drafted a short e-mail to him and was pleasantly surprised when he responded.

We met for dinner soon after that. There was an unpretentious calmness about him that was very appealing to me. As we talked, I didn't feel the need to sell myself. He laughed and smiled at appropriate times and asked thoughtful questions. Midway through the meal, I remember thinking, *I could spend a lot of time with this guy.* Dinner led to frozen yogurt afterward. I didn't want the date to end. When the date was over, I texted him to say I had a great time and breathed a sigh of relief when he immediately texted the same back to me.

And then I didn't hear from him for another week. Trusting Maya, I summoned the courage to send him another text: "Hey, you want to do something this weekend?" His response indicated he had plans, but that he'd be back in touch.

And then I didn't hear from him for two more weeks. I had heard the "I'll be in touch" line before. It's usually a nice way to brush someone off. So, I deleted his contact information.

Two weeks after that, I received a text. He explained that he had been in China on business and wanted to know if I was free the following weekend. On our first date after he returned from his trip, he held me in his arms as we danced at an outside concert. Hearing Maya's words in my head, I allowed myself to start to fall.

More than five years later, my heart still races at the sound of his voice, and I get a warm feeling at the touch of his hand. Today, as we build a life and future together, it feels so right. We have such a strong bond and a true partnership that is supportive and caring. The puzzle pieces of my life finally fit together.

Dating later in life isn't for the faint of heart. Sometimes, it can feel like a never-ending gauntlet of rejection and avoidance. As we age, the baggage we carry sometimes gets heavier. But the baggage we carry makes us who we are.

From my vantage point, falling in love at this stage has been a fulfilling and wonderful process. There's something so serene yet invigorating about finding love now. We have created a relationship grounded in love and respect that feels different from any other I have experienced.

We aren't in a rush to get married and start a family, and we aren't distracted by material things or overly focused on moving up the corporate ladder. We are seasoned at life and can prioritize what's important. We have the maturity that comes with living a long life that had several bumps in the road. Neither of us needs to be right all the time, and both of us listen to what the other has to say. And, taking nothing for granted, both of us appreciate each other and the "we" that we have become.

People often comment how happy I look. I must admit that my happiness is hard to contain. I feel so blessed that life's journey has led me to a place of such joy. I am grateful every day for what we have, knowing it was a lesson in perseverance to get to where we are. And I am grateful that I never gave up hope.

The advice I give my single friends is the same advice I took from Maya: "Have enough courage to trust love one more time and always one more time."

Thank you, Maya.

— Michelle Paris —

Embrace Your Years

75

Adventures in the Unknown

I saw that you were perfect, and so I loved you.
Then I saw that you were not perfect
and I loved you even more.
~Angelita Lim

knew by age twenty that travel is what I would work for — the big payoff. I wouldn't need a boat, fancy car, big house, jewels or furs. I wanted all the variety I could get in my one life by seeing different kinds of beauty and experiencing other cultures.

But after taking business trips alone in my twenties and thirties to Cannes and Maui, I tapered off. I postponed the glorious unknowns of the Outback, taking shorter trips to see friends and family in the U.S. and work in Canadian cities. Europe would keep, I told myself in my forties and fifties.

Then, at sixty-four, when I felt even stronger and more fit, physically and mentally, I found the belated, beloved travel mate of my dreams to share every adventure. We had the good fortune of marrying just in time to benefit from Medicare and pensions. With some savings, and hard-earned Social Security about to trickle into my bank account, I could attack the list of places I wanted to see.

We vowed we'd venture farther and wilder on each vacation. As a wife for the very first time in my life, I felt a rush of confidence as I pored over websites with pictures of exotic locales.

On our first trip, we are checking in at LAX to fly off to our honeymoon suite in Barcelona. And as Handsome bent over to put a tag on his bag, I saw it.

My face had a hot flash. I'd not seen him at this angle before. Maybe it was just an illusion born of gravity and the forelock at the crown of his head. I looked more closely. Unmistakable.

My husband had a bald spot.

It wasn't the spot that shook me up. It wasn't that he was less adorable. It was what it signified. Our map was already changing. A life-sized landmark had emerged early in our journey.

Then he straightened up and smiled, boyish and joyous. Gravity restored his hair and head, and all returned to normal. Except now, as we buckled into coach for an all-night flight, I was chastising myself.

I'd seen aging in myself, certainly. I'd lost an inch in height. The skin on my thighs was no longer taut. My face, which used to be my calling card, was a falling card. Certain signs of decay no longer went away with a good night's sleep, exercise, or my hairdresser's talents.

Marrying late, we signed up for it all. We looked in each other's eyes, evaluated the attraction, the humor, the extras, and the so-whats, and knew this person was the one. All the milestones of most marriages that might have taken place over many decades will be compressed into a few decades. All too soon, he and I will get old together. And, if we're lucky, we'll die together at the exact same second.

I reminded myself that, on a sane and sober day, I found forever in his face. I knew I'd want to look at him every morning, even when he made me mad. Of all the men in the world, I married only this one, knowing that the grief of losing each other would be worth it for the joy we'd have. I knew that sharing the center of the narrowing loop of our lives was the best fate I could imagine.

We landed in Spain, and as we pulled our bags from the carousel, I was already excited by foreign accents saying, "Excuse me." Then, Mr. Delicious bent over to get out his jacket, and I saw it again. I'd almost forgotten it.

Funny how the journey of aging—with its sudden turns into the unknown, its new language that only medical professionals will translate for us, and the adaptations that will be demanded of us as time flies by—is so much less welcome than the other surprises I will so treasure on our journeys to new places. Where the hell was my embrace of spontaneity, my openness to growth, to coping with the unknowns along the way?

I started having unproductive thoughts. Could his hair maybe grow back and cover up the bald spot? Had it just dried funny? Could hair loss be happening to me, too? Has he noticed and protected me as I would protect him? No. He's so kind that he only notices good things, and I have a fleet of intimate workers with whom I consult expensively who can negotiate workarounds on my hair, at least for a little while longer.

I wouldn't want him to work around. I dislike workarounds on men—comb-overs, plugs like bristle brushes, toupees, dye jobs—although I admire the workarounds on women and the artists who accomplish them. I have a big double standard. I like my man au naturel, courageously facing the unknown, protecting me from my vain fears of aging, which I've had since I was twelve. That part of me has never changed. My husband will be my brave explorer. I know he will carry this emblem with grace and lead me forward at every age.

In that moment, I fall deeply in love with the bald spot atop him, and I decide to adopt it. It's a whole new thing about him to cherish. It will be my new pet, a hidden motherless child I didn't know existed. It's young, vulnerable, and innocent, like an infant's derriere. Dear little spot.

He straightens up, hoisting his bag, and begins one of his world-illuminating grins, surprised to see me gazing so tenderly at him, tears in my eyes. "What is it?" he asks.

"Nothing," I say. "I love you."

"I love you, too," he says. "Here we go!"

—Melanie Chartoff—

76

Rebel

I'm a real rebel with a cause.
~Nina Simone

To hell with being
a little old lady
who wears muted pastels
and white gloves
and always dresses appropriately.

I shall wear a volunteer T-shirt
in a garish bright colour
with a huge cartoon motif
emblazoned across my chest.

I shall stand tall,
a living billboard for the arts festival
or the folk festival
or the symphony.

And, when I am gone,
you are forbidden
to wear black to my funeral.

Wear peacock blue
or exuberant orange
or emerald green!

Leave black for those
who have led colourless lives.

—Marion Young—

77

You're How Old?

*How old would you be if you didn't know
how old you are?*
~Satchel Paige

On my twenty-fifth birthday, I remember a friend asking, "How does it feel to be a quarter of a century old?" It caught me off-guard at the time. I had never considered age in those terms before. I must admit that for the very first time, I felt older than my twenty-five years, and that feeling stuck with me for a while.

As the years marched on, I grew very comfortable with my age. I was healthy and active, and the number came to mean very little to me. I sometimes had to actually stop and think when someone asked me how old I was. I would do a quick calculation in my head, subtracting the year I was born from the year we were in at the moment.

Then, for no apparent reason, I began to round up my age to the next decade. For example, when I was fifty-four, I would say I was sixty. My friends found this annoying because we were all close in age, but I just laughed it off. My patent remark was, "Age is just a number. Pick one you like."

People who didn't know me as well would respond, "Wow, you look great for your age!" It made me feel terrific, even though I knew it was a little white lie. And so, for the better part of my life, I have rounded up my age to the next decade.

Several years ago, my sister-in-law organized an amazing family holiday on a five-masted sailing ship to celebrate her fiftieth birthday. Her actual birthday had been about six months earlier, and she had already thrown herself a huge party. The trip was to take place the week following Christmas, which included my actual birthday. Unbeknown to me, my two children decided to plan a birthday celebration for me onboard the ship. They felt turning sixty was a big deal and needed to be recognized. Everyone was in on the surprise except me.

The morning of my birthday, I wandered into the dining room for breakfast and was met with a resounding chorus of "Surprise!" Our group was crowded around a table waiting to regale me with birthday wishes. I graciously accepted their comments and birthday cards. After breakfast, as I opened each card, I became more and more perplexed and guilt-ridden. Each one wished me a "Happy Sixtieth." And therein was the problem. I wasn't sixty. I was actually fifty-nine, but I had been rounding up for so long that even my family had lost track of my real age. I really wasn't sure how to handle the situation. Should I say nothing and just accept the well wishes, or should I admit the truth?

As the day wore on, I decided to keep the truth to myself. After all, it was my birthday. That part was true. Did the number really matter all that much?

Word on our ship spread, and several other passengers wished me well and bought me drinks throughout the afternoon. I truly felt special.

Each evening, we dressed up for a lovely dinner in the dining room, and this evening was no different. That night, however, our group of eighteen was seated at a large table in the centre of the room, and we were served from a special menu chosen especially for the occasion. Prime rib and all the trimmings... my favorite! I was embarrassed by all the fuss that had been made.

After an amazing meal, the chef placed a beautifully decorated cake complete with sixty, yes, sixty candles in front of me. The entire dining room sang to me. I was so conflicted but kept my secret to myself.

Later that same evening, my children presented me with a stunningly beautiful, black-pearl pendant to symbolize the milestone. I was so emotional that I could not continue with the lie. Tears filled my eyes. Everyone had gone out of their way to make my sixtieth birthday special, and I felt like a jerk for not coming clean sooner.

I took a deep breath and looked at my kids. "I'm so sorry," I blurted out.

"Sorry for what?" my daughter asked.

"It's not my sixtieth birthday," I whispered.

"What did you say?" she replied.

"It's not my sixtieth birthday," I repeated, louder this time.

Both my kids burst out laughing. My son responded first. "Oh, Mom," he chided, "you've rounded up your age for so long that you don't even know how old you are." They both giggled uncontrollably, but I remained solemn.

"I do know my real age, and it is not sixty; it is fifty-nine. Do the math! I was born in 1948."

They suddenly fell silent and stared at me. Realisation sunk in. I was telling them the truth.

My daughter broke the moment. "Well, don't expect another party next year then."

The three of us collapsed in gales of laughter.

I suppose I should have learned my lesson after that, but I have continued to round up my age. I am currently seventy-two years old, but if you ask me, I will tell you that I am eighty.

— Penny Fedorczenko —

78

Openly Gray

*You cannot swim for new horizons until
you have courage to lose sight of the shore.*
~William Faulkner

I was not happy with my reflection in the mirror. My normally clear skin displayed age spots. Wrinkles surrounded my eyes. Large pores appeared on top of my nose. Rogue hairs sprouted out of my chin like *Three Billy Goats Gruff*. My eyebrow hairs progressively turned white. My long and lush eyelashes from yesteryear had diminished. My normally pouty lips had grown thin. Another loss was the pink flush from my rosy cheeks.

Age was an unapologetic thief, slowly stealing my self-confidence and what was left of my beauty. Applying moisturizing creams, serums, and facial masks became my ritual. I never left the house without wearing bullet-proof eyebrow pencil, voluminous mascara, and plumping lip gloss.

After menopause, my body began to change. My hourglass figure contained a little more sand than usual. My waist grew larger, and calling that new feature a muffin top didn't make it any sweeter. Aging changes your body in ways you could never imagine. High heels became a thing of the past because arthritis pain invaded my previously perfect joints… no more beautiful stilettos or strappy sandals.

Dyeing my naturally brunette hair a light auburn every six weeks was becoming a burden. The bathroom linen closet always had a box of L'Oréal do-it-yourself hair color on the shelf. There were no gray hairs on my watch. But lately, I'd had to color my hair more often. Every time I looked into a mirror, the silver roots were shining like a beacon. I began parting my hair in a zigzag. It was an ingenious disguise for the silver scoundrels. It gave my short hairstyle a little sass and served a purpose at the same time. I suddenly felt like a magician using smoke and mirrors with a little sleight of hand.

It got worse, and to cover those annoying roots, I was forced to dye my hair more often. Now I was coloring every three weeks. I began to ponder giving up the fight. Gray was becoming a trend among the younger generation. Celebrities were suddenly coloring their hair gray by choice. If Pink, Katy Perry, and Adam Levine could do it, so could I.

But I didn't want to grow my hair out slowly. It would take entirely too long. What if I got the color stripped out? Then no one would be the wiser. My daughters knew a master hair colorist whom they trusted. Nicole's naturally soft brunette locks sported golden highlights, and Laura's naturally auburn tresses were tinted a bright fiery red reminiscent of the Disney princess Ariel. Their hair turned out spectacular, so maybe she could help me.

I weighed the pros and cons for several weeks. If I hated it, I could just recolor it again…. right? Would I look stylishly trendy? Or would I look old and tired? Not buying hair dye would save tons of money. It would also save valuable time. I definitely wouldn't miss cleaning messy stains off the bathroom sink and ruining white towels. This was a difficult decision. Finally, I built up enough courage to book the appointment and for the next few weeks, I stopped dyeing my hair. I let the color fade to make it easier to remove.

The half-hour drive to the salon was nerve-wracking. For moral support, my girls accompanied me. I was anxious but excited at the same time. I sat tentatively in the chair as Sara, my tattoo-covered stylist, applied the stripping compound to my auburn hair with what looked like an ordinary paintbrush. She wrapped my head in foil and plastic and left me to "cook." I felt like a baked potato. As I waited, my mind raced. She checked my progress every fifteen minutes to see if the color was lifting. After about an hour, she announced it was reveal time. She rinsed out all the gooey mess. I stepped back into the chair and looked in the mirror. My hair was completely and totally white. The sudden shock sucked all the breath out of my lungs. She saw the frightened look on my face and asked if everything was okay. At that moment, I wasn't sure if I liked it. In fact, I hated it... and I was trying to remember if I had a coupon for another box of hair color.

She continued to razor my hair into the cute style I had pointed out on Pinterest. Then she rinsed my hair again and applied toner along with a purple conditioner to remove any brassiness. She confidently wielded curling irons and hairspray like magic wands. The woman in the mirror who was looking back at me was a totally different person. Was it shocking? Yes. Did I like it? Absolutely! My hair was a lovely, rich silver tone.

On the drive home, I worried what my husband was going to say. Would he love it or hate it? When I walked into the house, he loved my new look and gave me a much-needed, stress-relieving hug.

The first thing I did was post a selfie on Facebook. I bravely announced that I had officially quit dying my hair. I was "openly gray." I wasn't sure how everyone was going to react to the transformation. Comments on social media could be brutally honest at times, so I sat back and nervously waited. My phone kept dinging with dozens of comments. They were all genuinely positive. Everyone loved the change. Reading all the kind and uplifting comments just reinforced the decision I made.

The next few weeks were interesting. Everywhere I went, the compliments followed. People would approach me completely out of the blue... in the freezer section of the grocery store... in line at the bank... at the accountant's office... and even while I was pumping gas. My husband would just shake his head and laugh because we couldn't go anywhere without someone telling me how beautiful my hair color was. It was crazy. If it had been friends or family being polite, I could understand it. But these wonderful folks were total strangers.

For me, the unspoken assumption that gray hair automatically means unattractive is shattered. I get more compliments now than I did for the entire thirty-five years I colored my hair. It has been almost two years since I made the decision to succumb to my God-given hair color. I have never regretted my decision or looked back. My gleaming sterling-silver hair will forever be my signature. Now I smile when I see my reflection in a mirror because, according to the kindness of strangers, I am beautiful at any age.

— Robin Howard Will —

79

Company Along the Way

Walking with your hand in mine and mine in yours,
that's exactly where I want to be always.
~Author Unknown

After thirty-five years of marriage, my husband Don and I do many things well. Organized sports are not among them. We can't be relied upon to catch a ball or return a volley. Swinging bats, clubs, or rackets seldom results in a connection with a ball. It's not that we've never tried. We have. We've embarrassed ourselves on many occasions.

I was once convinced by a friend to join her at a community recreation centre where a group of women was meeting to play volleyball. "Nothing serious," she said. "It's going to be fun!" Old enough to know better but young enough to foster the glimmer of hope that I might be a late bloomer, I agreed to give it a try.

These women weren't there to have fun. These women were dead serious. I was told to take my position in the front row, likely because at 5'8" people assume I have skills.

I faced the intense blue eyes of my opponent. This was not going to end well. The first volley whizzed past my ear and sent me spinning headfirst into the net. Despite the fact my hands were flapping at a phenomenal rate that surprised even me, the second volley whizzed by, too. For the rest of the game, I zigged, zagged, ducked, and dodged.

Anything to avoid the ball.

When there was a pause in the action I glanced over my shoulder. The women on my team were staring at me — mouths agape. I'd like to think it was because they'd never before witnessed such agility on the court. Probably not the case. When I inadvertently made contact with the ball, the inevitable happened — a loud snapping sound came from my wrists! A collective gasp arose from both sides of the net. Nothing was broken, but it hurt.

To my huge relief, I wasn't invited back. It was a setback in my athletic career. I feel I accepted it valiantly.

A few years later, Don and I joined an adults' badminton team. We were actually not terrible. It was quite meditative watching the birdie float back and forth, back and forth, back and forth. Then another couple suggested we try doubles. "Sure!" we said, buoyed by the confidence that comes from discovering a new skill. Don and I ran to one side of the net, and bounced in place like experienced players. We had this! The birdie was released. So lovely: back and forth, back and forth, back and forth, THWACK.

Well, that was uncalled for.

Then in quick succession — THWACK, THWACK, THWACK. We didn't stand a chance. The game ended soon after. The other couple sprinted on to their next victims as we gathered our deflated egos like parachutes at our feet. They called out a cheerful, "Good game!" as they departed.

Don and I are simply not competitive people. We don't care who wins or loses, which is the last thing a team captain wants to hear when she's keeping score and grunting orders. That doesn't mean we haven't remained active; we just have very specific criteria. We prefer activities that allow us to enjoy the scenery while participating. Have a conversation. Activities that don't involve flying objects. Biking, hiking, canoeing, kayaking in the summer: wonderful! In the winter, skating and, once upon a time, cross-country skiing.

Don and I used to cross-country ski all the time. It was the perfect fit for two people with limited dexterity. Sifting through fresh powder, sun glistening like diamonds on the snow, breath hanging in tufts on the icy air. Bliss.

When our sons were old enough, they joined us, outfitted with mini skis and poles from the church yard sale. Remnants of purchases made by other well-meaning parents who thought skiing with toddlers was a good idea. Parents who, like us, realized too late that the highlight of the adventure for the little ones was hot chocolate with marshmallows at the end of the day — once snowsuits were peeled off, and boots and snow-encrusted mittens were placed on the drying rack.

As our boys got older, they preferred crazy carpets, GT Racers, downhill skiing and snowboards — all of which caused us considerable angst given the gene pool from which they drew their athletic prowess. Don and I became spectators in our boys' lives. We stored the cross-country gear in the garage, determined to get back to it one day. That was twenty-one years ago.

You can imagine my surprise when friends invited us to go cross-country skiing recently, and my husband accepted their invitation enthusiastically. "Oh, it will be fun," he said. Uh-huh. These friends don't share our criteria for outdoor activities. They move with speed, agility, finesse. They have "fitness goals." Foreign concepts to us.

We went. The day was going well; the sun was shining; the conditions were great. We encouraged our friends to go ahead if we were holding them back. They insisted we weren't. Then we came to the top of a long, steep hill. Darn. I could have cried. Our friends went first. They were magnificent. Conquering the hill with the ease and grace of seasoned professionals. I considered removing my skis and walking. Instead, I snowplowed my way down. Huh. Not bad. Not bad at all! If I wasn't acutely aware of the growing line-up of skiers behind me, patiently waiting their turn, I might have been impressed with myself.

Then I heard the frantic shouts from my husband: "Get outta the way! Get outta the way!" He was *not* snowplowing; rather, he was coming straight toward me, painfully aware that the only way he wouldn't hit me was if I was able to get out of his way. I stood like a deer in headlights. His only recourse was to fling himself into the snowbank. I fell in tandem from sheer shock. There was a moment of silence. Two awkward snow angels. Then we started laughing hysterically. Our friends rushed back to assess the damage.

No broken bones. Always a good thing. However, the toe of Don's vintage boot, its leather dry and brittle from years in storage, was completely torn away. It was firmly entrapped in the ski binding of the ski that was making its way down the hill. The top of Don's boot, partially detached from the sole, exposed Don's heavy wool sock with each step.

We told our friends to go ahead and finish their run. We would meet them at the car. Don and I walked together, skis and poles over our shoulders, chuckling with each flop of Don's boot. How did we get here again? And did it even matter? We are never going to be the hares in the race, always the tortoises, and that's just fine with us. We like how that story ends. We're enjoying the journey and the company along the way.

— Florence Niven —

80

There's a Girl in Here

Do one thing every day that scares you.
~Eleanor Roosevelt

With the temperature at eighty-five degrees, I'd opted for a shaded trail. Several years back, I'd ascended a towering Montana mountain, so, if anyone called me a slacker, I'd mention that.

Meanwhile, my husband had headed back to our truck to grab water for me while I rested. More than one younger passerby asked if I was okay, and I always nodded and smiled. Still, had I pushed myself too hard?

This wasn't the first challenge I had undertaken at an age when people were questioning whether I was "too old." At age sixty, I'd signed on for my first Class 5 whitewater rafting adventure in West Virginia. My husband had wanted to make this trip for years, so I'd finally said, "Okay, but it better not be scary." Scotty had grinned as if to say "piece of cake," when he should have mentioned water cresting higher than my head. Still, we'd ended up with a highly skilled guide. Within minutes, I realized she could be trusted — until she added, "But if you do go over the side?"

If we what? I stared at my sheepish-looking husband.

"Remember," our guide continued, "your helmet and vest will protect you." Then she explained how to "walk" along the bottom of our raft. "If you get caught," she added, "you should pop right up, so not to worry."

I laughed now, thinking about that whitewater rafting trip. Scott returned with the water and I reminded him of it. "Remember how scared I was?" Scotty nodded. "But I made it." Not only under the boat but back out. "Popped up!" I sang. "Just like our guide predicted." Mission accomplished. No additional adventures necessary.

However, the following year, my pregnant daughter, her husband, and our eleven-year-old granddaughter wanted to do the river with us. I wanted to shriek, "No!" Instead, I shrugged. Meanwhile, we discovered that some people in our group would float individually in what they called "duckies" while our son-in-law would come along in his kayak. The rest would "man" a larger raft with our guide. "At least this time I'm not afraid," I whispered to my husband.

We'd floated halfway to our destination when our guide announced we were approaching a rock as tall as a house. Behind that rock would be a climbing place for anyone who wanted to jump. The "anyone" would definitely not include me. I'd turned sixty-one, for heaven's sake. But my granddaughter wanted someone to go with her.

Go with her? Our raft had begun to reel and spin, first left and then right. I might be directionally challenged, but I knew we could be in serious trouble! Did this child not see how old I was? I heard myself saying, like I didn't have an ounce of good sense in my head, "Okay… I'll go."

Within minutes, our guide had maneuvered our raft behind the enormous rock, and now she was shouting how she couldn't hang on in that place much longer. Anyone "wanting" to jump would have to hop out "ASAP!" and start climbing. She also shouted it could be "very slick," so we'd need to be very cautious. "Or," she said, "if you don't want to do this…"

"I don't want to…" I bleated while, without batting an eye, three boys and a thirty-something man were already over the side with my granddaughter right behind them! "Come on, Mom-Mom!" she called. "We'll jump together! This will be THE MOST FUN EVER!"

Jump together? This will be fun? Wouldn't lying in the sun be more fun? Roasting marshmallows could be fun. But jumping? "I'm coming," I sang, forcing myself to sound brave.

At the top, all three teens seemed to be flying as they jumped. The thirty-something man followed. We were now down to just Morgan Grace and me.

"We don't have to be embarrassed to go back," I whispered, my knees and teeth shaking.

"You've got to be kidding, Mom-Mom! You can do this!"

I wanted to exclaim, "Just one minute! I attended one of the largest universities in this country *and* did so as a young mother *and* graduated cum laude!" I'd learned to ski late. But, oh, how I did not want to do this. But I was already clinging to an unforgiving rock with one hand and sliding one vacillating foot into a narrow niche. "Maybe we could do this another day…" I'd barely spit out the words when my granddaughter — her arms becoming wings — was suddenly airborne, while the others bobbed on the churning water.

I don't know if I shrieked or not. I only know I was suddenly mid-air. Hitting the water and fearing I'd never touch bottom as I descended, my feet finally sank into oozy silt. I shifted into survival mode, pushed off and, within seconds, broke the surface where my laughing granddaughter was giving me a thumbs-up. Others were doing the same, while my daughter continued to shake her head.

For the next several years, I acted my age — until I turned sixty-eight and suggested we travel with an RV and build Habitat for Humanity homes for struggling families. Scotty liked the idea, so we sold our home, disposed of seventy-five percent of what we owned, and stuffed our remaining possessions into a condo. For six-plus years, I climbed ladders, ran a chop saw, put up siding, installed cabinets, laid flooring, learned to mud, tape, and spackle, and heeded the Deep South warnings about alligators.

"Okay," a friend recently said, "you did all that and give the impression you're much younger, but now that you've celebrated your eightieth birthday, it's time you slowed down and…"

I shook my head. "Wrong," I said. "Slowing down is for grandmothers who don't leap tall buildings." I laughed. "My body may be old, and some mornings I do ratchet myself out of bed, but I'm not ready to stop living." Scotty and I would be taking up hiking. "This, I can do," I declared.

Until the morning we decided on a full-sun mountain hike — and it hit me that I really was eighty. Eighty and grateful for occasional shade. Eighty and needing an occasional rest. Eighty and longing for the non-existent restroom. "Remember, though…" I took my husband's hand. "My body may be slowing down, but there's still a girl in here."

— Nancy Hoag —

81

Goals for Growing Older

If you want to be happy, set a goal that commands
your thoughts, liberates your energy
and inspires your hopes.
~Andrew Carnegie

'm running half-way across Canada—some 2,200 miles—for
my seventy-fifth birthday. It's a long way, for sure, but I have two
years to get there. And if my knees hold up, it'll be a great way to
celebrate this milestone birthday.

To be more precise, this cross-country jog will be mostly around
my neighbourhood in Ottawa. It is the distance by air to Vancouver
on the west coast that a friend and I are doing. That's 3,550 kilometers
(in Canada we use metric) but it's far no matter how you measure it.

If we reach our goal, my friend Louise Rachlis, whose birthday
is just a month before mine, and I will get on a plane and actually fly
to Vancouver the year we turn seventy-five. We want to run in one of
the BMO Vancouver Marathon weekend races in May. Likely that'll be
the eight-kilometer (five-mile) race and not the marathon distance.

We may not win medals, but for sure we'll have cake at the finish
line.

I should be clear that neither of us is an elite runner, nor do we
love the sport the way good runners do. Although it has its moments,
sometimes it's a hard, slow slog.

We've modified some rules to help account for this. We can count the distances of longer, fast walks. But the walk has to last for at least thirty minutes and get your blood pumping. So we can't count steps at the shopping mall, dog walking or strolls to the corner store.

So far, I'm finding that averaging three miles a day, nearly ninety miles a month is very hard for a natural couch potato like me.

Still, the point is to do something that's really challenging so we can revel in our accomplishment as we hit our birthday goal.

This build-up to big birthdays represents an enormous change for me. I used to hate birthdays, especially those milestone ones. Even when I turned thirty, I remember feeling low because I wasn't married yet. At forty, I was married with kids but hated that milestone because I no longer felt young.

Turning fifty was the worst — I was divorced, had moved to a new city where I had few friends and was struggling to raise three children on my own, after returning to work. That birthday two friends took me to lunch at a fancy hotel. I am still grateful for that act of kindness, which helped me though a particularly dark day.

Perhaps it was the memory of that awful birthday that helped shape a change in attitude as I approached my sixtieth birthday. But I also have to credit Louise, who suggested setting goals to mark milestone birthdays.

"That way you are looking forward to something, not dreading it," she pointed out. It was wise advice.

By setting goals that expand my world or demand new skills, I can feel myself growing, not shrinking, as I hit those special birthdays.

For my sixtieth, I got it into my head that I should do an Olympic distance triathlon. This was no small feat for me. The race involved swimming 1500 meters (close to a mile), biking forty kilometers (twenty-five miles) and running ten kilometers (six miles).

I had not been athletic in my younger years — I took up running and open lake swimming in my fifties. So, as my goal began to take shape, I took both spinning and swimming classes from a triathlete training club. I also signed up for a weight loss program and dropped thirty-five pounds.

It was exhilarating to cross the finish line with an enthusiastic group of friends cheering loudly. After more than four hours on the course, I was last among the ninety-five competitors. But I was the oldest woman competing, so that made me first in my age category.

Ever since that day, I've looked at birthdays as a reason to celebrate. Milestone birthdays, especially, are a call for trying something different.

For my sixty-fifth birthday, I went with a friend to Disney World to run in the Princess Half Marathon, the longest distance I had ever done. I wore a T-shirt that said: "Never Too Old To Be A Princess — Running for my 65th."

I got many birthday wishes and one "Happy Birthday" serenade as other runners passed me. There were also several inspiring moments when women ran up to me to say they had passed that sixty-fifth milestone some years before and were still going strong. I loved that.

Approaching seventy was a different journey. Again, Louise had a role to play in this. We were talking about the benefits of learning something new to keep our minds sharp and attitudes young.

So, we promised each other we would do seven activities that would take us out of our "comfort zone" during the year we turned seventy. (In truth I jumped the gun and did two of them in the months leading up to our milestone year but I counted them anyway.)

Louise and I did only one of our goals together. We signed up for a tap-dancing class for older adults. It was fun and excellent brain-body training. But it was tough for both of us first-time tappers. Louise finished two fourteen-week sessions, but I only made it through one and a half. After missing a few weeks, I found it too hard to catch up, so I bailed out. Kudos to Louise, who danced right to the end and continued the following year.

Another time, I agreed to let a friend introduce me to a guy she thought I'd like. Going out on a date for the first time in decades took me way out of my comfort zone. But it was fun and good for my self-esteem, even though we parted ways after a few dates.

In the year before my seventieth, I took a trip to India to practice yoga and meditation at ashrams. The next year I went to China, where I climbed on the Great Wall and hiked in the awesome Yellow Mountains.

My other projects involved going to a paint night at a bar, when I've always been embarrassed by my lack of artistic ability; collecting donations for the Salvation Army, when I hate to ask for anything from others; and finally, solving an issue that weighed on my conscience for more than a decade. I had inherited a valuable set of antique silverware from a dear friend and mentor, but I never used it. I put off the inevitable for years, but finally sold the set at auction and donated the proceeds to cancer research.

I know that I'm fortunate to have already celebrated so many birthdays in good health and good spirits, so whether I succeed in running to Vancouver or not, I am grateful for the opportunity to try.

One thing I've learned in taking up these challenges to mark my milestone birthdays, is that there are lots of possibilities for new adventures and achievements, even as we grow older.

And that's a gift worth celebrating every day of every year.

— Kristin Goff —

82

Two Merry Christmas Widows

Shared joy is a double joy; shared sorrow
is half a sorrow.
~Swedish Proverb

In October 2017, after three years of learning to cope with my husband's death, I decided to sell my home in Panama City Beach, Florida and move to a new town 200 miles away. Although my best friend Marsha, also a widow, remained behind, we agreed we would always visit one another.

We had created a close bond since being introduced by a couple who knew both of us and believed we would find comfort in sharing our grief and coping with our "new normal" after decades of marriage. Marsha and I, both retired, became cruise buddies and sounding boards for each other.

After Thanksgiving 2017, in my new hometown of Biloxi, Mississippi, where Marsha and I had spent a few days at Christmas and Thanksgiving 2016, I meandered through Walmart. After selecting a few Christmas arrangements to brighten my new apartment, I noticed Christmas attire in the women's department. An above-the-knee, soft, A-line sweater dress particularly caught my eye. Its candy-cane-striped long sleeves, white-and-green bodice and flared skirt with a wide black belt sewn in reminded me of what Santa's elves might wear. *This is adorable and will look so cute with black leggings and knee boots!* I thought to myself.

I bought two!

Then I found a red Christmas derby that I had no doubt would look great on Marsha and a headband with candy canes for me.

Marsha and I had already agreed that she would drive to Biloxi the day before Christmas Eve and stay until Christmas Day. We planned to see the Christmas ice-skating show, have brunch and dinner, and press a few buttons at the MGM Beau Rivage Resort & Casino.

"Girlfriend, do I have a surprise for you!" I told Marsha on our next phone call.

"What is it?"

"I can't tell you!" I said. "You'll have to wait and see. But it's going to bring us lots of fun!"

After Marsha arrived at my apartment on December twenty-third, I couldn't wait to show her our matching outfits.

"Oh, my gosh! These are awesome! But where are we going to wear them?"

"We're dressing up for Christmas Eve! We are going to smile brightly this year and make others smile!"

On Christmas Eve, Marsha and I dressed in our elf dresses, black leggings, and knee boots. We added Christmas earrings, bracelets and necklaces. Marsha looked just as adorable as I knew she would with the red derby placed on top of her beautiful, silky white hair brushed down straight over her ears. I dressed, pulled my long brunette hair into a ponytail, and added my headband with bouncy candy canes. We looked each other over, laughed and agreed we were the cutest over-sixty elves in Biloxi.

Inside the MGM Beau Rivage, families snapped photos of one another among all the Christmas decorations and activities, including visits with Santa. Marsha and I, feeling happy and full of Christmas spirit, almost skipped down the hallway like children. Heads turned and smiles came our way. "You both look adorable!" said one person after another.

Just after dark, a lady approached us with a big smile.

"Hey, you two, aren't you supposed to be out helping Santa tonight?"

Marsha and I stopped for a moment. "Oh, Santa has released us for the rest of the evening. Our work is done at the toy shop till the new year! We're headed to dinner now."

"Well, you both look absolutely fabulous! Merry Christmas!"

We thanked her and looked at one another.

"This is so much fun!" Marsha said. "I'm glad you came up with this idea. It keeps my mind off past Christmases with Charlie."

"I know. Me, too," I said. "I'm so glad we have each other."

Marsha and I walked toward the restaurant for dinner. A couple stopped us.

"Are you with the ice-skating show?"

Again, Marsha and I smiled, feeling that we had really outdone ourselves with our Christmas Eve attire.

"No, we are just two best friends and widows making our way through the holiday without our husbands," I said with a smile.

"Oh, our condolences," they said. "But it's wonderful that you have one another and are able to do something like this to get through it." The couple smiled.

"We are very fortunate to have each other," Marsha said. "No one can make a grief journey alone."

"When you both wake up on Christmas morning," I said to the couple, "let your Christmas presents to one another be to look at each other, give great big smiles, hugs, and kisses, and say 'I love you.' Because no couple knows how long they'll share life together."

They both nodded in agreement. "You're right. We hope you both have a wonderful Christmas, especially given your circumstances," said the husband.

At dinner, where we continued to receive smiles and compliments, Marsha and I spoke excitedly to one another about how fabulous our Christmas Eve day had been.

"We've received a lot of smiles and sweet comments," Marsha said. "It sure makes a person feel good."

"Yes, it does. And we've provided smiles to others," I said. "It's a good health benefit, you know. Lowers stress and blood pressure, and puts people in a better mood."

Marsha said, "So, I guess we gave out lots of gifts today. And got some back!"

I agreed, and with a little laugh, I said, "You know, we have to make this an annual event and call ourselves the two Merry Christmas widows!"

Marsha agreed as we toasted one another, grateful that this Christmas was just a bit easier because we chose to do something unique in the holiday season to ease our grieving hearts.

— Deborah Tainsh —

Celebrating Sixty

The life you have left is a gift. Cherish it. Enjoy it now,
to the fullest. Do what matters, now.
~Leo Babauta

t was totally out of character for me. I had never worried about getting older. I had always embraced birthdays. They had been times for rejoicing and celebrating what was and what was to be. But sixty was different; it just seemed so old. It meant that my life was undeniably more than half over.

On the night of my fifty-ninth birthday my darling husband, Michael, was clearing the table after a lovely dinner, including ice cream and cake.

"Oh, dear," I sighed.

As he picked up dishes, he said, "What's wrong? Didn't you enjoy your birthday dinner?"

"Yes, I did. It was wonderful. But you know what tonight means?"

"No, I don't."

"It means, well, it means that next year at this time, I will be officially old. I will be sixty!" I stated emphatically.

"Ah, no sympathy from me," Michael said. "I have been there for a few years already."

"Yes, but at sixty, women start to wear orthopedic shoes, and the wrinkles start coming fast and furious. It's hard to find pants with buttons and zippers, which means I might have to wear pants with elastic waistbands."

"Perhaps, but I will always love you, clodhoppers and all," he said as he leaned in to kiss me.

The year leading to my sixtieth birthday progressed. Often, I found myself thinking about my next birthday with trepidation. I kept asking myself questions. How would my life change? How would I deal with what I saw as old age? Was it the unknown that caused me to be fearful?

Then the call came that made me stop fretting. It was the Saturday after Thanksgiving. I looked down at my phone and recognized the name of my old friend, Norma Mae, who grew up three doors down from me. We shared a birthday. She was exactly one year older than me. We had gone through school together, including college. While our lives took different paths, we had managed to keep in touch, so her call wasn't a surprise. What she said was.

Norma Mae had been diagnosed with terminal brain cancer. She was undergoing treatment but had been given about six months to live. Being a kind of take-charge person, Norma had decided to call all her friends to tell them herself while she was still able.

"I didn't want you to hear about this from anyone else. I wanted you to know that I am sick and probably won't get better. I am having to come to terms with it. You know that I am going to be sixty-one this year. I have decided to have the biggest and bestest birthday party for myself. I wanted to invite you."

"Oh, Norma Mae, of course I'll be there," I answered, holding back the tears. "Just tell me where and when."

We chatted for a few more minutes. She tired easily and told me she had other calls to make. I hung up, promptly bursting into tears. Michael came running in.

"What's wrong?" he asked.

"That was Norma Mae. She has been diagnosed with brain cancer. It's terminal." I sobbed. "I just can't grasp it. She is so young. She is only sixty years old. It is just so unfair."

As soon as the words slipped out of my mouth, I realized what I had said. Me, who had been so concerned about hitting my sixth decade, had just said that sixty was young. Wouldn't that make me still young when I turned sixty?

"Michael," I stammered. "I will still be young when I turn sixty with lots of time to do the things I want to. But Norma won't have those opportunities."

My dear, ill friend had pulled me up short. It put a whole new spin on things and what sixty really meant. Sixty was young, not old. I had much to look forward to. There was no need for obsessing about growing old. At least I would have the privilege of growing old. I knew my life would work out.

That year, I went to two parties. The first was for Norma. She held it a few months before her actual birthday. As she promised, it was the "biggest and bestest" party. She was a convivial hostess, making everyone comfortable in what could have been a rather macabre situation. The life of the party, she donned a colorful rainbow wig to disguise the baldness caused by her cancer treatments. She told funny stories about her life. It was a joyful, uplifting afternoon. I left with a renewed appreciation of my own impending birthday.

The second party was one that I decided to throw for myself. I invited sixty women. Each woman represented one year of my life. I gathered them into my cozy living room. I had everyone bring a book that was donated to a local charity.

My friends told stories about me. I laughed as I remembered what a fabulous life I have had. Looking around my living room, I saw small groups of women huddled together, talking intently, champagne glasses in their hands and huge smiles on their faces. These were the women in my life who had helped make my sixty years what they were. It was just how I envisioned it. I was bursting with joy.

I asked my guests to raise their glasses and join me in a toast to my recently departed friend Norma Mae, who taught me how to celebrate being sixty.

— Ina Massler Levin —

Second Wind

Rebuilding a Life

*Some people say you are going the wrong way, when
it's simply a way of your own.*
~Angelina Jolie

My decision to turn our 2,400-square-foot home into a 4,000-square-foot home, fully renovated and with three new additions, met with an interesting variety of opinions. Evidently, empty nesters in their early sixties weren't supposed to need a larger house, especially when the husband was being overtaken by dementia that began in his fifties.

We'd enjoyed living on our lovely, tree-lined country acreage in a traditional two-story home for the past seventeen years. I'd often tried to get my husband interested in adding on a room — or two or three — but that was never his thing. So, I paused my dream of getting to build a house in my lifetime, but I never abandoned it.

People around me offered up all the usual commentary in response to this aggressive and unique plan I was drawing up: Why don't you just build a new house for yourself somewhere, rather than go through all that tearing-up mess? Do you really need all that space to yourself? Why aren't you selling out and moving into a retirement community like I did?

My response to that last one stopped that person short. "Because my life isn't over yet. I still have things I want to do."

I ride the bike trails, mow our acreage, and do my own housework. I need to move, to get my hands dirty in flower gardens and generally stir the pot, trying new and different things.

When my husband's psychologist laid out the picture of what life was going to look like as his illness advanced, I saw our future die. The future we'd worked and saved for was never going to be.

I'd have to create a new life for myself without him.

As I contemplated the realities of it all, I knew I would not wait until I was too old, too sick or too tired to do something I'd been dreaming of for years. Ever since I was a small child, I'd loved Victorian-style turrets. There was a mystical uniqueness to the architectural form, and I'd always wanted one — or more — to be part of a house I lived in. They seemed like a space that a writer and reader should have.

As we didn't live in a historical neighborhood, the true Victorian turret wasn't going to work for our house, but my designer and I put together plans that included three new additions — and all of them would have a contemporary, hexagonal flavor. These would get me as close to having turrets as I could, and I was eager for the work to begin.

This was not a frivolous house design, however. I knew it needed to be a smart build, and we incorporated features that would make it easier for me to remain living here on my own as I aged.

As we'd had no bedroom on the first floor, I added a large master suite as one of the additions, complete with a zero-entry, walk-in shower, wider-entrance hallways and pocket doors. It's far easier to slide a door out of one's way when a walker or a wheelchair is part of the equation. Adult-height toilets were installed in every bathroom in the house.

The kitchen was gutted with plenty of maneuvering room left around the island. Pull-out shelves in all the lower cabinets were installed for easy access. A security system was added.

We lived on-site throughout the whole process — something else people thought I was nuts to do, but I wanted to watch my dream being built. To protect my husband from the chaos, I hired professional caregivers to come and take him out of the house every afternoon while I stayed behind to be accessible to the contractors, and sweep up and dust the small areas we lived in during the process.

It was a happy time for me to be around the action. This was going to be the only chance I'd have to do something like this, and I wasn't about to miss out on any of it.

Sometimes, I think my decision to build my dream house was my way of sassing back at The Universe for taking everything I'd assumed would be as we aged together. Perhaps it was my way of saying, "Oh, yeah? Just watch me. You aren't going to keep me from building my house."

I believe now The Universe was on my side. I was blessed with a talented and capable general contractor who took on the difficult build and hired the right crews — many who, over the eight months of construction, became friends of mine. We'd talk about their kids' activities, and they'd watch out for my husband if he was around. They showed concern for me when we had bad days.

Amidst all the drilling, hammering and sheetrock dust was this joy of a dream going up before me, juxtaposed against my husband's degrading health and a future together erased. It is a complicated dichotomy that the casual bystander cannot comprehend unless they stand in my shoes.

I wasn't going to be able to continue living in our home space the way it had been when we were a couple. I couldn't live in what had been. I had to make it new for the changing life happening to me.

My new home has become a sanctuary, not only for me but for family and friends, and new memories are made on a weekly basis.

I've come to realize there are expectations for women of a certain age who are alone. I want to shout from the top of my new turreted office to anyone who will listen: Do not wait. Do it your way. Let no one tell you how you "should be" at your age.

Building the house saved me in the year that was the hardest of my life. My husband's disease advanced quickly, and I was afraid I wouldn't get the house finished before I had to move him into a care facility, but we made it. He lived in the new house for a few months with me before that day arrived, and I'll always be glad that he did, even though he no longer remembers any of it.

— R'becca Groff —

New Recruits Wanted

*Choose a job you love. You will never have to work
a day in your life.*
~Author Unknown

"**N**ew Recruits Wanted." The sign caught my eye and revived my dream of becoming a firefighter. But, just as quickly, I reminded myself that I was getting close to sixty and was probably not the picture-book image of a firefighter. Forty years in construction had taken its toll on my body, but the decades spent as a Level 3 First Aid Attendant had built a certain "rescue mentality" in me that gave me the confidence to visit the fire hall and fill out an application.

A few years earlier, on my way to work, I had assisted at a roadside motor-vehicle accident. It was a head-on collision with one vehicle submerged in a water-filled ditch. I helped a police officer rescue the driver, but she was in cardiac arrest. I was able to start her heart with CPR and save her life. This powerful experience forever changed my appreciation for first responders and the role they play. And though I understand that not everyone can do this kind of work, I believe that those of us who can need to step forward.

My dream of becoming a firefighter began when I watched the television show *Rescue 8*, filmed with the cooperation of the Los Angeles Fire Department. Each week, the two specialists on the *Rescue 8* truck performed all manner of daring rescues and medical calls, as well as attended fires with the regular crews. At an early age, I knew what I wanted to do, and the theme song from that show stuck in my head for years.

Unfortunately, life doesn't always follow the dreams of young boys. A career in construction, a family to raise, and many other factors got in the way of volunteering with the local fire department when I was younger. Now, in anticipation of retirement, my wife and I had just relocated to a beautiful village on a lake about four hours north of Seattle, Washington. I was new in town; I had time to give; I knew I could contribute; I filled out the application and introduced myself to the Chief.

To my delight, I was accepted for training. Yes, I was the oldest recruit. Yes, it was tough. There were five of us in that recruit class. Two of us made it through the training and became firefighters. Three dropped out, one by one, over the weeks of training required. I'm not sure if my maturity gave me the stamina required to hang in there when younger guys were dropping out or if it was just the realization that I would never get another chance.

But I almost quit. I remember that day. We were practicing rescue in a darkened structure. We were crawling around with sixty pounds of gear on our backs, searching for victims in the dark. Afterwards, my poor old knees were screaming, my back was aching, and I wasn't sure I had the right stuff to complete my training. I was ready to give up and let the younger guys do it.

When I got home from practice, some friends were over. I cleaned up and was going to let everyone know that I couldn't do it anymore. But it was Christmas, and my friend, who is an author and inspirational speaker, had a small gift for me. It was a book. But not just any book. It was a beautifully illustrated book of firefighters in action by Vancouver photographer Allan de la Plante. And it was signed by the author with a personalized message of inspiration, encouraging me to follow my dream. As I leafed through the pages with tears in my eyes, I marvelled at the courage and dedication of these brave individuals captured on film. It gave me the inspiration and strength I needed to carry on and complete my training. I knew then that my age didn't matter. What mattered was my attitude and perseverance.

Over the next few weeks, the training continued to be intense, but I never lost focus again. I lost twenty pounds, but at last I was certified as a firefighter. It was almost surreal. And when the tones went off and we responded with lights and siren, there was a song playing in my head. It took me a few years to figure out what it was. I finally Googled the old TV show, and I knew as soon as I heard it. The theme song from *Rescue 8* was playing in my head when we responded to calls. It had been buried deep but never went away. And it gave me courage.

I am currently a trainer with the department. I certify drivers to drive fire apparatus and operate fire pumps. I love to drive the big red trucks and serve my community. And, yes, the theme song from *Rescue 8* still plays in my head every time I drive with lights and siren. I found a place where I fit in with the department despite my age. I am a medical first responder, firefighter, driver, pump operator, trainer and member of the Critical Incident Stress Management team. And at a time when most of my friends are retiring, I have found a new career that I love.

My proudest moment with the department came in 2014. Each year, the members of our department fill out secret ballots to choose the firefighter who most exemplifies the highest work standards and dedication to service among us. In 2014, my peers voted me Firefighter of the Year. It was not a gift to the old guy. It was in recognition for the hard work I had put into building our department.

It's been almost ten years since I walked into the fire hall in trepidation, worried and wondering if I was being foolish. Here I am, rapidly approaching seventy, and I now know that you are never too old to redefine your life; never too old to take on new challenges; never too old to follow your dreams. I don't run into burning buildings or climb ladders anymore. But I am still proud to drive the pumper or the rescue truck to the scene. Yes, with the *Rescue 8* theme song playing in my head. And I am very proud to teach the next generation of firefighters the skills they will need to keep our village safe and save lives. Their decision to become a first responder will be one of the most challenging but rewarding decisions they will ever make. I know it has been mine.

—Fred Webber—

86

My Ping-Ponging Parents

We don't stop playing because we grow old;
we grow old because we stop playing.
~George Bernard Shaw

When I called my dad in Florida, he sounded a bit worked up on the phone. He told me an ad had said a ping-pong table was on sale, with free delivery, but at the store they said he was a day late and the sale price no longer applied. His heart had been set on the ping-pong table, so he decided to buy it anyway and figured he'd haul it home on the roof rack on his car. The clerks at the store, however, refused to load the 300-pound table onto the roof rack, and Dad conceded that it was just as well because he wasn't sure how he'd unload the table once he got home. But when they tried to charge him one hundred fifty dollars for delivery, Dad had marched back into the store and asked for his money back. He sounded disappointed to go home empty-handed.

As he related his tale of woe, I wondered where this idea had come from. Dad was eighty-three years old! My parents' younger friend, Bev, plays ping-pong at the senior center, so I figured maybe they got the idea from her. But my parents don't get out as much, so, at the respective ages of eighty-three and eighty-one, they decided they needed their own ping-pong table at home! This seemed odd to me, considering Mom's current state of health.

Mom had fallen and hit her head the year before and had lost much of her short-term memory. Her previously diligent habits of eating healthful foods, walking, and swimming regularly were forgotten. Although she seemed to think she was still doing these things every day, she was not.

High-school sweethearts, my parents have been together for almost seventy years and married for over sixty of them. When Mom lost her memory, Dad had to take on many of the tasks Mom had always managed, like keeping the calendar, getting to appointments on time, paying the bills, shopping for groceries, doing the laundry, and more. Not that Dad had never helped with these things before, but many were definitely Mom's niche, things that Dad hadn't needed to take charge of.

Mom was mostly cheerful but had lost interest in many of the things she used to do. Dad was stressed over having to take on all the extra responsibilities. I was concerned that Mom wasn't as engaged or active as she used to be, and her good health appeared to be declining. She seemed to be shrinking before our very eyes.

But when my parents went to Florida for the winter from their summer home in Wisconsin, they got this crazy idea to play ping-pong. Dad had planned to put the table out on their lanai, where they could play in the fresh air under the cover of a roof. After he came home empty-handed, I told him maybe they just needed a net, a ball, and some paddles, and they could play on their dining-room table.

To be honest, every time I thought of my parents playing ping-pong, I felt a little burst of joy. So I checked online and found a "pop-up" ping-pong table that fit into its own box. Weighing only fifty pounds, it came with a net, ball, and paddles. It was available from the same store at less than one-third the price of the 300-pound tournament table. The website claimed that the pop-up table could also be set up in less than five minutes with no tools!

The following day was Cyber Monday, and I could order the pop-up table online at twenty-five percent off, but there was no delivery option. I called Mom and Dad and told them all about it. I told Dad that if Mom wasn't interested, he could fold this table and hit the ball to himself. But Mom exclaimed in the background, "I know how to play ping-pong! We used to play it in my grandma's basement when I was a little girl!" She sounded as excited about the table as Dad. I offered to order it for them if they would pick it up at the store. We wondered why the clerks hadn't mentioned this other table, which was in stock, to Dad the other day. But Dad forgave them for their ineptness and jumped at my offer. I ordered the table and sent the receipt to his phone.

The next day, I received an e-mail receipt that my order had been picked up. I called and left a message for my folks, joking that they must be too busy playing ping-pong to answer the phone. Later, Dad left me a message back. In a genuinely giddy voice, he said, "We did get the table, and we are out there playing ping-pong on it. We'll probably be so good that you won't want to play with us when Christmas comes!" I could hear the mirth in his voice. And I could picture my parents out there playing like the pair of teenagers they were when they first met. My ping-ponging parents had discovered a new way to play, a way to make life fun again!

— Jenny Pavlovic —

87

Still Miles to Go

To find joy in work is to discover the fountain of youth.
~Pearl S. Buck

My husband Tom came through the front door with a huge grin on his face. He held his arms wide and announced, "I'm retired!" It was official. After working for the U.S. Postal Service for thirty-three years, Tom could stop setting his alarm for 4:30 a.m. He was free to sleep in. And there would be no more checking the next day's weather on the evening news.

Tom had enough years in to qualify for retirement at age fifty-five. The first thing we did was move from Illinois to South Carolina. Moving is a lot of work, and unpacking and organizing kept us both busy. We enjoyed exploring our new town. But as time went by, I could tell that Tom was getting bored. He was used to full and busy days, where he was responsible for much more than bringing in the mail or mowing the lawn. He began to pace like a lion, glancing out the windows. I knew what he was searching for. I did the same searching when the children "left the nest" and I had filled the void by providing drop-in childcare for neighbors.

"I think I'll look for a part-time job," Tom informed me one day. I felt instant relief. The lion would cease his circling, and I could vacuum in peace. We both kept our eyes open for job opportunities. "Something will come along," I told him confidently. A few days later, something did come along in the shape of a large yellow school bus that we were following down a road. It was 3 p.m., and as our car crept behind, we watched the flashing lights signal each impending stop. The stop sign would pop out, the doors would open, and a child would jump from the high step.

"You could drive that bus," I remarked casually to Tom. I knew he liked to drive and seemed to savor the times when we had to rent a truck to move something. He had driven us over the mountains to our new home, through driving rainstorms on winding roads. Behind the wheel, he seemed fearless.

"Of course, I could drive that bus," he answered back. "But could I drive it with forty-five children bouncing and yelling in the back?" We both laughed at the thought. As we finally passed the bus, I glanced in the windows. "They're not all bouncing. Most of them are sitting quietly." I didn't mention the child with his face pressed against the window. The one with the runny nose.

When I was a child, my mother would tell me to "get the bee out of your bonnet" when I seemed obsessed about something. That black-and-yellow bus became the bumblebee that buzzed around me. I pictured Tom happily going off to work again, climbing behind that giant steering wheel and setting off on his daily route. My enthusiasm must have intrigued Tom because I overheard him on the phone one day with the transportation department of our local school system.

He was hired, providing he could pass the physical performance test and acquire the school bus commercial driver's license. This was no easy task, and he spent hours studying manuals and learning to maneuver the bus down narrow streets and through heavy traffic. He had to train for evacuation, dragging a heavy load down the bus aisle and jumping from the emergency door.

He was proud the day he got his commercial driver's license. The very next morning, he was given a bus and a route sheet. The bus had a wheelchair lift. His passengers would be special-needs children. He would drive high-school students and then make another run for pre-kindergarten, the four-year-olds.

I'm sure he was nervous, but Tom will accept any mission. Driving the bus turned out to be rewarding, and Tom is thriving in his new role. I think he likes being the "big guy" on the road. He now knows every street in our town, where the potholes are, and which intersections get backed up. He's back to checking the weather, and the alarm is set for 4:30 a.m. again.

The day he got his route, he also got a new name and, in many ways, a new identity. He is now "Mr. Tom" to his riders and their parents. I don't have the privilege of observing from a bus seat while Mr. Tom is in action, but I hear he is quite amazing. He greets the children with high-fives and compliments. He waits patiently while one high-schooler performs a security routine, turning around three times before he can sit. He listens carefully to the ones who have speaking issues, and he tucks blankets around the girl in the wheelchair since the back of the bus can be cold. He wipes the runny noses and wishes the kids a good day when they arrive at school.

When the pre-K children are dismissed and climb aboard, he straps them into car seats while they reach for his glasses and tug on his name badge. Then he leads them in a quick and fun activity. They know the routine and look forward to it. "Reach your hands up high. Now touch your ears. Touch your knees," he instructs. Then comes their favorite part, where they get to shout after hours spent in their quiet classroom. "Goodbye, teachers!" yells Mr. Tom. The little ones repeat it. "Goodbye, school!" Again, they repeat, joyfully. Mr. Tom then yells out the last two lines, and the children laugh and repeat at the top of their lungs, "Let's go, Mr. Tom! What are ya waitin' for?"

And with that, Mr. Tom checks the mirrors and steps carefully on the gas. He has been driving the bus now for seven years. He gets lots of notes from grateful parents, thanking him for keeping their child safe and well-cared for. Sometimes, while I'm out running errands, a school bus passes me on the road. It always warms my heart when the driver is the one I'm hoping to see and I catch the kiss he blows me.

— Marianne Fosnow —

88

Repurpose Your Life

Though no one can go back and make a brand-new start,
anyone can start from now and make a brand-new ending.
~Carl Bard

t started like any other Monday. I had worked both Saturday and Sunday, preparing for a meeting with my new boss. She had been on medical leave for several weeks. She asked me to brief her on what transpired in the marketing communications department I led while she was out.

I pulled together a comprehensive report, several visual aids, and a short list of items that required immediate action and headed to her office. As vice president of marketing, I assumed she would use my presentation to update the president later that day.

When I entered the room, she was waiting for me. However, sitting to her right at the guest table was a representative from Human Resources. That's when I knew I was being fired.

I set down my materials and paused, giving my boss the courtesy to formally introduce me to the elephant in the room. It didn't take long.

"Jim, have you met Monica from HR?"

I shot a sideward glance at Monica. "I certainly know Monica. What's up?"

"Well, effective immediately, your job has been eliminated. Monica will explain the details."

"Just a second. I've worked here seventeen years. I've been a high-performing employee. Why is my job being eliminated?"

My boss gave me a blank look. "Your job has been eliminated due to duplication."

"Really? What duplication?"

"Your job has been eliminated due to duplication," she repeated robotically.

"I heard you the first time. What duplication?"

She repeated herself again verbatim.

It finally sank in. This was a cost-saving measure, and she was literally echoing the company line. "Job duplication." They're safe words to hide behind, disguise intentions, and prevent lawsuits.

My head started to spin, and my career flickered through my mind like an old black-and-white silent film. Before I could regain my perspective, it was Monica's turn.

"Let's go through your severance package, Jim."

This is when I felt the out-of-body experience. This happened to other people, not me. After everything I had contributed over the years? And such high performance reviews?

I slipped back to reality for a moment. "Monica, is everything you're about to say in writing?"

"Yes, I will review it with you now, and you can take it home, read it, sign it, and get it back to me."

Her comment gave me permission to check out of the conversation. Everything started to slow down. I was lost in another galaxy far, far away.

When I finally left the room, I collected my thoughts and called my staff into my office to inform them. I encouraged them to stay positive and continue to achieve our goals for the balance of the year. I cleaned out my desk, but unlike others who were escorted out of the building, I stayed the balance of the day to say goodbye to many of my long-term colleagues.

I arrived home at about 5:30 p.m. and sat down with my wife, Karen. "I want to talk to you about something that happened at work today."

"What happened?"

"I lost my job."

"Yeah, right."

"No, really, I lost my job."

She shifted her weight on the couch and leaned toward me. "Very funny. What really happened?"

"My job was eliminated."

"How could they eliminate your job after all your accomplishments?"

"It's corporate America. Everyone's expendable."

"Did you really lose your job?" She looked at my expression. "You're serious!"

"Very."

"Why would they do that to you?"

I paused, watching her process the news. She always saw a silver lining. I loved that about her. She quickly transitioned from shock to anger to what's next.

After talking for thirty minutes, she said, "I guess we'll have to get ready for God's next great adventure for us." Her attitude lifted my spirits and gave me hope.

She leaned back. "So, what do you want to do now, Jim?"

"Well, I have a Plan A, B, and C. Plan A is to find something similar to what I was doing. Plan B is to start my own business again as a freelance advertising copywriter and executive speechwriter like I did before. Plan C is to retire outright if our financial planner thinks we're ready. I'm leaning toward Plan A."

"Are you sure you want to keep doing what you were doing?"

"Yeah. I love marketing communications. I've been doing it for forty-one years."

"Forty-one years? Do you need forty-two?" The simplicity of her question was powerful and profound, and it stunned me.

"Ah, well, it's all I know…"

She paused for a moment and then hit me again with the blunt force of a two-by-four to my forehead. "Forty-one years? When is the right time to do something different with your life?"

"Ah, now… I guess."

I would learn later that my severance package included outplacement assistance with a leading career-transition firm. As an older worker, near retirement, I embraced this service, became actively involved in my job search, and learned the most effective résumé, networking, and interviewing techniques to find employment in today's job market.

My job search was long and lonely. On one of the darkest days, I penned a creed to restore my perspective. A portion stated:

When I'm discouraged, I will remember:
I lost my position, not my skills.
I lost my salary, not my value.
I lost my benefits, not my health.
I lost my colleagues, not my friends.
I lost my role, not my reputation.
I lost my duties, not my identity.
I lost my livelihood, not my life.

Before I completed my outplacement training program, Debbie, the senior vice president of the career-transition firm, asked me to consider Plan D in my job search. Plan D was to join their career-transition firm as a part-time consultant and spend my off time writing the articles and books I had planned for full retirement.

Today, I'm a consultant for the largest career-transition firm in the world — and I've never been so fulfilled. I love helping professional people navigate through today's complicated job-search process. Training and coaching job candidates to land better jobs than they had before is gratifying for me — and life-changing for them.

It's a second career that brings help and hope to people when they need it most. And, in the meantime, my nonfiction articles are being published, and my first novel, *The Glimpse*, is now available online.

In Max Lucado's book, *Cure for the Common Life*, he says, "We need to know how to step away from the game. We need regular recalibrations." While I wasn't happy when my previous job was eliminated, I understand why it was important for me to step away from the game, recalibrate, and do something different with my life.

In the end, for me, it wasn't about finding a new job; it was about charting a new direction, a repurposed life.

—James C. Magruder—

89

The Accidental Historian

I have found that if you love life,
life will love you back.
~Arthur Rubinstein

never intended to become the town historian — it just sort of happened! After having lived in other cities for twenty-seven years, we had moved back to our previous hometown — Winona Lake, Indiana — in August 2003. I had a sketchy knowledge of the town's history but only a layman's interest in the historical details. I knew that it had once been a Chautauqua center, drawing huge crowds, and later it became known as the home of the world's largest Bible conference. I knew the world-famous evangelist Billy Sunday lived there, and that the town was the launching point for Billy Graham's ministry in the late 1940s.

Somewhere about 2010 or 2011, it came to my attention that the town had been incorporated in June 1913. That meant we would soon be approaching the 100th anniversary. I asked around. Was anyone planning a celebration? Had anyone updated the town history, which by now was about fifty years out of date?

Nothing was happening. So, I started collecting data. I pored through the Indiana Room of our local public library to glean all I could about local history. My wife faithfully prowled the Friday and Saturday garage sales around town. When she found scrapbooks with clippings of the town's history, she purchased them. I started interviewing longtime residents of the community.

Soon, I realized I had a major project on my hands — updating and re-writing the town's history — and I was racing against the deadline of June 2013 to kick off a year of events we had created to draw attention to the Centennial.

"Winona at 100: Third Wave Rising" appeared in June 2013, just in time for our annual juried art fair. I felt the town's history neatly divided into three segments. The first was the Spring Fountain Park and Chautauqua Days (1881–1895), the second was the era of the Bible conference (1895–1968), and the third was the modern Village at Winona, which today is a delightful tourist destination. The subtitle "Third Wave Rising" suggested that the town's third phase was by no means done, and was, in fact, "rising" to even better days ahead.

While selling the book at festivals, fairs and other events, I jokingly referred to it as "354 pages of absolutely useless trivia about Winona Lake." But there was local interest in it — lots of local interest.

Pretty soon, I started getting invitations to speak on the town's history to service clubs. So I created a PowerPoint presentation entitled "Winona at 100... and Counting" and started making the rounds. Rotary. Kiwanis. Optimists. Retired teachers. Literary Club. I'd speak anywhere, for whatever length they desired, for anyone who asked.

Then the local college, which was in charge of the town museum and the home of famous resident Billy Sunday, invited me to become the chief docent, giving talks, walking tours of the town, and bus tours as requested. So the History Center became my office, complete with Wi-Fi and all other necessary communication equipment so I could work on projects when there were no visitors to the museum.

One of the unintended side effects was the steady flow of visitors who had stories to tell and artifacts to donate. They told about visiting their grandparents' cabin on the lake. Or they told about coming in the summers for camps or Youth for Christ conventions. Or they had been students at the college and worked in local hotels. The donated artifacts ranged widely, from photos to souvenir bats (Billy Sunday had been a professional baseball player), to furniture, to metal artifacts dredged up from the silt at the town beach.

Soon, it was time to create a new presentation since most everyone in town had heard the first one. This presentation became "Bibles, Booze, and Billy." It focused on the Bible conference years, the temperance movement in northern Indiana (Winona Lake was headquarters for the Prohibition Party), and the two Billys whose ministries were associated with the town—Billy Sunday, who moved here in 1911 at the height of his popularity, and Billy Graham, whose ministry was launched from an all-night prayer meeting in the Rainbow Room of the Westminster Hotel in July 1949, just before his Los Angeles crusade.

Other invitations led to the development of specialized invitations. The Rodeheaver Concert Series commissioned a presentation on Homer Rodeheaver, who was Billy Sunday's song leader and choir director, and later founded the Rodeheaver Hall-Mack Publishing Co., which became the largest gospel music publisher in the world at one time.

Some happy coincidences have made it easy. The Chicago Cubs finally won the World Series in 2016. The only other time they had won was in 1907 and 1908. Billy Sunday, a pro baseball player before he became an evangelist, played for the Chicago White Stockings, which eventually became the Cubs, but left the team a few years before the Series win. So that developed into an article and presentation entitled, "The Cubs Won the World Series and Billy Sunday Just Missed It!"

Some of the other town legends developed nicely into modules we could use with children and school groups. One of these was Jerry, the waterskiing lion. There is actual YouTube footage of Jerry skimming along behind a Chris-Craft speedboat on Winona Lake! Another was the story of the local ghost—Phoebe—and her caring for the illegitimate child of a marriage that never happened. And, of course, there are local tragedies, such as airplane crashes and drownings that elicit strong human interest.

For children and high-school students, we developed a ten-question scavenger hunt. The answers to all the questions (What was Billy Sunday's lifetime batting average?) are all on the walls of the museum somewhere, and the prize was a free ticket for a ride on the Winona Queen excursion boat.

We also have the delight of working with many scholars who are doing historical research or are working on books, articles, or dissertations. Right now, the "in-production" piece is an authoritative biography of Homer Rodeheaver, Billy Sunday's trombone-playing song leader. One of the co-authors was a trombonist with the Boston Symphony Orchestra for several decades. Working with elite scholars is a terrific perk of the job!

So, at age seventy, when I thought I was about to retire, this whole new career appeared and has come to be one of the greatest joys of my life. We feed historical information regularly into the Facebook pages of the Winona History Center and the Town of Winona Lake and invite anyone interested or who is passing through northern Indiana to visit us at the Winona History Center.

— Terry White —

90

Second Take on a New Restaurant

Passion is oxygen for the soul.
~Author Unknown

was reading in my living room in Buffalo on a cold December day when my husband Steve yelled, "There's a Facebook post that says Lewis' Restaurant is making a comeback."

"It must be a joke," I said.

But when I called my Uncle Rich, the restaurant's former owner, he said yes, it was happening. And when I texted my family members, we all had the same reaction.

What?

My uncle Rich had sold our family's restaurant four years earlier. He was turning seventy in a few months, and he had Parkinson's disease. It seemed that if he was going to have a second act, it should involve enjoying his grandchildren and fishing and boating at his lake house, not the stress of running a restaurant.

In the tiny upstate New York village of Sherburne, Lewis' was started by my grandparents in the 1940s. My grandfather rented an Esso gas station and lived upstairs with my grandmother and their six children while they ran the service station. They started selling food and added a bar, and eventually the gas tanks were removed to make more room for the thriving restaurant.

On any given night, you could find multiple generations of Sherburne residents enjoying chicken cordon bleu, pizzas, and sizzling steak dinners. The whole town showed up wearing green shirts and glittery hats on St. Patrick's Day. If you wanted a drink, you could count on a warm welcome at the enormous curved wooden bar. My grandmother could be found sitting in a corner window crocheting afghans. She greeted everyone by name as they walked in, and if she didn't know you when you walked in, she did by the time you walked out.

We loved the restaurant so much as kids. We'd swipe cheesecake from the coolers and beg the cooks to make us fresh-cut French fries and the famous Lewis' garlic pizza strips, dripping with mozzarella cheese.

I spent two summers there waiting tables while in college. When my cousin Kelley got married, she even insisted on coming up from Florida and having her wedding reception there.

As Uncle Rich aged, we worried about what would happen to the restaurant since his two daughters were not interested in taking it over. When he was diagnosed with Parkinson's, no one was surprised that he decided to sell. But we were still heartbroken because this treasured piece of family history was slipping through our fingers. There were tears, last visits, and a lot of sadness when, after seventy years, Lewis' had new owners and a new name.

But Rich couldn't quite let everything go. He saved, in his barn, the long, wooden bar top, which represented the heart of Lewis'.

Over the next few years, my uncle indeed enjoyed his retirement and his grandchildren, even as he struggled with Parkinson's. We organized a family reunion at his beloved lake house in 2016. And as we water-skied and prepared large dinners, we all wondered if it would be the last reunion with him.

But things are not always what they seem. It turns out that my uncle had seller's remorse and some verve left in him after all. He searched for another restaurant to buy but couldn't find anything that fit the bill.

In 2017, he heard that the restaurant's owners were struggling financially. Instead of buying a new place, Uncle Rich wondered—could he somehow buy back the old one?

But before he tried to put a deal together, he needed to know that this was something he could manage. He knew he needed just the right actors to make this happen, people he could trust. Who could he call? His old crew!

First, he contacted his cook, Russell. Would he be willing to work again for my uncle? Then he called his head waitress, Linda, who was retired. In Florida. Linda and Russell, along with five other former employees, came back to work for my uncle in Sherburne.

If I had known he was going to do this, I probably would have paid him a visit and tried to talk some sense into him. But determined not to let a pesky thing like a seventieth birthday get in the way, my uncle soldiered on, planning the grand re-opening of Lewis' in May.

I visited just before the big day, and I was shocked. In a good way. My uncle, all smiles, was thrilled to show off the renovations. He was doing exactly what he wanted to do, where he wanted to do it.

And the restaurant? I was amazed that it still had the same shape and kitchen we used to run in and out of as kids. But the bar area was more spacious, the walls were painted rich shades of mustard, burgundy and blue, and right at the entrance sat the old bar top, gleaming on a new, barnwood-sided base.

My uncle was nervous, hoping the turnout would be worth all the work he put into the old place. Turns out his worries were groundless, as the place was mobbed from the moment the doors opened. His challenge became not finding more business but finding more employees. When my sister visited, she said it was as if the locals realized they'd lost something special and were grateful to have it back. He'd made the right choice by reopening it, and I was happy no one had tried to change his mind.

Fast forward to the COVID-19 quarantine. Rich let everyone know that Lewis' would switch to take-out only and try to help their employees and the town the best they could. They posted their specials, manned the phones, crossed their fingers, and waited. And wouldn't you know it? Business went crazy. Specials sold out in an hour. The phones were so tied up that people suggested they put in another line. (They said no. They were busy enough!) Some people bought gift cards as an investment in the future. But the most touching gesture came from a longtime patron who walked in, put a large amount of cash on the bar, and asked Rich to distribute it to his staff.

As I ponder my own second act as I retire and move to South Carolina, the enormous change and uncertainty can feel overwhelming. But then I think about Uncle Rich. He wanted a second act, and he bravely forged one where he could live out the rest of his life serving his beloved community. And when the situation wasn't quite what he had planned, he rolled up his sleeves, took a deep breath, and did the best he could. That community, touched by the selfless service he provided, showed my uncle how much they loved him right back. That inspiration fills me with hope and the courage to dream and plan my own second act, wherever it may take me.

— Karen Lewis Jackson —

91

My Film Debut

There is a whole new kind of life ahead,
full of experiences just waiting to happen.
~Betty Sullivan

"**B**ackground! Action!" That was my cue to quietly chat with the guy sitting on the couch with me, as if we were having a fascinating conversation. I was one of twenty background actors in the atrium of a historical southern Indiana hotel, the setting for the film. This was my first day on the set and the first time I had done anything like this.

Six months ago, I had retired. Colleagues kept asking me, "What are you going to do now?" My husband Tim suggested that I say, "Anything I want to do!" More than anything, I wanted to be available for new opportunities that came along.

When I read in the newspaper that a film was going to be made in one of the hotels, just seven miles away, my fantasy of being in show business resurfaced.

Growing up in the 1960s, I watched TV constantly and imagined myself becoming famous. I would sit on my porch in Missouri on the off chance that Buz and Tod from TV would drive by in their Corvette, even though I lived nowhere near Route 66. One Christmas, I received a pair of go-go boots and practiced for *American Bandstand*. From the teen magazines, I read about Twiggy and, even though I was just five feet tall, I imagined myself as a model. Soon, I would be "discovered" and make many guest appearances on *The Tonight Show Starring*

Johnny Carson.

None of that happened. I trained for a different sort of role-playing and modeling: I became a teacher. For forty years, I taught a wide span of age groups, preschoolers to adults.

When I filled out the application to be an unpaid extra in the film, I came to the question about acting experience. I had none, but my husband Tim said, "Write down that you had forty years of teaching." I thought he might also have a creative response for the question about my age. He said, "That's just a number." I wasn't sure if he was being literal or clever.

The following week, I received a reply. I had been chosen for filming that began in just two days! There was no time to lose ten pounds or grow seven inches in height. I was to report to the set for twelve hours, from 5 p.m. to 5 a.m. I hadn't stayed up that late since... well, never. The e-mail advised me to be on time and follow directions. That's the same advice I would have given my students.

Before reporting to the set, the costume designer requested that I submit photos of myself wearing outfits appropriate for the scenes. This was my chance to show off my modeling potential. Tim, my photographer, used a blank wall as a backdrop for the photoshoot, but no fan to blow my hair and look glamorous. For one outfit, I was to dress as a server with a white shirt and black pants. Tim handed me a tray so I would look the part. He took one photo and said it was okay. For the second outfit, I dressed as a classy hotel guest, with a jacket and dress slacks. I chose my comfy, retired-teacher shoes, since I figured I would be on my feet for much of the filming. Tim took the photo, and we were done.

On the day of the filming, I packed like I was going to a sleepover—a bag of snacks, water, books, a blanket, pillow and my outfits. Twenty of us background actors were kept in a "holding room" until the director was ready for us. We waited for seven hours and passed the time by eating, playing cards, reading and napping.

The best part for me was getting to know the other background volunteers. Several of the women were discussing their previous gigs on other well-known films and TV shows. One guy described the make-up required when he had played a zombie on a show. Another had been in a movie made by the same film company and had walked the red carpet at the grand premiere.

At midnight, we were called to the set. We wore our classy hotel-guest outfits, along with accessories provided by the costume designer. I was thrilled when we were told the make-up artist would take care of us on set. She applied hairspray and a bit of powder on my nose. I felt like a star ready for a closeup.

The background actors were paired up to stand at the bar, sit at a table or walk across the lobby. I was directed to the atrium where I sat on the couch with one of the guys (not the zombie one). We were quite a distance from the stars of the movie, but we could hear the dialogue. On cue, we talked, pointed at our surroundings and looked up at the beautiful glass dome. During each take, we used different facial expressions, laughs and gestures. After numerous takes, we were old pros at background acting.

This was certainly less stressful than my teaching job had been. First of all, I wasn't in charge, so I didn't have to direct anyone about where to go or what to do. Plus, making sure everyone got along wasn't my responsibility anymore. Best of all, I didn't have to confront the actors about doing their homework.

At the end of the day's work, the director allowed us to see a few of the scenes from the camera's viewpoint. The movie's release date was not announced, but when you go see the movie, which was filmed at an historical southern Indiana hotel, look for the scene in the atrium. Notice the couch, and you'll see *my* shoe on camera — size five and a half, brown, the comfy, retired-teacher one.

— Glenda Ferguson —

92

The Kid Who Hated English

It's a very cool thing to be a writer.
~Bryan Hutchinson

By the time I reached third grade, I was convinced English was for nerdy girls and sissies. God made real boys for more important stuff.

Diagramming sentences was a punishment akin to being forced to eat lettuce, carrots, and asparagus. "Close enough is close enough" was my attitude with regard to spelling. Commas, periods, and paragraphs were useless conventions invented by people who tortured children and sustained by knuckle-rapping teachers.

I entered ninth grade with no working knowledge of nouns, verbs, adjectives, adverbs, pronouns, or conjunctions, and I had no intention of ever figuring them out. I thought a predicate was a chubby woman with a baby in her tummy, and if it wasn't, that was okay because people laughed when I said it.

Ninth-grade English started out just like every other English class, with more of the rules, do's and don'ts I was sick of. I'd blown off English since first grade, and I saw no reason to change. Then, without warning, my teacher slammed the textbook shut and said, "That's enough of the rules. Now I'm going to teach you to hear English correctly." For the first time in my life, an English teacher had my full attention.

I'd always been a storyteller. I liked making people laugh, and when I could spin a bigger yarn than the other guys, it felt like I'd won the World Series. Now, with the shortcuts and tricks Miss Pffisner was teaching us, I'd be able to write my stories.

By the time I reached college, I was filling notebooks with my ideas and stories. I thought I was pretty good, but the red marks all over my returned assignments resembled a bad case of acne. Still, I continued to fill notebooks with my writing, I couldn't get it on paper fast enough. Every word I wrote shined a light into my soul.

In 1998, I discovered the existence of a new thing: a writer's conference. There was one of these conferences just forty miles from my home. Unfortunately, I was too late to register for that year's conference, but I resolved to go the following July.

From the moment I walked into the 1999 Montrose Christian Writers Conference, I knew there was something different about this place. It felt like home. As the days passed that week, I began to realize this place was full of wonderful, albeit slightly odd, people who were a lot like me, except most of them knew how to diagram sentences and thought it was important. Was I too late to be a real writer? Could I ever catch up?

I took an armload of my handwritten stories to my first writer's conference. No publishers lined up to print them. But on the last day of the conference, Patti Souder, the conference director, approached me and said, "I love your stories, Ed. Now make them sing." These words of encouragement saved my day, but at the same time it was a charge to improve my writing. I knew that involved rewriting, rewriting, and more rewriting until I got it as good as I could make it. Yet I was reluctant, oh so very reluctant, to touch the precious words that illuminated my soul. Ultimately, though, I knew rewriting was absolutely necessary.

That same year, my boss insisted I not only discover where the power button on my computer was located, but she expected me to use the darn thing. She was serious. Without explanation or apology, she eliminated my clerical support. I had to either retire or get with the program. While my clerical support was gone, my boss hired the best computer teacher to ever grace Planet Earth to teach me how to use my dusty PC. She also said, "If you have any questions, you can ask any member of my staff to help you."

I've continued to go to the conference in Montrose every year since that first phenomenal but challenging year. Surprise of surprises, I've grown to love the rewriting process. Yes, that kid, the same one who hated English, is now a writer, not only in his own mind but also in the eyes of a number of other writers.

I retired in 2009 and have sat at my desk, keyboarding, for thousands of hours since I've been freed from the rigors of showing up at work. I take great joy in writing and rewriting my stories. Yet I come to this field with a handicap. Those English rules I hated as a boy are still difficult. Still, my love of story coupled with the technical help of my editor and friend, Marsha Hubler, have bolstered my energy, confidence, and competence. To be sure, I'm not a bestseller and probably never will be. The miracle is, the thing I hated most is the thing I've conscientiously chosen to spend my retirement years actively doing. To date, I have four previously published stories by my friends at Chicken Soup for the Soul, and I've published one book. I've written two screenplays, and I have three more books in the works.

The one writing job I resist is drafting our grocery list. My wife Linda, however, insists it's my responsibility because I'm the writer in the family.

— Ed VanDeMark —

So Much to Give

93

Double Dutch

*Step through new doors. The majority of the time
there's something fantastic on the other side.*
~Oprah Winfrey

Okay, let's get four Black women, all over fifty, and send them to Russia — to jump Double Dutch. What? Okay, let me back up. Twelve years earlier, I established a Double Dutch program. *Established a program* sounds too pretentious. Let's say, I put the word out for anyone who wanted to jump rope to come out to the recreation center in my Washington, D.C., neighborhood.

That started what would become DC Retro Jumpers. We're a team of adult jumpers who do exhibitions and give lessons all over the metropolitan area — and now the world.

DC Retro Jumpers is a broad collection of people, but there are four core members (including me). Myra is a slim, trim, retired high-school counselor. She blows away audiences with her signature stunt — jumping Double Dutch while jumping single simultaneously, negotiating two different rhythms at the same time. CeeCee holds it down as a master turner. She's steady and precise and knows how to keep a jumper in the rope. Robbin is the coach. She's developed a method for teaching anybody and everybody to learn Double Dutch instantly. It doesn't matter if you're four or ninety-four. If you have feet, she can get those feet jumping. Or even just one foot — but more about that later.

The real beginning of the idea took place years before in the early

1990s. "Hey, everybody," I asked my co-workers, "why don't we exercise by jumping Double Dutch during lunch?" How to lose weight was a constant topic in the office. However, nobody was willing to do anything new. "Girl, I'm too old to jump," seemed to be the general consensus. But the idea stuck with me. So, instead of actually jumping rope, I jump-started my imagination. I wrote a play, *Outdoor Recess*, about a group of adult women who form a Double Dutch team. In the play, the team jumps outdoors every day downtown. One day, a *Washington Post* reporter sees them and does a story. They become sought after, showing off Double Dutch to audiences all over. Cute idea for a story, right? But not something grown folks in real life would do…

Anyway, I wrote the play, and eventually it got produced. While promoting it, someone suggested that I actually offer Double Dutch to grown-ups who want to relive a little childhood fun. And that's when the call went out for anybody who wanted to jump. But by 2017, I had grown tired of Double Dutch. Over time, the Friday night sessions at the recreation center were more hit-and-miss than fun and games. Sometimes, the only person who would show up was Myra. You need three people at a bare minimum to do Double Dutch. So, I suspended the recreation-center sessions. Robbin and CeeCee continued to teach at a school, and the rest of us would come together to do demonstrations when requests came in.

At one community festival where we gave a demonstration, a man attended with his wife and kids. He got infected with the Double Dutch bug. It was his first time trying Double Dutch, and he experienced that rush that comes from propelling yourself up and down. Turns out he was a *Washington Post* reporter, and he wrote a story about the group in the fall of 2017. The story was read by Mary McBride, an arts advocate who arranged tours for others, usually musicians, to entertain audiences around the world. Double Dutch appealed to her because, unlike a band, there were no bulky instruments, heavy amplifiers or sensitive mics to transport. No stage or auditorium needed. All that was required was a rope and some open space. She contacted me and asked, "How would you like to go to Russia?"

It sounded exciting, but as 2017 rolled into 2018, it sounded scary. Russia was prominent in the news but always for something sketchy. There were reports that Russia had influenced the election. A Russian woman attending grad school in Washington was accused of being a spy. An American visiting Moscow for a wedding was arrested for espionage. Staffers at the respective embassies in both countries were sent home. Was it safe for us to travel? And once I got there, how would we be received?

The June date that had been set was cancelled. Paradoxically, despite my trepidation, I was disappointed. I wanted to see Red Square, eat beef stroganoff, and share my own culture with others. Were we ever going to get there?

Then, as plans began to solidify, other fears arose. Jumping rope was something I did for fun and only for fun. Could I produce an entertaining presentation for people who didn't grow up knowing about the sport? And my age — most athletes are in their twenties and hang it up in their thirties. At sixty-three, could I reasonably perform as an athlete? What if I injured myself and had to go to the hospital and no one spoke English?

Back in the 1980s, my pastor had gone on a ministry tour of the Soviet Union. I pulled him aside one Sunday and asked him to pray for me regarding my trip. His response was to have me stand before the congregation and ask the whole church to pray for me. To my surprise, several different people in the small Baptist church I belong to told me that they had visited Russia before, and I had nothing to worry about.

And so, we were off. We took a three-city tour to Moscow, St. Petersburg and Belgorod, Russia in September 2018. We performed at music festivals, schools, an orphanage, and the U.S. Embassy in Moscow. I rode a cross-country Russian train by night, sleeping in a cramped but cozy overhead bunk. We hung out with Russian beat-boys who breakdanced to hip-hop jams. I fell in love with the balalaika, a guitar-like folk instrument. At Perspektiva, a Moscow center for the disabled, Robbin even taught a man with no arms and just one leg how to jump.

DC Retro Jumpers still offers remarkable experiences to others, albeit close to home. One of the most heartening parts of doing Double Dutch exhibitions is when I see someone watching us from the sidelines. "I want to jump!" is written all over the watcher's face. If it's a guy, he looks dubious — is Double Dutch for men? If it's a grown woman she's hesitant, wondering if she's too old to remember how or too old to learn now. Then, she sees us mature ladies jumping, grinning and chanting childhood rhymes. He decides he wants to get in on the fun, too — so what if he looks foolish? And so the reluctant one jumps in, and exhilaration fills the face that had been pinched with doubt moments before.

Once, a woman started crying after jumping — not because she had hurt herself, but because it had been so long since she had felt so much joy.

And that's what Double Dutch reminds me to do: to keep jumping into life no matter my age. The very word defines how we should proceed — to jump means to propel forward; to pass over an obstacle; to be lively. Jump for fitness, jump for joy, jump for life!

— Joy Jones —

Editor's note: To see video of Joy's trip to Russia and her group's work in the States as well, visit www.dcretrojumpers.com.

94

Little Fighters

*As you grow older, you will discover that you
have two hands, one for helping yourself,
the other for helping others.*
~Audrey Hepburn

"There is a baby for you to hold in Room 29," the unit secretary said as she quickly passed by. I stood at the white hospital scrub sink and washed my hands and arms, keeping my eye on the clock. The three-minute scrub from fingertips to elbows in water 84 to 104 degrees felt pleasantly warm. I was minutes into a four-hour shift, offering my heart and soul to tiny babies in the Neonatal Intensive Care Unit (NICU).

Seven years earlier, I stood at the golden gate of retirement. As I pondered what I wanted to do next, I recalled a volunteer role called "baby cuddler" in the NICU at one of the local hospitals. I had long desired to be one but just never had the time. I had always loved the healthcare environment, both in work and volunteer settings. Wanting to be a nurse when I was younger but never realizing the dream only helped fuel my enthusiasm.

As a brand-new volunteer, I started out a little on the nervous side, and it showed. My first day on duty, I forgot where the sinks were for hand washing—and I walked right past them. If a baby I held cried, I would just rock faster. I sang every nursery rhyme I could remember, and the babies rewarded me by crying louder.

I thought back to my earliest baby-holding days when I was only six years old and held my first little nephew. I was thrilled to be trusted. By age twenty, I had nine nieces and nephews. So, whenever I picked up a baby in the NICU, something in my brain went back to those childhood days. I would sometimes whisper to the little one at hand, "You are in good hands. I've had a lot of experience holding babies." And it seemed to work. They may have fussed a little, but when they sensed my confidence, they quickly settled down and drifted off to sleep.

As I walked down the long hallway that divided the two sides of the NICU, the sounds of cardiac monitors, feeding pumps, milk warmers, baby cries and adult voices drifted out from the various rooms. I was heading to Room 29, known as the "Quiet Room," where noise is kept to a minimum, and the lighting is dim, too. This room is for newborn babies who were exposed to addictive drugs while still in their mothers' wombs.

I greeted the nurse on duty and, once given the okay, I very gently and quietly picked up a little one. "Shhh," I whispered. While carefully tucking in the baby's pacifier, I eased into the rocker. There, I firmly held the baby. Not rocking. Not singing. Not questioning. Not judging. It was heart-and-soul time. I was just there in that little baby's time and space, easing him along in the process of withdrawal, helping him to sleep so that he could heal and grow.

I, too, have grown as a volunteer. Gone are my nerve-filled, forgetful days as a new volunteer. I am now frequently asked to have a new volunteer shadow me as I work. I am happy to share all I have learned. I openly share my shortcomings, saying, "You don't want to do what I did." And I share the joys. "This is the perfect volunteer job for me. I absolutely love volunteering here!"

I may have lived most of my life, but here I am helping these special babies begin theirs. These little babies are such fighters. Their human spirit, even in its tiniest shapes and forms, has given me new hope and encouragement to keep going through my retirement years.

— Marilyn Ibach —

95

Life After Work

The unselfish effort to bring cheer to others will be the
beginning of a happier life for ourselves.
~Helen Keller

Although I enjoyed my new life and the time it freed up, there always seemed to be something missing. Initially, I thought it was a result of going from a high-activity career to a life of leisure. The retirement honeymoon lasted for one whole enjoyable year. Golf took up most of my summer, curling in the winter, and hiking filled the times between.

At the end of that first year, I was asked by a friend to help out at a local church that ran a winter soup kitchen. The commitment was not too onerous. It started out to be only one day a week and took just four hours of my time. The task involved going to the local food bank, loading up my car with preselected food items, and driving them to the church hall in preparation for the weekend. The person who had been doing the job up to then had to stop due to health concerns. He wanted to pass the torch to someone else. At least, that was how it started.

Within a few weeks, I was also helping to sort out the food I was bringing to the church. This soon expanded into preparing the cutlery and dishes for the weekend event. I must have done a good job as I then found myself on the roster for weekends.

My duties were never the same from one week to the next, which kept things interesting. Sometimes, I would help serve meals; other days, I could be on security or dishwashing. I sometimes filled in for sandwich makers or soft-drink servers who hadn't turned up for their shifts. Different groups of volunteers would come each week to serve the meals. One week, it could be a dozen or so people from another church or a synagogue. Other weeks, it might be a group of university students offering their services.

For me, the most remarkable person involved in the process was the lady in charge of preparing the three-course meal for upwards of one hundred and fifty people. It never failed to amaze me that, although she might not know what food was available until the very last minute, she was always able to pull together the most wonderful, nutritious meals.

The clients who came for the free meals were multifarious. Some were homeless and living on the street. Others were individuals and young families who had fallen on hard times. One day, when I was on front-door security duty, I saw a guy head outside for a smoke between courses. It was way below freezing, and he was not wearing an outdoor coat. I mentioned to him that he would find it too cold to be outdoors dressed that way. Without a hint of bitterness, he pointed out to me that as he slept under a bridge at night, he would probably manage in the cold just outside the church. It made me feel quite humble.

The common thing uniting all the guests was their gratitude toward the volunteers. At the end of the day, most diners would take the time to individually thank the people with whom they had come into contact during the meal. That was a wonderful reward for our efforts.

The event was opened each week by a group of volunteer musicians who would begin playing before the first course and continue right through dessert. A communal prayer was offered up before the meal began, given by the inspirational minister of the church. Despite not being a member of his parish, I always felt privileged to work alongside this charismatic individual. The only thing I ever heard him demand of the clients was mutual respect. His naturally inclusive leadership style allowed everyone to feel an important part of the event. Each participant, whether volunteer or diner, took ownership of the process.

The food for the dinner came from a number of sources as well as the local food bank. Local merchants donated large amounts of meats, poultry, fruit and fresh vegetables each week. The wonderful thing was that their gifts were given selflessly. There was never any expectation of public recognition for their donations; they just did it.

As time passed, I saw there was also a need for volunteers at the food bank's central location. The main duty there was to unload and sort boxes and bags of donated food. These donations also came from many sources. Every week loaded skids would arrive from food wholesalers and from the individual packages that people had dropped off in collection baskets at supermarkets. I threw myself enthusiastically into this task, enjoying the physical side of the work as well as the friendly competition with the other volunteers. We fed off one another's energy. Before too long, we were being hailed as the most productive group of volunteers they ever had at the food bank.

My volunteering duties have now grown to encompass two partial days at the food bank plus a day for the Saturday dinner. It is easy for me to work my week's activities around this schedule, and my time spent volunteering has positive results. I can safely say that I get much more personal satisfaction out of this type of activity and interaction than I ever managed to get from any round of golf or game of curling.

It takes time and commitment to be a successful volunteer, but the personal rewards are tremendous. I heard a quote once that went something like "a life lived without purpose is a life poorly lived." Volunteers cannot be accused of lacking purpose in their lives. I have found a wonderful way to enrich two lives: the life of the recipient and mine. I get way more satisfaction and personal reward from my volunteering than I ever got from working.

—James A. Gemmell—

96

The Popsicle Kids

Caring about others, running the risk of feeling, and
leaving an impact on people, brings happiness.
~Harold Kushner

A nearly empty box of Popsicles in the freezer, left from a grandchild's visit, caught my attention. My first inclination was to toss it out. In her infinite wisdom, my wife suggested we give the few remaining in the box to the neighborhood children.

Her suggestion altered our lives and led us to a future full of "Popsicle Kids."

My wife and I, a couple of decades into our retirement on Social Security, reside in an apartment complex. After careers in sales and nursing, our lives evolved into worry about our aches and pains. The major topic of any day was what to fix for dinner. We occasionally looked at one another and wondered: What good were we to the world?

That changed dramatically after we gave away the first Popsicle.

Minutes after watching a neighbor boy, a second grader, walk away with an icy treat, our doorbell rang. An adorable blond girl, about six, smiled sweetly. "Is it true you're giving away Popsicles?"

I'd barely settled into my easy chair when the doorbell chimed again. There were two somewhat younger, dirty-faced boys voicing the same question.

With the box empty, we returned to our aches and pains and worrying about dinner.

Early the next morning, the doorbell rang repeatedly. Standing on our porch were the four children from yesterday. Like hungry young birds in a nest, they vocalized their wants. "We want Popsicles! We want Popsicles!"

Between us, we'd raised seven children, so we recognized a teaching opportunity. Looking into the eager young faces, thoughts and ideas free-wheeled through my mind: *What have I started? What can I do about it? Don't these children have any sense of proper behavior? But they're all so cute. What if they were my grandchildren?*

The last question sealed the deal. My grandchildren wouldn't behave like this.

First, I didn't like the idea of just handing out free Popsicles. There shouldn't be any "free lunches." I held up my hand to quiet their chattering. "Here's how it's going to work, kids. If we give you Popsicles, you have to follow some rules. Understand?"

Sensing a victory, they nodded eagerly.

"First of all, when you come here, you ring the bell once. One ring! No knocks. You can have only one per day."

Whenever it's necessary to talk about a rule, it's the most important at the time. Hence, all Rules of Popsicle are #1.

They stared at me, concern on their young faces.

"I'm not giving out treats for free. You have to give me something in return."

Their thin shoulders drooped in disappointment....

I came to the rescue. "You have to tell me something good about your day. Maybe telling me what you've learned at school or how you've helped another student. And I'll ask you every time, 'Have you told your parents today that you love them?'" I've even asked them to recite the Pledge of Allegiance.

Over time, new rules were added: Popsicle Rule Number 1 now includes "Ladies first," "Don't interrupt when someone else is talking," and "Put your Popsicle sticks in the trash — not on the ground."

On holidays, they get to express their understanding of why the day is celebrated.

Over the years, there have been about fifty youngsters at our door.

Some have inserted themselves into my life, which I never anticipated that first day.

One morning, the doorbell rang at 7:30. Startled to see one of the kids, I asked, "Aiden, are you here for a Popsicle this early?"

"No, my bird died." His shoulders slumped. In tears, he stepped through the door, wrapped his arms around my waist and sobbed.

"Let's sit out on the steps and talk about it," I said as his tears continued. "Why did you love your bird so much?"

"She sang to me every morning."

We talked about life and death, the inevitability of dying, and ways to be the best we can be every day. I told him I was proud of him for feeling such sorrow over the loss of his pet and how it proved what a good person he was. Eventually, his sobs subsided, and his tears dried. He thanked me and left for home with a sad smile.

A week later, he invited me to watch him ride in a BMX race. I stood a few feet away from his family. He won the first heat, rode directly to me and got a high-five. I moved away to let his family gather around.

One spring, I sat with four kids on the steps and read *Where the Red Fern Grows*. We discussed how to catch crawdads, loving our pets, and relationships within the main character's family. It was a special time for me, and the kids seemed to enjoy our sessions.

One night, after dark, another boy appeared at the door. "I don't want a Popsicle; I just need to talk."

It amazes me that these kids, generally six to ten years old, want to talk to an old man.

"Sounds like trouble at home," I suggested.

A nod confirmed my guess. "My sister thinks she can boss me around."

"What does your mother say?"

"She's not home."

A light dawned. Sister was in charge while Mom was out. "What does your sister want you to do?"

"Clean my room."

"Is your room messy?"

A mumbled affirmative and a bowed head were his response.

"Maybe your sister hasn't yet learned how to phrase her requests properly. The real question is: Why did you have to be reminded to clean your room? You know your responsibility. Take care of it without being told, and your sister problem is solved. Right?" He wasn't smiling when he left, but I think he had a better understanding of his role in the family.

Over the years, I've learned the majority of these kids live in single-parent homes, generally with the mother. These mothers are struggling to provide shelter, food and clothing in proper measure. I see a hundred ways the "Popsicle Kids" are loved at home.

I've sensed it's more than Popsicles that bring these kids to our door. Sometimes, they're more eager to share that they are not understanding an assignment or that they're being bullied.

The "Popsicle Kids" have given me a new sense of purpose. We're de facto grandparents. We've dried tears, bandaged scrapes, broken up fights and hopefully been another source of love in their lives. And, just maybe, we've helped establish some positive attitudes they can use throughout their lives. There're still no quotas to meet, but when the doorbell rings, we answer. Our lives are now full once more. Another kid needs attention. What we receive from these kids is worth far more than the cost of a few treats.

—D. Lincoln Jones—

97

How Many Books Can You Read?

Passion is energy. Feel the power that
comes from focusing on what excites you.
~Oprah Winfrey

had just finished my mostly heartfelt thank-you speech at my retirement party when my friend Donna approached and asked what I was planning to do with my newfound leisure time. Donna and I were in the same book club and shared a serious love of novels. As I shrugged my shoulders, she asked me two questions that I scoffed at when I first heard them.

"What's next for you? After all, how many books can you read?" she wondered.

"I can't count that high," I naively replied.

I read everything on the bestseller list. I re-read my favorite classics. I was knocking off about three books a week. But about six months into this strange new animal called retirement, I began to grow restless. After all, for the past fifty years, I'd belonged to "Workaholics Anonymous," a club for people whose lives revolved around the next project, deadline, or great idea. I had been a speechwriter, journalist, and college professor specializing in public relations.

Now, I really wanted to find something new to do.

I never had a hobby. It wasn't that I didn't try. I was just really awful at everything. My knitting was lopsided and unwearable. My attempts at drawing or painting resulted in piles of expensive, unused art supplies. At the end of my first semester of jewelry making, when all my classmates were moving on to intermediate level, my teacher pulled me aside and suggested I might like to repeat the beginner class. I had also tried macramé, hooking rugs, sewing, embroidery, ethnic cooking, piano, guitar, acting and a laundry list of other subjects best forgotten. So, when reading began to give me eye strain and leave me forgetting a book two days after I finished it, I panicked.

I decided it was time to spread my wings and do some glamorous things I had always wanted to do. Fortunately, I live in Los Angeles, so I began to explore what was available in the world of entertainment. Perhaps I could be an "extra." I did some Googling and learned the name of the best extras casting agency in town. I had the required headshots taken at Costco, and off I went to the "extra orientation."

I learned that my photos would be kept in their files. Each day, I could learn about potential jobs from online postings. Once I saw a job description that fit my profile, I was to telephone the casting agent who would look up my headshot in the file and let me know if I fit the bill. Easy enough, right?

Nothing but disappointment greeted me for the first few weeks. Almost all the jobs sought "Asian bikini models" or "yoga instructors." I took the plunge and tried for one that sought "parents dropping off children at school." That could be me, right?

Now, a new hurdle arose. I had to actually get my phone call through to the casting agent. I soon learned I wasn't the only person in town applying for this opportunity. I got busy signals for about an hour. I hit redial until I got blisters before I finally got someone on the line. She asked my name and looked me up. In under five seconds, she was back on the phone. "No, thanks," she said and hung up. No explanation. I guess my gray hair (which I erroneously thought could look blond under certain lights) was a dead giveaway that I was no longer credible as "parent dropping off children at school."

The day after my initial rejection, I saw an ad for "all types" for a new sitcom called *Mom*. It was searching for extras to play diners at an upscale restaurant where the star was a waitress. I could do that! I was an "all type." I went to restaurants. I knew how to properly hold a knife and fork. I dialed for an hour and reached the casting agent. After she looked me up, she told me to report to the studio the following day at 7 a.m. with three cocktail-type dresses. Wow! I had passed. I would receive free parking plus minimum wage.

When I got there, I noticed that everyone else in the extras pool seemed to be unemployed actors hoping to be discovered. They were "slashers," meaning they were a waiter/actor or an Uber-driver/actress, and so on. I was the only person in the room not looking for stardom. I just wanted to find something interesting and fun to do. I soon learned it wasn't fun at all. It was boring. After sitting in the bleachers all morning, we finally broke for lunch. I spent more money at the commissary than I would make all day.

Finally, about 3 p.m., they called my name, and I took my three dresses to the costume department. They selected a dress, told me to put it on, and then sent me to hair and make-up. When I was all gorgeous, they sat me at a pretend bar with my back to the audience and told me to silently pretend to drink and chat with the actor/bartender. I did this for another few hours and was finally dismissed. A few months later, my husband and I watched my back on CBS. I knew it was me because I recognized the dress. So much for my career as an extra.

Still anxious to be a part of the glitz, I decided to try to be a temp in any office related to show business. I figured after a few weeks of secretarial work, my bosses would recognize my brilliance and promote me to a position of authority. I went to an employment agency, sure that my fifty years of professional experience would impress the pants off any interviewer. But first, just as a formality, I had to take a secretarial test. I did not pass. I was fine with the typing portion, but when they asked me to do a "mail merge," they might as well have been asking me to run the New York Marathon. I realized I didn't know how to be a secretary. I'd had a secretary for my entire career. Another idea down the dream drain.

My last attempt at finding something cool and fun to do was to become a "secret shopper," someone who poses as a customer while secretly evaluating the quality of service provided by the store's employees. I thought at least I could get some delicious, free meals at fancy restaurants. Unfortunately, my first assignment was to pretend to buy a new car. I went to the assigned lot, asked the required questions and found myself waiting outside for half an hour in the 110-degree summer heat for the salesman to get me some paperwork that I would never complete. Another idea shattered.

Maybe I shouldn't look for a job, I decided. Maybe I could volunteer. I went to my local library and offered to read to preschoolers. They wanted a commitment that I would be there every week so I wouldn't disappoint the kids. My grandchildren live 3,000 miles away, and I like to visit them. When I told them my travel plans, they rejected me. I also tried working at a few nonprofits. All of them were delighted to meet me and promptly assigned me to the fundraising department where I was to dial numbers, read a speech and ask for money. I hate those people when they call me. I did not want to become one of them.

Then, Providence struck. One of my friends invited me to a play at a local community theater where her sister-in-law worked. I went and was introduced to the director. When she learned that I was a retired journalist, she asked me if I would like to volunteer and start a public-relations program, as they had never been able to afford one. I told her I didn't really want to do that anymore. I wanted to do something different. Could I work backstage or even try playwriting? She said, "Sure, as long as you do our PR, too." I agreed. Soon, I fell in love with the people, the place and even the scope of my work. I'm learning to write plays, and two of my short pieces were actually produced.

It's not Hollywood, and I won't help someone win an Emmy, but I found a way to link what I am good at with what interests me. I think that's the secret of retirement. That, and always having a good book close at hand.

— Maureen Shubow Rubin —

98

A Ladder to Light

When we give cheerfully and accept gratefully,
everyone is blessed.
~Maya Angelou

had just turned sixty-five and I yearned for a new purpose in life. Then, one Sunday, our youth pastor at church approached me. "Hey, did you ever think about volunteering with the youth department? The high-school group needs help."

"Really? Don't you have a bunch of parents willing to help?"

"Not really. I'd love to have a few mature volunteers who can do some mentoring. Think about it."

I went home to convince my husband this was something we should do together.

"Just think, sweetheart, this could be fun, even keep us young." I chuckled remembering the youth pastor's comment about needing a mature person.

My husband peered over the top of his glasses. He gave me one of those "you've got to be kidding" looks. But I knew I'd win in the long run. So, together we started to meet with the Sunday school youth Bible class and also the youth events on Sunday evenings. It was a time filled with silly games, raucous music, fellowship and scripture study.

Little did I know how much this generation gap, this look at the life of teens today, would change me. When I took on the challenge of mentoring teenagers, some of whom lived in difficult home situations, I never expected I'd learn something from them. I didn't expect to feel joy and excitement while I watched them walk across a graduation stage. I didn't believe I could stay up on New Year's Eve until 2 a.m. and rejoice to teen exuberance.

I watched teens learn to care about the homeless, the needy, and the blind, and I realized they willingly took part in making a difference in someone else's life. I trailed behind teens who walked or jogged for a cancer cure or a right-to-life event.

When our youth pastor asked if I'd like to be a leader at the annual summer-camp trip, I jumped at the chance. By this time, I felt fully accepted as the oldest youth leader.

As I started to pack my blood-pressure medicine, Tylenol and extra-long Bermuda shorts, I laughed out loud and questioned whether I'd lost my mind to take a week-long trip to the mountains with fifty teens.

I reached to massage my aching hip as I took the first step up into the waiting bus, which was already filled with shouting, overzealous teens. One of the boys put out his hand. "Here, Mrs. K. Let me help you. I saved a seat for you in the front. It will be easier for you to get out."

I didn't know whether I wanted to hit him or hug him. His big smile softened my heart. I just said, "Thank you."

I walked to my seat, looked around and sighed. Every student held an iPad, iPhone, or tablet. They typed away frantically. I glanced down at my bag. My tattered crossword-puzzle book peeked out from a side pocket. Did I remember to bring my pencil sharpener? I felt my shoulders slump before I chuckled.

Ten hours later, we arrived at our destination. I found myself gasping for breath as I trudged up a long hill to the girls' dorm. Must be the altitude, I guessed!

I hoped I had prepared myself for the drama that almost always plagues teen girls at camp. I had. I soothed tears. I prayed for and with girls about their hopes and dreams, fears and choices. I provided the listening ear, and an arm around a shoulder. I became their cheerleader when they needed it.

The next morning after worship, the youth had free time, and they eagerly signed up for the zipline over a deep canyon. I had no idea my role as supporter could take a twist, that I might be the one who needed a listening ear, an arm around the shoulder, and a battery of cheerleaders.

I watched with fascination as, one by one, our teens ascended a mountainside to zipline across a canyon. I didn't share with them how terrified I am of heights.

One of the camp leaders geared up the last teen and then announced, "Any of you leaders who want to zip can gear up after this last one goes."

One teen boy ran toward me. "Come on, Mrs. K. It's your turn."

"No, no thanks. It's not my cup of tea. I don't exactly like heights."

"Aw, come on, Mrs. K. You can do this. Anything is possible with God." Then he laughed and gave me a wink.

"Don't pull that God thing on me. I'm certain God doesn't want me to zipline."

Another leader stepped by my side and nudged my shoulder. "I'll go with you. They zip two at a time. I'll be right there with you, right along with God." Then she winked at me.

Somehow, I found myself geared up, and we started the ascent to the tower. Even with encouragement, I needed to stop many times to catch my breath and try not to cry.

A thirty-five-foot ladder loomed in front of me. Four steps up, my legs wobbled. Ten steps more, and bile collected in the back of my throat. Voices from above chanted, "You're almost here. We'll help you." Three young men stood at the top of the platform with their hands stretched toward me.

Once I planted my feet on the platform, I said, "I can't do this."

The clip snapped onto the zipline, and Julie hollered, "One, two, three, let her rip."

Suddenly, I flew through the air. The leader yelled, "Look at you, Alice. You're flying. You've got this." She held her hand out with a thumbs-up gesture.

I opened my eyes and heard my own screaming voice. I looked up, and suddenly a peace settled over me. I waved to the leader and began to sob. I scanned the incredible beauty of God's creation.

I felt a tug before I dangled above the world and waited to be helped down on yet another tall ladder. The gallery of teens I had mentored and cared for offered their support and cheers for me.

I volunteered to be a light in the lives of a teen youth group, but the truth is, I walked away seven years later with the best deal from the relationship. Volunteering brought new meaning to this old gal.

—Alice Klies—

99

Chicken Soup
for the *Soul*

Back in Business

Children make your life important.
~Erma Bombeck

Our family was eager to move away from the cold and snowy Midwest when my husband Tom retired. We chose South Carolina and found a house in a quiet town. The first few weeks after moving day, we were busy from dawn to dusk unpacking boxes. Venturing outdoors, we drove on unfamiliar streets in search of a grocery store. We located City Hall and the post office, and we chose a bank. We explored parks and tried out restaurants. We waved to neighbors, but aside from quick introductions, we hadn't really made connections.

As time went by, I missed our former neighbors. It had been nice to know names and share friendly conversation. Our long-established neighborhood had many people in our age range. There weren't many young couples, probably because the houses were older. They lacked the modern kitchens and large garages that younger folks desire.

Our new subdivision was just the opposite. Homes were being built all around us. The residents were mostly young professionals with small children. We rarely saw anyone outside, and if we did, they were mowing the lawn or jogging. It's hard to chat when people are busy. I continued to wave and hoped that we'd meet people soon.

We had a community page online that I checked often. It informed us of HOA meetings and other news of the subdivision. People would post if they had a sofa for sale or needed a recommendation for a painter. I usually scanned it quickly, but one day a post from a young mother caught my eye.

She had an appointment that afternoon and couldn't find a babysitter. Being a school day, there were no teenagers available. Could anyone help? I had run a home daycare for many years when my children were small, and I enjoyed it very much. I started to type a reply to this woman, but I caught myself. Perhaps I shouldn't answer her call. After all, it had been over ten years since I had cared for a little one. I was well "over the hill" and certainly not as spry as I once was.

Then again, it was just a quick appointment. I really should be neighborly and help her out. I typed a message to her and gave her my phone number. She called immediately. "You are a lifesaver!" was the greeting I got when I answered. She was just two blocks away, so I walked over to meet her. She opened the door with a smiley fourteen-month-old in her arms. "This is Macy," she informed me. She then quickly rattled off a list of instructions, handed me a sippy cup and Macy, and rushed out the door. The child felt heavy in my arms. "It's been a long time since I carried a baby," I told Macy. I set her down, and we looked at each other. "Show me your toys," I suggested.

Macy proudly handed me a stuffed bunny with a soggy ear. "You must be getting a tooth," I said. I thought back to my childcare days and the brilliant white of a newly erupted tooth. I spotted a basket filled with toddler books. Picking out a few, I invited both Macy and her bunny to sit with me. We spent the next half-hour snuggled together. What a surprise to find a copy of a classic book I had read repeatedly many years ago. Turning the pages and pointing at the pictures, I recited it from memory.

I was a little rusty when it came time to refill the sippy cup. They are much more complicated now, as they have made them magically spill-proof. Again, my mind drifted back to the days of wiping milk off the floor, table and little chins.

Before I knew it, Macy's mother was back, and I was walking home again. I'd had such an enjoyable afternoon. Macy's antics had kept me laughing. I didn't realize how much I missed the children. Perhaps I could find some children here in South Carolina to care for. I was available during the day. My mind began to swirl with possibilities. Perhaps here, in our new neighborhood, there may be a need for my services. I brought the idea up to Tom.

"Have you forgotten that you're no spring chicken anymore?" he replied. I pondered that. It was true that I was less physically fit. I was certainly slower, especially when it came to climbing stairs. But I could rock a baby and change a diaper. "I want to try," I told Tom with determination.

That conversation was eight years ago. Since then, I have developed a thriving little business. I watch children of all ages. I sometimes walk to their homes, but usually they come to me. Our dining room is now a playroom. My closets hold games, and my bookshelves hold picture books.

I've developed better arm muscles and quicker reflexes. I spend a lot of time sitting on the floor building castles out of blocks. I don't jump back on my feet like the children do, but they are patient with me. Once again, I'm spooning baby food into tiny mouths and shaking sand out of little sneakers. I laugh a lot. Kids are funny—like little Jack, who handed me a basketball that he failed to sink in the child-sized hoop. "Here," he told me after several tries. "This thing doesn't work!"

One little boy told me he needed a second cup of juice because the first cup had made him thirsty. As I played "hospital" with a little girl, she told me that I needed surgery so she would have to put me to sleep. How I smiled when she started singing "Rock-a-Bye Baby" in my ear!

Besides the joy that the children bring, there's another benefit. I've met so many neighbors now. It's nice to know them by name. I have a wonderful collection of new friends to greet me. It warms my heart when I open my front door, see a sweet, little face, and hear, "Good morning, Ms. Mary!"

— Marianne Fosnow —

100

Animal Therapy

Sit with animals quietly and they will show
you their hearts. Sit with them kindly
and they will help you locate yours.
~Author Unknown

For many years, I'd enjoyed painting as well as making jewelry and garden art. On weekends, I'd set up my tent and tables and display my items at craft fairs. It was a lot of work setting up, unloading, taking everything down, loading it, driving home, unloading, etc. But I enjoyed it, so I didn't find it difficult.

But two years ago, in July, right in the middle of a fair, I started feeling ill. I thought it was the flu, but when I kept feeling worse by the day, I went to the doctor. I had blood tests, CT scans, MRIs, and on and on. Everything came back "normal." I was "in perfect health." It was suggested that I see a psychiatrist when the symptoms led to depression, anxiety and insomnia. More tests. Still no diagnosis. I was unable to get out of bed many days. I lost twenty-five pounds in eight months.

Finally, after nine months, an integrative doctor had me tested for Lyme disease. I was dumfounded. Lyme? In Michigan? I thought Lyme only happened to people on the East Coast. So, I began treatment and gradually started getting better. But, at seventy-one, I was so weakened by the disease, there was no way I could go back to vending. This broke my heart, and I became depressed and withdrawn. I had no interest in painting or making anything. My doctor and therapist both told me that I needed to find something to do, or I'd only get worse. "Try something new," they said. But what would that be?

We live in a very rural area with many horse farms. I noticed that one of them, about a mile from my house, had a new sign. I slowed my car and read it: OATS — Alternative Therapy with Smiles. Alternative therapy? Was this a place to learn horse whispering?

I drove past OATS many times on my way to get groceries or to the pharmacy. I was still feeling sad and lacked purpose. So, I called OATS and asked what it was about. It was a place where they offered "animal therapy" to people with autism, cerebral palsy, etc. It was a way of learning about animals and enjoying nature while receiving physical and emotional therapy.

I asked the owner if they needed volunteers, and she sent me the forms. When I read the part that said you must be able to walk or run for at least twenty minutes and be physically sound, my heart sank. But I called and explained my health issues. Beth, the owner of the farm, assured me they'd find something for me to do.

I drove there the next morning at 9:30 to find a circle of children and adults singing a song. I was nervous and felt out of place. Then a woman named Dee tapped my arm and said, "You're working with me today." As it turns out, OATS was in the middle of four weeks of day camp for disabled children and adults, and she was the arts-and-crafts lady! I was thrilled to help. She was so organized and brought all the supplies for the crafts. All I had to do was assist the campers. I fell in love with them. They were all so sweet and funny. We thoroughly enjoyed decorating little birdhouses, painting pictures, and creating fun works of art.

I continued volunteering every weekday for the next two weeks. Half of the campers were taken on slow, gentle walks on horseback while being led by trained volunteers. The joy on the campers' faces was wonderful. I started feeling healthier and stronger every day. Often, I went home and took a long nap — it was exhausting work, but in a good way.

I started to worry about what I'd do at the end of Day Camp. I was enjoying it so much and really wanted to continue volunteering. Beth came to me on the last day of camp and asked if I'd like to come back. I said yes, but I didn't think I was up to handling a two-thousand-pound animal, no matter how much I love them! So, they taught me how to feed the other animals: goats, chickens, ducks, two donkeys and two mini-horses. This I could do. What fun! I volunteered to "muck out stalls" (remove poop piles from the stalls while the horses were in the pasture). My energy and mood improved immensely. My duties only took about two hours, so it wasn't too taxing for me.

Then one day I was told that I'd be leading horses from the pasture to their stalls. Yikes! I wasn't afraid of the horses, but the responsibility was rather daunting. But they started me off with the gentlest horses and the closest pasture to the barn. Soon, I was feeding the small animals and harnessing horses, leading them to and from the barn to the pasture and back. I'd never spent any time with horses or even thought about them. But I learned that I was very good at working with them and had found a new purpose and identity. It was a truly healing experience.

— Patricia Merewether —

The Payoff

Gratitude makes sense of our past, brings peace
for today, and creates a vision for tomorrow.
~Melody Beattie

The smell of grilled hamburgers wafted in through the half-open back door, and I hurried to put the salad together. A cake sat, newly frosted, on the kitchen counter. I ran a fingertip through the white whipped-cream icing and put my finger to my tongue. That's when the back door slammed open, and my husband Charlie stumbled into the kitchen crying.

"Do you know who that is out there?"

I barely understood him and shook my head. Outside on the patio were three guests who had joined us for church and then lunch. I knew exactly who they were: the father and brother of a former foster child and the brother's girlfriend. That was nothing to cry about.

"She asked about the tree."

What tree? The catalpa that shaded the yard? No, the ponderosa pine that grew against the fence... the one our first foster child had planted on Arbor Day years ago.

"That's Cindy." Charlie grabbed my shoulders and said again, "Cindy."

I rushed outside and searched the girl's face. Fifteen years had passed, but her eyes had the same twinkle. The same dimple flashed in her smile. Yes, it was Cindy. The years melted away, and I wrapped her in my arms.

We had agreed to foster one child in 2000, but she was more like family — the younger sister of our daughter's fiancé. A week after that girl came into our home, the Department of Human Services called us. There was a little girl from another county who needed placement. It was an emergency. Would we take her? That was a hard decision to make. We weren't young people. Our last child had recently moved out, and we briefly experienced the freedom of an empty nest: no need to rush home from an afternoon of golf to fix a meal. The child for whom we became certified was a teenager and didn't need a lot of supervision, but this girl was six.

We said yes and welcomed Cindy into our home. She came wearing an oversized, dirty sweat suit and carrying another one wadded in a plastic grocery bag. There were clothes and toys to buy, followed by tap shoes and a tutu. We had Cindy for nearly a year before she was placed in the custody of her grandmother. Within a month, we had another foster child, and then another.

People have asked what the biggest challenge of being a foster parent at our age was. Here's the thing. Getting up at 2 a.m. to fix a bottle for a three-month-old baby is not easy; older people need their sleep. Driving kids to counseling appointments and parental visits is an imposition; we have a life, too. Agreeing to allow the county into our home at a moment's notice feels like an invasion of privacy.

The hardest part of fostering as a senior citizen, however, is going to parent-teacher conferences. Older people stay far longer with the teachers than their younger counterparts. It is not that we are more interested in the child's progress or the teacher's prowess. It is because we cannot think of how to get ourselves out of those tiny desks once we have wedged ourselves into them.

We endured the conferences, though, and sat through endless flag-football games and fifth-grade band concerts. We scheduled our own appointments around the schedules of the children. We endured the allegations when a disgruntled parent accused us of abuse and cried when we had to have a child removed because we could not deal with his violent behaviors. We cried with two of our kids when they lost their parent to addiction. We often mourned the loss when a child returned home or was placed with family, and we sometimes breathed sighs of relief when the caseworkers drove away, taking a difficult child back home.

Sixteen years of fostering passed. Our hair got grayer, and our energy lagged, but we seldom said no when the phone rang and the county was on the other end.

As a matter of fact, we were pretty good at that fostering thing. Older parents understand the value in children weeding the garden or cleaning out the dog kennel. We know no child has ever died because he didn't eat his vegetables or snuck a second piece of German chocolate cake. We knew that covering a child, and ourselves, in prayer was a good thing to do.

Then Charlie got bad news. He had lung cancer. It was harder to schedule the kids' appointments around his doctor visits, and we finally told the county we would no longer be certified. By that time, we had fostered nearly seventy children and adopted three. Charlie's surgery was successful and his cancer was gone, but so was our time as foster parents.

That all led back to that moment — standing with a sobbing young woman held tightly in my arms.

"Didn't you know me, Mom?"

I just smiled.

"They said you didn't want me anymore."

"Who said that?"

"My family."

I remembered the day they drove away with Cindy in their car, who was twisting to get a last glimpse of me and the house she had called home for a year. She was the first to leave but not the last.

I told her, holding Grown-Up Cindy, that Charlie and I had offered to adopt her if she ever became available. She hadn't, but we had wanted her.

The hamburgers had grown black and dry, but we hardly tasted them. The cake frosting melted. We ate it anyway. Older people may forget where they put their car keys or what they intended to get at the market. They are really good, however, at remembering the sweet moments of life. Like this one. Like the moment we got the payoff for years of foster care.

— Caryl Harvey —

Meet Our Contributors

Violetta Armour is a former bookstore owner. She has published four books, including the award-winning *I'll Always Be with You* and sequel *Still with You* in addition to *A Mahjongg Mystery* and *S'mores Can Be Deadly*. She lives in Sun Lakes, AZ where she enjoys an active retirement lifestyle, including pickleball.

Speaker and author, **Peg Arnold**, brings stories to life through her engaging drama ministry that encourages all to embrace their God-given values. As a church leader, wife, mom, and nana to five, she freely shares her joys and challenges of these life experiences in her writing and speaking. Learn more at www.pegarnold.org.

Elizabeth Atwater lives in a small southern town with her husband Joe. She discovered the joy of reading in first grade and that naturally seemed to evolve into a joy of writing. Writing brings her so much pleasure that she cannot imagine ever stopping. Elizabeth sold her first story to a romance magazine when she was seventeen years old.

Barbara Bartocci is an author and speaker, a mother of three and grandmother of seven. She married the love of her life, John Bartocci, after he graduated from the Naval Academy. He became a fighter pilot and, sadly, was killed in combat. She has published nine books and gives inspirational, motivational talks to women's groups.

D.J. Baumgardner retired after forty-three years in the water treatment industry. He has been married to wife, Dodi, for thirty-eight years and has two daughters ages thirty-three and thirty-five. He enjoys gardening and doing home improvements. D.J. plans on living long enough to be a great-grandparent. E-mail him at santaclausisded@gmail.com.

Barbara Bennett is the author of *Anchored Nowhere: A Navy Wife's Story* about their twenty-six moves in seventeen years. This is her fourth story published in the *Chicken Soup for the Soul* series. Born in Rochester, NY, she now lives in Raleigh, NC, and is the mother of two, grandmother of seven, and proud great-grandmother of one.

Danie Botha was born in Zambia and completed his school education and medical training in South Africa where he later specialized in anesthesia. He has called Canada home for the past twenty-one years. He has published three novels and a poetry collection. Danie loves cycling, land paddling, kayaking and cross-country skiing.

Beverly Burmeier has enjoyed careers in education and journalism, using the M.A. degree in English she earned. Now, she documents her travels to more than 120 countries and her adventures such as skydiving, hang gliding, hot air ballooning, paragliding, ziplining, and river hiking on her blog, www.goingonadventures.com.

Jill Burns lives in the mountains of West Virginia with her wonderful family. She's a retired piano teacher and performer. She enjoys writing, music, gardening, nature, and spending time with her grandchildren.

Louise Butler is a retired educator with advanced degrees in administration and economics. She was a speaker at the Global Summit on Science and Science Education. She now enjoys the life of a writer. Louisa is active in her community where she enjoys good books, golf, playing bridge and mahjong.

Felicia Carparelli is a retired Chicago public school teacher, caregiver and writer. She lives with her dogs and birds and is learning to tap dance and play jazz piano. This piece was originally written on her website www.lifeaftermedicare.com. You can find her fiction book online.

Since 1996, **Jane Cassie's** articles have appeared in more than 7,000 publications as well as sharing travel stories with armchair adventurers. She frequently escapes to her cottage in British Columbia's Cariboo where more stories unfold. She is also co-owner/editor of *Travel Writers*. Learn more at travelwriterstales.com.

Melanie Chartoff is an actor who's been featured on Broadway, and in series like *Newhart*, *Seinfeld*, and *Rugrats*. She has been published in *Five on the Fifth*, *Glint*, *Entropy*, *Verdad*, *Bluestem*, *Mused*, *Defenestration*, *McSweeney's*, *Medium*, *Evening Street Press*, *The Jewish Journal*, and *Funny Times*. Her first book, *Odd Woman Out*, will be available on Amazon in 2021. Visit her at melaniechartoff.com.

Sherri Daley has been writing freelance for national and regional publications for many years, including *MORE* magazine, *Car and Driver*, and *The New York Times*. She is the author of a book about commodities traders and a ghostwriter for business motivational texts. She has established herself as someone who will write about anything. Read more at sherridaley.com.

Betty Johnson Dalrymple is a freelance writer of inspirational devotions and stories. Her work has been published in *The Upper Room*, *Chicken Soup for the Soul* books, *Guideposts* books, and Jim Bell compilations. She loves spending time with her large family, golfing with friends, and knitting afghans for her ten grandchildren.

Kathy Dickie is the proud grandmother of two amazing granddaughters who fill her life with never ending adventures. She enjoys globetrotting with her husband, family visits, quilting, research, and writing. Kathy and her husband live in South Surrey, British Columbia.

Christine Dubois is a widely published writer/editor and popular writing instructor. She lives with her husband near Seattle, WA and is the mother of two fabulous millennial sons. In her spare time, she likes to go birding. She's excited to be in the same book as her mother, Jean Dubois. Learn more at www.christinedubois.com.

Jean H. Dubois is a poet, photographer, birder, and gourmet — with two lit degrees and an expired teaching certificate. She's the daughter and wife of university professors, mother of three (all writers), and grandmother of six. Now ninety-four, she's happiest when she has several creative projects going at once.

Penny Fedorczenko is a retired teacher and mother of two. She lives in Ontario, Canada. In her spare time she enjoys writing, reading, gardening, and traveling with friends. She writes a blog about the humor of aging called thesensationalsingleseniorblog.com.

Valorie Fenton, aka Valorie J. Wells, Ph.D., is a clinical hypnotherapist in Kansas City. She and her husband Kenny enjoy traveling for his fine art landscape photography hobby. Valorie is proud of their eighty-year-old bungalow and cottage gardens, which are a certified urban wildlife habitat on the line between Kansas and Missouri.

Glenda Ferguson received her education degrees from College of the Ozarks in Missouri, where the closest she came to acting was an internship as a summer theater usher. Since retiring from a forty-year teaching career, she volunteers as a tour guide at two historical hotels in southern Indiana and writes nonfiction and devotionals.

Diana Fischer-Woods is a mother and grandmother who, as a retiree, loves trying new things such as learning the flute and submitting a story to the *Chicken Soup for the Soul* series. When she's not spending time with family and friends, she volunteers for the Chicago Architecture Center, as well as for a stable that works with individuals with disabilities.

Marianne Fosnow is still madly in love with her husband, Mr. Tom, the bus driver. They share a cozy home in Fort Mill, SC and take good care of each other.

Betsy Franz is a freelance writer and photographer specializing in nature, wildlife, the environment and both humorous and inspirational human-interest topics. Learn more at www.betsyfranz.com or e-mail her at backyarder1@earthlink.net.

Paula S. Freeman, MSW, is founder and former executive director of Hope's Promise, a Colorado adoption and orphan care ministry and author of *A Place I Didn't Belong: Hope for Adoptive Moms*. Widowed with seven grown children, she lives in Colorado but gets to the beach as often as she can. Learn more at www.paulasfreeman.com.

M. Elizabeth Gage, with her husband of thirty-five years, makes her home in the Deep South. On most days she can be located outdoors, working in her gardens. When the weather refuses to cooperate, she whiles away the day with her old friends (Chopin and Schumann) at the piano.

Heidi Gaul loves good food, good friends and good books. Her work can be found in several *Guideposts* and *Upper Room* devotionals and in ten *Chicken Soup for the Soul* anthologies. Connect with her at www.HeidiGaul.com or www.Facebook.com/HeidiGaulAuthor.

Renny Gehman majored in creative writing at the University of North Texas and graduated at sixty-seven. She has been published in magazines as diverse as *Today's Christian Woman* and *Bird Watcher's Digest*. Renny lives in Gunter, TX with her husband. She has two married daughters, six grandchildren, and is working on her first novel.

A father of two grown children and grandfather of three, **James A. Gemmell's** main hobbies are hiking, writing and guitar playing. Travel has always been an interest and seems to increase as time goes on. James has a love of all things Spanish and enjoys being in that country at every opportunity.

Kristin Goff is a retired journalist, grandmother of five, plodding runner and outdoor enthusiast (when she can force herself off the sofa). She enjoys traveling, trying new things and is grateful for the support of friends and family, who may laugh with her but not at her.

R'becca Groff is a former administrative assistant turned independent content provider. She has written on the topics of healthcare, business and financial trends, as well as local interest stories for her community, in addition to writing personal nonfiction stories for national anthologies and magazines.

Carol Emmons Hartsoe writes from her home in coastal Bear Creek, NC. A retired teaching assistant, she enjoys writing nonfiction and children's stories. She and her husband of forty-seven years are fortunate to have children and grandchildren living nearby and treasure time spent with them.

Caryl Harvey is a retired foster parent who now is a freelance writer and living history presenter. She performs as Margaret (Molly) Brown, Helen Keller, an Irish Victorian maid and a pioneer woman.

Marilyn Helmer is the award-winning author of many children's books as well as short stories, poetry and articles. She recently self-published a collection of her short adult fiction titled *Birdsong on a Summer Evening* and contributed to *Stories to Chew On,* a book of fifty-word stories published by her writers' group, the Wellies.

Nancy Hoag is the author of 1,100-plus stories, articles, and columns.

She has also written four nonfiction, inspirational books including *Good Morning! Isn't It a Fabulous Day!*, *Storms Pass, So Hang On!* (Beacon Hill Press of Kansas City) and *The Fingerprints of God: Seeing His Hand in the Unexpected* (Baker Books/Fleming H. Revell).

Darrell Horwitz settled in Charlotte, NC after leaving Chicago and is currently writing restaurant reviews for the *Queen City Nerve*. He is an officer in the Charlotte Writers' Club and Toastmasters. His hope is to broaden his speaking career to help young people. E-mail him at darrellhorwitz@gmail.com.

After retiring from a successful corporate career **Kathy Humenik** decided to explore her more creative side. She launched a small vintage furniture company, embarked on adventurous travel and turned to writing to express experiences and opinions that are inspired by a well-lived life.

Marilyn Ibach has a Bachelor of Arts degree, with honors, in elementary education from Cardinal Stritch University. Traveling, taking creative writing classes, volunteering, and being Grammy to four fun-loving grandchildren fill her retirement. She and husband Bill live in southeastern Wisconsin. She plans to write a memoir.

Geneva Cobb Iijima has published two children's picture books and two origami books. She is finishing a book about heroes who saved Jews and others threatened by Hitler during World War II. Learn more at www.genevacobbiijima.com or e-mail her at geneva@iijima.us.

Jennie Ivey lives and writes in Tennessee. She is the author of numerous works of fiction and nonfiction, including many stories in the *Chicken Soup for the Soul* series. Learn more at jennieivey.com.

Karen Lewis Jackson shares homes in Buffalo and South Carolina with her newly retired husband. While relishing their empty nest, they miss their three way-too-independent children scattered around the U.S. Karen writes, plays the Irish flute, and tries not to volunteer too much. Find her on Facebook at karenfifer.facebook.com.

Following a career in sales and sales management, **D. Lincoln Jones** turned first to painting in his retirement and then to writing. He is the author of two post-Civil War books and is writing a third about World War II, all based loosely on family history.

Joy Jones loves the written and spoken word. She is the author of several books including *Fearless Public Speaking*, and *Jayla Jumps In*, a novel about a girl who starts a Double Dutch team. Keep up with her at www.joyjonesonline.com or with her Double Dutch team at www.DCRetroJumpers.com.

Tassie Kalas writes humorous short stories, based on her big fat Greek life, about growing up and growing older and laughing without fear of the future. A native Houstonian, she enjoys making people laugh, visiting her three grown children and taking road trips with her husband.

Learn more at TassieTypes.com.

Ellen Kennedy, aka E.E. Kennedy, is the author of the Miss Prentice cozy mystery series about a high school English teacher. The titles include *Irregardless of Murder*, *Death Dangles a Participle*, *Murder in the Past Tense* and *Incomplete Sentence*. She leads a weekly writers' critique/encouragement group in North Carolina.

Alice Klies has a passion for wanting her stories to bring smiles, tears, and laughter to her readers. This is her eleventh story in the *Chicken Soup for the Soul* series, and she is humbled to be included. Her novel, *Pebbles In My Way* is available online. Alice is president of Northern Arizona Word Weavers. Learn more at aliceklies.com.

Helen Krasner has a degree in psychology from the University of Edinburgh. Over the years she has had a number of different careers including being an occupational psychologist, helicopter instructor, and freelance writer. She lives in Derbyshire, in the middle of England, with her partner David and their five cats.

Leesa Lawson is an award-winning advertising copywriter and essayist. Her essay "Garden Vigilantes" was chosen for The Prairie Home Companion website. She's appeared in *Greenprints* and *Berkshire Homestyle*. She received three top awards from the Garden Writers association. One judge said, "Her writing made me laugh out loud."

Carole Lazar is a retired provincial court judge who now resides in Surrey, BC. She was an avid backpacker when she was younger and still enjoys long treks, though now she usually opts for a nice B&B rather than a tent at the end of the day.

John J. Lesjack starred in baseball in 1953 and 1954 for E. Detroit High School with Bill Rattenbury, Jim Koresky and Dick Koelzer. He's still in touch with his teammates and August 5, 2003 they were with him in spirit. E-mail John at jlesjack@gmail.com.

Ina Massler Levin was a middle school teacher and later the editor-in-chief at an educational publishing house. In retirement, she has been indulging her love of travel and ballroom dancing with her husband Michael. Ina also loves spending time with her family, especially her granddaughter, Elianna Mae.

Linda Loegel was born and bred in New England. She moved to San Diego, CA for thirty years before moving to North Carolina in 2013. She writes historical fiction as well as a guide for beginning writers. She recently married at age seventy-nine, proving it's never too late to find true love. She still loves to fly high.

Barbara LoMonaco received her B.S. from the University of Southern California's School of Education. She has worked for Chicken Soup for the Soul since 1998, wearing many hats, including that of Senior Editor. She has one husband, three sons, three daughters-in-law, two grandsons and lots of Corvettes!

Patricia Lorenz is the author of fourteen books and hundreds of stories, articles and essays. She has written devotionals for the annual *Daily Guideposts* books for thirty-one years and has been published in sixty *Chicken Soup for the Soul* books. To hire Patricia as a professional speaker contact her at patricialorenz4@gmail.com.

Queen Lori, aka Dancing Grammie, is ninety-one, a mother of seven, grandmother of twenty-two, and two-time contributor to the *Chicken Soup for the Soul* series. She began writing after being crowned queen of the 2016 Erma Bombeck Writers Workshop. Lori leads and tap dances with the Prime Life Follies. Follow her at DancingGrammie.com.

James C. Magruder is the author of *The Glimpse*, an inspirational novel, and many reflective essays. He has been published in eight *Chicken Soup for the Soul* books and many national publications. Visit jamescmagruder.com to read his blog and sign up for his popular newsletter, "Pause More. Rush Less."

Jan Mann's early years were devoted to marriage, three daughters, and a career. However, she found ways to keep her passions alive. After retiring she pursued them with gusto, publishing *Cruising Connecticut With a Picnic Basket* and *How I Won the West: A Journey of Discovery*. Jan recently settled down in South Carolina. E-mail her at janamann02@att.net.

Timothy Martin is the author of *Fast Pitch* (Cedar Grove Books), *Rez Rock* (Damnation Books), *There's Nothing Funny About Running* (Marathon Publishers), and *Summer With Dad* (Eternal Press). His multicultural novel *Scout's Oaf* is due out in 2021 (Cedar Grove). Tim has contributed to twenty-five *Chicken Soup for the Soul* books.

Jane McBride is a wife, mother, grandmother, and author. During the recent COVID-19 pandemic, Jane decided to dye her hair blue. It's the most excitement she's had in years!

Barbara McCourtney is an award-winning author and speaker. Her first book, *Does This Diet Make My Butt Look Fat?*, has all five-star reviews on Amazon. Currently, she is working on a series of books that teach children life skills in an amusing way. Her books help children and adults become the best they can be.

Patricia Merewether lives in the country and tries to save stray cats, dogs, needy plants, feral neighbors (just kidding, they don't have many neighbors). Painting, writing, gardening, and volunteering keep her busy and sane and also keep her supplied with a long list of projects.

Laurie Muender obtained her Master's in Psychology after raising three children in a blended family. She is now the proud grandmother of three. Laurie enjoys drawing, writing, walking in nature, dancing, and conversation with loved ones. She and her lifetime partner, Mark, live in Carmel Valley, CA. E-mail her at Lindleymuender@gmail.com.

Nell Musolf, wife and mom, lives in the upper Midwest with her husband, two dogs and two cats. She enjoys writing fiction and nonfiction.

Sandra R. Nachlinger enjoys sewing, quilting, writing, reading, photography, spending time with her granddaughter, and hiking in the beautiful Pacific Northwest. She blogs about all these things and more at SandraNachlinger.blogspot.com.

A glass artist and graphic designer, **Florence Niven's** creativity also extends to the written page. Florence enjoys the challenge of writing — finding the humor in the everyday. She and her husband Don have no illusions about their athletic prowess — and they are fine with that.

Phyllis Nordstrom spent most of her adult years in education in addition to being a pastor's wife. This is her third publication in the *Chicken Soup for the Soul* series. Currently she is working on a book of memoirs to be presented to her twelve grandchildren. To keep her mind and body fit, she swims, reads, travels, and volunteers.

Judy Opdycke is a retired teacher, who now spends her days writing, enjoying extended family, helping care for grandchildren, and reading a wide variety of books and novels.

Nancy Emmick Panko is a retired pediatric nurse with sixteen *Chicken Soup for the Soul* stories to her credit. The author of award-winning *Guiding Missal*, Panko recently published *Sheltering Angels*, the story of a little girl who can see and talk to her guardian angel. Nancy is a mother and grandmother who loves to be in or on the water with her family.

Michelle Paris is a Maryland writer who is enjoying chapter two with her fiancé Kevin and their two cats. Her first full-length novel, *New Normal*, is loosely based on her own life as a young widow.

Jenny Pavlovic, Ph.D., is the author of two published books and several published stories. She lives in Wisconsin with her dogs Cayenne, Herbie, and Audrey, and her cat Junipurr. Her parents are doing well in their mid-eighties but had to leave their ping pong table in Florida while riding out the COVID-19 pandemic in Wisconsin.

Connie Kaseweter Pullen lives in rural Sandy, OR, near her five children and several grandchildren. She earned a B.A. degree, with honors, at the University of Portland in 2006, with a double major in psychology and sociology. Connie enjoys writing, photography and exploring nature. E-mail her at MyGrandmaPullen@aol.com.

Michelle Rahn is a wife, mother, grandmother, educator, entertainer, motivational speaker, Ms. Senior America 2004 and… the woman in the walk-in-tub commercial! She believes that choices are part of the legacy that we seniors demonstrate every single day.

Susan Randall is a hospice nurse in Montgomery County, MD. She writes heartwarming nonfiction stories of her experiences. This is her third story published in the *Chicken Soup for the Soul* series. She enjoys bicycling, walking her dog, and cruising on her moped. E-mail her at rnsue19020@aol.com.

Maureen Rogers is a transplanted Canadian who has lived in Seattle, WA most of her life. She has been writing fiction, poetry and nonfiction for over twenty years. Her work has appeared in newspapers, online publications, anthologies and various titles in the *Chicken Soup for the Soul* series. E-mail her at writeinseattle@hotmail.com.

Maureen Rubin is an emeritus professor of Journalism at California State University where she taught writing and served as an administrator. Prior to becoming a professor, she worked in the Carter White House and Congress as a public information specialist. She is now a freelance writer and community theater volunteer.

Nancy Saint John lives in California. She has worked as a publicist, radio writer/broadcaster and librarian. She formed a puppet troupe and music program for children. Her story, "Convicted Feline," appears in *Chicken Soup for the Soul: The Magic of Cats*. She actually met her love online.

Beverly LaHote Schwind had a TV show, *Patches and Pockets*, for eighteen years. She is a rehab teacher and wrote *Porch Theatre Devotions* for her class. She is active in Senior Olympics and has gold medals in golf, tennis, softball and basketball. She is a retired nurse and mother, grandmother, and wife to Jim for sixty-eight years.

Claudia P. Scott has been keeping a journal since she was eleven. She often writes about her experiences as a solo wanderer to soak up the sights, sounds and sensations of new places in North America and Europe. Her passion is visiting museums. She lives in Jacksonville, FL with her husband Barry. E-mail her at cipscott@comcast.net.

Caroline Sealey is blessed to be a mum, farm gramma, author and freelance writer. Her life consists of the four Fs — faith, family, farming and friends. Thrilled to be a third-time contributor to the *Chicken Soup for the Soul* series, Caroline also has had stories and articles published in magazines and newspapers.

Susan K. Shetler has earned a M.Ed. degree and is a certified educational administrator and yoga teacher. She has enjoyed a long career as a speech pathologist working with young children with special needs. She is currently working on publishing a memoir. Susan enjoys outdoor adventures and time with family and friends. Her blog can be found at www.susankshetler.com.

Barbara Shoner is an empty nester with wanderlust in her DNA and joy in her soul. She aspires to trek through this new season of life actively using her writing, photography, and travel experiences to inspire others to embark on life-changing journeys. The only thing she collects now is sand between her toes.

Bobbi Silva has loved to dance her entire life, becoming a dance teacher in the 1950s. She has continued to dance throughout the years, discovering clogging, a fast-moving style of dance, and becoming a member of the award-winning Country Knights Exhibition dance team in the 1990s. Currently, she enjoys dancing at One Generation Senior Center.

Lynda Simmons grew up reading Greek mythology, bringing home stray cats, and making up stories about bodies in the basement. Everyone knew she would either be a writer or the old lady with a hundred cats. As luck would have it, she married a man with allergies, so writing it was. Learn more at www.lyndasimmons.com.

Deborah Tainsh, widow of a U.S. marine and mom to two sons, the oldest KIA in Iraq, is a published author of four military family books and one children's book. She enjoys giving inspirational talks, teaching writing workshops, mentoring at-risk youth, traveling, camping, hiking and continued writing and learning.

Donny Thrasher received his B.S. from the University of Central Arkansas in 1976, his MDiv from Southwestern Theological Seminary in 1984, and his M.S. from Kansas State University in 1994. Donny retired from the U.S. Army in 2006. He now enjoys full-time travel with his wife Joyce and their two cats in their motorhome.

Ed VanDeMark retired after being a local government administrator for thirty-five years. His full-time career consisted of numerous part-time jobs no one else wanted to do. Ed and his wife Linda have been married for forty-six years. He is the father of three adult children and grandfather of nine wonderful young people.

Donna Volkenannt is a wife, mother, grandmother, and volunteer. Winner of the Erma Bombeck Humor award and the Pikes Peak NLAPW flash fiction award, she was also a finalist in the Steinbeck short story competition. Donna divides her time between suburban Saint Peters and rural Osage County, MO.

Nick Walker is a meteorologist, speaker, singer, writer and voice-over narrator with more than forty years' experience in broadcasting, most recently appearing on *The Weather Channel*. As the Weather Dude, he teaches weather to young people through educational songs. Learn more at nickwalkerblog.com.

Fred Webber holds the British Columbia Provincial Instructors Diploma and still teaches part-time for the Laborers' Union. He plays bass in a popular classic rock band and writes and records original music. He lives with his beautiful wife of forty years and a black Lab named Becky, in Harrison Hot Springs, BC.

Valerie Hansen Whisenand has written nearly eighty novels and is currently concentrating on the Christian line, *Love Inspired Suspense*. She is a *USA Today* and *Publishers Weekly* best-selling author and is eagerly anticipating being an extra for the filming of "The Sermon on the Mount" for the TV series, *The Chosen.*

Lettie Kirkpatrick Whisman is still enjoying marriage and texting Jim while also writing and speaking. Her newest book, *God's Extravagant Grace for Extraordinary Grief: Devotions from the Refiner's Fire*, offers encouragement to both those who are caregivers and those dealing with loss. E-mail her at Lettiejk@gmail.com.

Terry White's career has included teaching at all levels, pastoring in churches, working in prison ministry, serving as church musician, and writing/photography. Living in historic Winona Lake, IN, he has become the unofficial town historian and hosts museum visitors, lectures, and researches aspects of Winona's history.

BJ Whitley received her Bachelor of Arts degree in English, Writing, and Editing from North Carolina State University in 1984. Her work has appeared in newspapers, healthcare publications and the Florida Air Museum blog. When not riding her bike, she can be found working on a book of essays about aging in America.

Robin Will lives in rural Pennsylvania with her husband of almost forty years. She is the mother of two beautiful daughters, and Gigi to the sweetest granddaughter ever. She loves writing, reading, sewing, crafting, baking, and upcycling things that other people throw away. She is currently writing an inspirational memoir.

Ferida Wolff has been a teacher, yoga instructor, journalist, and is the author of books for children and adults. Her latest book for middle graders, *Rachel's Roses*, came out last year and she is working on a sequel. She loves writing essays that explore our everyday experiences.

Marvin Yanke received his Master of Science in Clinical Psychology from Eastern Kentucky University in 1981. He has worked in various clinical settings as a psychotherapist and has been a life coach since 1999. He volunteers in the individual care ministry at his church.

Marion Young lives in Regina, Saskatchewan under a big beautiful prairie sky. Her interests include reading, writing, photography and volunteering; she has a massive collection of volunteer T-shirts from past summer arts festivals.

S. Nadja Zajdman is the author of the short story collection *Bent Branches*. In 2021 Bridgehouse Publishing in England will publish Zajdman's second work of fiction, *The Memory Keeper*. Zajdman has completed work on a memoir of her mother, the pioneering Holocaust educator and activist Renata Skotnicka-Zajdman.

Jerry Zezima writes a syndicated humor column for Hearst Connecticut Media Group and is the author of five books: *Leave It to Boomer*, *The Empty Nest Chronicles*, *Grandfather Knows Best*, *Nini and Poppie's Excellent Adventures* and *Every Day Is Saturday*. E-mail him at JerryZ111@optonline. net or read his blog at jerryzezima.blogspot.com.

Meet Amy Newmark

Amy Newmark is the bestselling author, editor-in-chief, and publisher of the *Chicken Soup for the Soul* book series. Since 2008, she has published 168 new books, most of them national bestsellers in the U.S. and Canada, more than doubling the number of Chicken Soup for the Soul titles in print today. She is also the author of *Simply Happy*, a crash course in Chicken Soup for the Soul advice and wisdom that is filled with easy-to-implement, practical tips for enjoying a better life.

Amy is credited with revitalizing the Chicken Soup for the Soul brand, which has been a publishing industry phenomenon since the first book came out in 1993. By compiling inspirational and aspirational true stories curated from ordinary people who have had extraordinary experiences, Amy has kept the twenty-seven-year-old Chicken Soup for the Soul brand fresh and relevant.

Amy graduated *magna cum laude* from Harvard University where she majored in Portuguese and minored in French. She then embarked on a three-decade career as a Wall Street analyst, a hedge fund manager, and a corporate executive in the technology field. She is a Chartered Financial Analyst.

Her return to literary pursuits was inevitable, as her honors thesis in college involved traveling throughout Brazil's impoverished northeast region, collecting stories from regular people. She is delighted to have come full circle in her writing career — from collecting stories "from the people" in Brazil as a twenty-year-old to, three decades later, collecting stories "from the people" for Chicken Soup for the Soul.

When Amy and her husband Bill, the CEO of Chicken Soup for the Soul, are not working, they are visiting their four grown children and their grandchildren.

Changing your life one story at a time®
www.chickensoup.com